MENTAL IMAGERY AND HUMAN MEMORY

MENTAL IMAGERY AND HUMAN MEMORY

JOHN T. E. RICHARDSON

St. Martin's Press   New York

First published in the United States of America in 1980
ISBN 0–312–52975–9

Library of Congress Cataloging in Publication Data

Richardson, John T E
 Mental imagery and human memory.

 Bibliography: p.
 Includes indexes.
 1. Memory. 2. Imagery (Psychology) I. Title.
BF371.R525 1980   153.1′32   79–26849
ISBN 0–312–52975–9

Dedicated to Sonia

Contents

Preface

Over the last eight years, I have carried out a variety of experimental investigations of the role of mental imagery in human memory. In common with many other research workers, I have found mental imagery to be a fascinating, yet extremely elusive phenomenon to study in the psychological laboratory. Under many circumstances, it is possible to demonstrate substantial empirical effects which may be attributed to the operation of mental imagery, as I shall explain in the central chapters of this book.

Be that as it may, our understanding of the significance of mental imagery for remembering in everyday life is still very limited. The obvious experiments, the easy, well-controlled studies of remembering under artificial conditions have now been done; the much more difficult problem of saying anything meaningful about the cognitive tasks which confront ordinary people in their everyday activities has yet to be faced. Nevertheless, the considerable amount of laboratory research which has been carried out to date may be seen as an important preliminary to the latter activity. In this book, I have tried to give a perspicuous summary of this research within a reasonable and reasoned theoretical context.

The experimentation on mental imagery has been heavily influenced by the behaviourist tradition in experimental psychology. To understand the research which has been carried out, it is necessary to understand that tradition, and to assess its conceptual adequacy as a scientific methodology for the investigation of personal experience. I hope that I have given a fair and balanced account of the behaviourist tradition, even though I believe its effects upon the development of cognitive psychology to have been largely detrimental. More generally, I hope that it will become clear to the reader that advances in human experimental psychology are likely to result from the combined use of empirical investigation and of conceptual analysis.

To the extent that this book is able to make any contribution to the development of our knowledge and understanding of the role of mental imagery in human memory, it is because I have been able to focus my training and research experience both in human experimental psychology and in philosophy. Accordingly, I am pleased to be able to acknowledge my gratitude to those who have been instrumental in determining such skills as I have in these areas. In particular, I would like to thank Alan Baddeley for his guidance and example when I began my research on mental imagery as a graduate student at the University of Sussex; Allan Paivio, for the inspiration of his writings, and for his continued encouragement of my own efforts; and Peter Hacker, for his patient instruction and specifically for his helpful advice on the conceptual problems discussed in this book. I am also grateful to my colleagues and students at Brunel University for their various reactions to my ideas over the last four years. Finally, I would like to thank my wife, Sonia, for her patience and tolerance during the months in which this book has been written, and for her careful reading of the final draft.

John T. E. Richardson

Department of Psychology
Brunel University
Uxbridge, Middlesex
April 1979

I

Introduction

Until a few years ago, research on the nature and function of mental imagery was one of the success stories of modern experimental psychology. A considerable amount of experimental work was carried out during the 1960s, and this appeared to implicate mental imagery not only as an empirical phenomenon of considerable predictive importance, but also at the theoretical level as a major representational system underlying human cognitive behaviour. Especially in North America, this research was widely hailed as reflecting a major change in the direction of experimental psychology, and a reaction against the excesses of the behaviourist tradition. Indeed, it was said that this change represented a shift in the scientific paradigm employed by experimental psychologists which made it possible for them to carry out a rigorous empirical investigation of an aspect of human experience which they had long neglected (see, for example, the papers by Holt, 1964; Kessel, 1972; and Neisser, 1972a, 1972b).

However, for the last six or seven years, the literature has manifested a perceptible disillusionment, and this has been engendered by several different factors. First, some of the experimental research has not demonstrated clear and unambiguous effects in accordance with the predictions of the prevalent theoretical approach. Moreover, some of the effects which *were* clear and unambiguous appeared to be open to alternative interpretations. Second, a variety of methodological procedures have been devised for investigating mental imagery in a laboratory setting, but they are so many and so diverse that it has become difficult to integrate the findings within a single framework. Third, the original success of the theories which identified mental imagery as a distinct cognitive mode was partly due to the patent inadequacy of the alternatives, which were based upon purely verbal representations in human memory. Nevertheless, several researchers began to develop more sophisticated, propositional theories of memory which were not subject to these limitations, and which seemed to encompass most of the empirical phenomena which had been explained by the imagery approach. Finally, these theoretical alternatives tend to be supported not so much by further empirical evidence, as by conceptual objections to mental imagery as a coherent format for mnemonic representation.

In the late 1970s, then, the interested though sceptical inquirer could perhaps be forgiven for thinking that research on mental imagery was empirically unsound, methodologically fragmented, theoretically outdated, and conceptually confused. It is certainly true that sections of the literature leave one 'half distressed and half confused', as Newell (1973) described his own reaction. Despite this, however, the field has continued to develop and expand at a remarkable pace. The percentage of publications in psychology which is devoted to mental imagery has increased in an exponential fashion (Paivio, 1975*d*), and in 1977 a *Journal of Mental Imagery* was established. There is clearly an urgent need to integrate and organise the research findings which are being produced. Indeed, this need was identified by Newell in 1973 and has recently been emphasised by Sheehan (1978). In this book, I hope to go some way towards satisfying this need. Specifically, my intentions are as follows: to spell out the major theoretical alternatives in understanding and explaining empirical findings on mental imagery; to consider the conceptual problems inherent in previous psychological research; to assess the methodological adequacy of the experimental procedures which have been employed; and to review the available empirical evidence in a manner which enables it to be integrated within a single theoretical framework.

Some remarks are in order concerning the areas of research which are not covered in this book. First, it will be concerned with mental imagery insofar as it contributes to human memory. It will not therefore be concerned with forms of mental imagery other than those which are involved in remembering. An obvious reason for this is that by far the greatest proportion of experimental research has been carried out in connection with human memory, and that, however fragmented this research might be, its links with studies of other forms of mental imagery are much more tenuous. An interesting account of after-imagery, dreaming imagery, hallucinatory imagery, and other forms has been given by Richardson (1969, chaps 2, 5). Second, this book will be concerned with human memory insofar as it is illuminated by the study of mental imagery. It will not therefore be concerned with other approaches to understanding human memory. Concepts such as primary and secondary memory, and the role of organisation in memory will be mentioned from time to time, but excellent discussions of these alternative approaches are readily available, and it would be redundant for me to discuss them in any detail.

I shall begin by giving a brief review of the attitudes which have been expressed by experimental psychologists since the beginning of this century towards the possibility of carrying out a scientific study of mental imagery. This will mainly involve a discussion of American behaviourism, and of the procedures adopted by the behaviourists for investigating apparently 'mentalistic' concepts. Chapter 2 will continue by contrasting the dual coding theory of imagery and verbal processes with the common coding theory of propositional representations. The experimental methods which have been employed in laboratory research were devised in order to handle the behaviourists' misgivings concerning the ordinary-language concept of mental imagery. Chapter 3 will consider the philosophical presuppositions of the classical behaviourist attitude; it will be argued that these were confused and ill-founded, and that they imposed unnecessary and perverse restrictions upon the nature of subsequent research. It will also be necessary to give a positive account of the ordinary-language concept of mental imagery, and to indicate the implications of this conceptual analysis for future research.

My account of the empirical evidence on mental imagery will begin in chapter 4. This will consider certain experimental situations which have only recently been investigated, yet which have been considered necessarily to implicate mental imagery. These are tests of immediate memory in which the subjects are required to represent, to maintain and to manipulate information concerning the spatial orientation and physical properties of perceptual objects. Similarly, chapter 5 will discuss the retention of pictorial information in long-term memory.

The remaining chapters of this book will consider the more traditional empirical approaches to understanding the role of mental imagery in human memory, and especially in long-term verbal memory. Chapter 6 will review the experimental evidence on the effects of instructions to subjects to use mental imagery in their learning. This sort of strategy for remembering is the basis of many of the ancient techniques for improving and helping memory, but it is important to consider the mnemonic efficacy of different sorts of instructions, and to relate them to theoretical accounts of the processes assumed to be involved in remembering. In chapters 7 and 8, I shall consider the properties of the material to be remembered which influence the use of mental imagery in learning. The role of stimulus imageability and concreteness will first be considered in conventional laboratory situations in which the subjects are merely required to learn individual, unrelated words. This evidence will then be used to consider the processes involved in remembering linguistically structured material, such as phrases, sentences and connected discourse.

Finally, chapter 9 will discuss the various methods and procedures which have been devised for discriminating between individual subjects in terms of their use of mental imagery. The laboratory methods of questionnaires and objective tests vary widely in their value for predicting performance in learning tasks. A different and more radical source of variation in human abilities is pathological, surgical or traumatic damage to the mechanisms of the brain which subserve those abilities. Therefore, I shall conclude my review of the empirical evidence by considering the use of neurological patients in order to test theories of cognitive function based upon the normal, intact subject.

I shall, of course, arrive at various theoretical conclusions in discussing specific topics in the experimental literature, and these conclusions will recur at different points in the book, supported by diverse sources of evidence. However, in chapter 10, I shall attempt to integrate these ideas into a single theoretical framework for studying mental imagery, for identifying the role of mental imagery in human memory, and for specifying the approximate cerebral localisation of the postulated psychological mechanisms.

2

Psychological Attitudes to Mental Imagery

It is not always easy to understand or to appreciate the various ways in which psychologists choose to investigate mental imagery. Their methods are often abstruse and are occasionally bizarre. In common with much of the research which is carried out in experimental psychology, it is typically difficult to relate their investigations of psychological processes to the familiar, everyday situations in which ordinary folk believe those processes to be operating. In order to achieve some kind of appreciation of the activities of contemporary psychologists, it is vitally important to understand the historical development of the discipline. In particular, it is essential to realise the conceptual and methodological origins of current psychological research into mental imagery, if, on the one hand, one wishes to gain a proper evaluation of that research, and if, on the other hand, one wishes to put forward apposite criticisms of its foundations.

Therefore, this chapter will attempt to introduce the reader to the psychological investigation of mental imagery by tracing the changing attitudes towards the concept since the beginning of this century. It will become evident that most of the important research to be considered in the later chapters of this book has been carried out within (and, indeed, has been dominated by) the conceptual framework of behaviourism. This has specified the nature of the research to be carried out, and it has prescribed the sorts of theoretical concept which might be legitimately employed in offering an explanation of the findings of that research. It will be indicated that behaviourism imposed rigorous limitations upon the extent to which psychologists might concern themselves with cognitive processes. (The coherence and force of these restrictions will be evaluated in chapter 3.) The influence of behaviourism in contemporary psychology will be considered, in order to determine whether any fundamental changes have occurred in the study of such processes. Finally, I shall describe the way in which psychologists have studied mental imagery within this sort of framework, and the attitudes which are prevalent today in psychological research which takes mental imagery as the object of investigation.

2.1 THE RISE OF BEHAVIOURIST PSYCHOLOGY

The early years of this century witnessed the heyday of introspectionist psychology. This was the outcome of a considerable amount of activity which had the explicit aim of establishing psychology as an objective, scientific discipline. Psychology was defined as the study of the mind and its contents; *introspection*, the careful observation of one's own mental processes, was regarded as the primary source of information. It is not surprising that mental imagery came to have a central significance in this approach to psychology. Of all the various thoughts, ideas, feelings and sensations which might be enumerated in a classification of the mind's contents, mental images are certainly among the most intriguing and most striking. More than this, mental images were identified as the most obvious elements or constituents into which the process of thought might be introspectively analysed (Holt, 1964). During this period, therefore, psychology was most emphatically the 'science of mental life', rather than the 'science of behaviour'.

For a variety of reasons, however, introspectionist psychology went into a severe decline. First, the methodology of introspection seemed to be inadequate to handle a variety of intrinsically interesting situations. It was reasonably satisfactory in studying images, sensations and other simple cognitive events. However, it was difficult to extract meaningful introspective reports, even from carefully trained subjects, in the case of emotions or motives, and quite impossible to do so in the case of complex problem-solving situations. Second, the data of introspection seemed to have the disadvantage of being 'private' to the subject himself, in the sense that only he was in a position to observe, to describe or to quantify his cognitions. Thus, the introspective method appeared to be inherently incapable of providing common, objective evidence for investigating mental processes. This led to the idea that psychology should consist, not in the careful introspective reporting of mental experience, but in the objective study and measurement of behaviour.

In North America, this reaction against introspectionism took an extreme form in the behaviourist movement. The behaviourists argued that mental phenomena, by their very nature, could not be the object of scientific investigation, and so the study of behaviour should be the sole aim of psychology. They argued, further, that since the very words which were used to describe mental experience could not be rigorously defined in terms of behaviour, then they should be excluded from all scientific discussion. Watson (1914, pp. 9, 27), the founder of the behaviourist school, expressed his position in the following terms:

> Psychology, as the behaviorist views it, is a purely objective, experimental branch of natural science, which needs introspection as little as do the sciences of chemistry and physics. It is granted that the behavior of animals can be investigated without appeal to consciousness. The position is taken here that the behavior of man and the behavior of animals must be considered on the same plane . . . .
>
> It is possible to define [psychology] as 'the science of behavior' and never to

go back upon the definition: never to use the terms consciousness, mental states, mind, content, will, imagery, and the like . . . .

Hebb (1960) described the rise of behaviourism as the American revolution of psychology. As Holt (1964) pointed out, like a political revolution it necessarily went to extremes. For a period of thirty or forty years (extending from the 1920s to the 1950s), concepts such as 'attention' and 'sensation' were systematically excluded both from psychological investigation and from psychological theorising. Whereas cognitive states and processes had previously been the focus of consideration for introspectionist psychologists, during this period they were virtually ignored. In particular, while mental imagery had been one of the central concepts of the previous era, it came to be regarded with intense suspicion. Watson (1913) proposed that mental images were nothing more than mere ghosts of sensations and of no functional significance whatsoever.

(As this last sentence implies, the early behaviourists presented both conceptual and empirical arguments against the psychological investigation of mental imagery. Strictly speaking, of course, the empirical arguments should have been redundant—indeed, meaningless—if the conceptual arguments had been adequate. If mental imagery cannot in principle exist, the question whether images are functionally important should be as senseless as the question whether the King of the U.S.A. is bald. Only if mental imagery is a possible object of investigation is the question of its functional significance relevant.)

2.2 CONTEMPORARY PSYCHOLOGICAL ACCOUNTS

The attitudes which I have just described dominated research in human experimental psychology for a considerable portion of the century. As Neisser (1972a) remarked: 'Introspective psychology disappeared, and the study of mental imagery vanished with it. For about 30 arid years respectable psychologists considered it almost indecent to speak of mental processes.' The behaviourist 'revolution' had its major impact in the U.S.A., but its influence extended to most other English-speaking countries. In particular, British psychologists had no coherent agreed conceptual framework with which to confront the behaviourist movement, and much experimental research (especially research conducted during the 1950s) shows the clear hallmarks of the behaviourist methodology.

Roughly twenty years ago, however, there were signs of a change, and behaviourists began to allow so-called mentalistic concepts back into their discussions. Hebb recognised the change as early as 1960, when he referred to it as a second phase in the behaviourist revolution. He wrote:

In the psychological revolution, the second phase is just now getting under way. The first banished thought, imagery, volition, attention, and other such seditious notions. The sedition of one period, however, may be the good sense of another. These notions relate to a vital problem in the understanding of man, and it is the task of the second phase to bring them back . . . .

These developments superficially involved a resurgence of interest in all kinds of mental experience, and especially a reconsideration of the role of mental imagery in psychological processing. The resulting methodology has been variously called 'behavioural mentalism', 'objective mentalism' and 'neomentalism' (Paivio, 1975*d*), and a similar approach has been recommended by Fodor, Bever, and Garrett (1974, p. xi) under the heading of 'experimental mentalism'. Paivio (1971*c*, p. iii; 1975*c*) claimed that neomentalism 'represents an integration of prebehavioristic and behavioristic views concerning the nature of thought'.

Nevertheless, as Neisser (1972*a*) pointed out, the approach to mental phenomena which is characteristic of the second phase of the behaviourist revolution is quite different from that of the prebehaviourist era: 'What contemporary . . . psychologists mean by "the mind", however, is very different from what their predecessors meant. The definition is no longer in terms of conscious, introspectively given phenomena. Instead, it is in terms of a flow of information in the organism.' Indeed, the crucial point about contemporary information-processing or cognitive approaches in psychology is that they do not identify mental concepts as empirical phenomena to be investigated in their own right; rather, they are introduced as explanatory constructs incorporated into theories of the processes which are hypothesised to be responsible for other, purely behavioural phenomena. Holt (1964) expressed this by saying that, in general, the methodological approach of behaviourist psychology changed so that it became possible to conceptualise subjective phenomena as part of the inner workings of a theoretical model. However, while this change involved some development in the range of concepts which might legitimately be incorporated into an adequate psychological theory, it involved essentially no modification at all in the range of phenomena which might legitimately be investigated in psychological research.

Neisser (1972*a*, 1972*b*; see also 1976, p. 5) suggested that contemporary cognitive psychology involves quite radical changes in psychological methodology, compared to that of earlier forms of behaviourism. He described these changes as a 'paradigm shift':

> The behaviorist taboos have been broken, and the mind suddenly seems worth studying after all. Ideas and images are once again discussed in respectable journals . . . . Because of this paradigm shift, contemporary psychologists feel able to attack crucial and long-neglected problems and have a new array of concepts with which to do so.

However, Neisser seems to have heavily overstated this point, since recent research in cognitive psychology has in fact involved relatively little conceptual and methodological innovation. The concept of a *paradigm* is of course taken from the analysis of scientific development given by Kuhn (1970, p. 10): it refers to a situation whereby 'some accepted examples of actual scientific practice— examples which include law, theory, application, and instrumentation together provide models from which spring particular coherent traditions of scientific research'. Although research in cognitive psychology has involved the use of terms which in everyday usage refer to mental states and processes, these terms are given systematically different meanings when they are incorporated into psychological theories, and they are defined in a manner which is entirely consistent with the canons of behaviourist psychology.

In particular, research on mental imagery does not seem to have given rise to any radically new sorts of law, theory, application or instrumentation. This is not to say that this research is not of great interest to anyone concerned with the nature of mind; only that the manner in which it has been conducted does not involve any radical break with tradition, nor any drastic change of attitude concerning the correct procedures to be followed in scientific research. To substantiate this charge, however, the development of research into mental imagery must be considered in more detail.

2.3   MENTAL IMAGERY IN CONTEMPORARY PSYCHOLOGY

The revival of interest in the concept of mental imagery among cognitive psychologists was dominated by the work of Allan Paivio. His early experiments set the pattern of most of the subsequent research on mental imagery, and his more recent publications defined the methodological foundations of that research more clearly (for example, Paivio, 1971*c*, 1975*b*, 1975*d*). It will therefore be appropriate to characterise contemporary approaches to the study of mental imagery with particular reference to Paivio's writings.

The basic problem with which all of Paivio's research has been concerned is that of discovering a way to study mental imagery which is consistent with the methodology of behaviourist psychology. His fundamental aim has been to demonstrate to behaviourist psychologists that the concept of mental imagery, while admittedly 'mentalistic', can nevertheless be of real scientific value (Paivio, 1971*c*, p. iii). His method has been to work within a systematic associationistic framework of the classical behaviourist variety (Neisser, 1972*a*), and to adopt a rigorous methodology which would satisfy even the strictest behaviourists (Sheikh, 1977). Yuille and Catchpole (1977) have recently suggested that Paivio was forced to 'adopt a defensive stance concerning the appropriateness of imagery as a psychological concept' to compensate for his 'radical departure from the theoretical tenets of his peers'. However, I do not believe that Paivio has ever questioned or deviated from a strict behaviourist methodology. It is clear that he has always accepted the behaviourists' scruples concerning the everyday concept of mental imagery (namely, that it is a mentalistic concept referring to a private experience, and that it requires a radically different sort of treatment if it is to become part of a scientific cognitive psychology). The theoretical framework described in Paivio's (1971c) *Imagery and Verbal Processes* assigned to mental imagery a status which was entirely equivalent to that granted to verbal mediation in standard classical association-ism (Neisser, 1972a). As Richardson (1974b) remarked in reviewing that book, although Paivio's aim was to show that mental imagery could be fitted into something which behaviourist psychologists would accept as a psychological theory, his own predilection for such an approach is quite obvious. It is this primarily which supports the judgement that contemporary psychological research into mental imagery, heavily influenced as it is by Paivio, his collaborators and his students, involves no 'paradigm shift', and indeed involves no major methodological deviation from traditional American behaviourism.

But how is the 'mentalistic' concept of imagery located within this sort of framework? Paivio's solution to this problem is to interpret mental imagery as a theoretical concept with behavioural, operational indicators (Paivio, 1975d). He thus adopts the approach characteristic of the second phase of the behaviourist revolution, that of identifying mental concepts as hypothetical constructs which are used to explain patterns of behaviour. Such a construct is to be defined by operational procedures which serve to specify an observable, measurable concept (Paivio, 1975b), and thus appear to solve the general problem of how to carry out an objective, scientific investigation of a subjective, private experience. Paivio himself certainly does not regard this approach as involving a 'paradigm shift' from the principles of behaviourist methodology, as the following remark makes clear: 'Operational procedures are devised to establish a link between hypothetical inner events and observable events, permitting inferences to be made about the former. There is nothing new about this principle, since it has been standard procedure for studying intervening variables and symbolic processes for at least 60 years . . .' (Paivio, 1975d).

Three sorts of operational procedure have constituted the basis of most of the experimental research into the psychological importance of mental imagery (Paivio, 1972, 1975d):

1. The use of instructions to experimental subjects to employ mental imagery in carrying out psychological tasks. By far the greatest interest has been in the effects of such instructions upon human learning and memory; this research will be discussed in chapter 6.

2. The measurement of the extent to which the stimulus material is reported to produce mental imagery by the experimental subjects, and the extent to which these reports predict variations in performance in psychological tasks with different samples of material. Again, a primary area of research has been the study of the relationship between such reports of the image-evoking potential of experimental material and the memorability of that material. This research will be discussed in chapters 7 and 8.

3. The comparison of different experimental subjects in terms of their reports of the subjective vividness of experienced mental imagery and in terms of their performance in tests of spatial manipulation ability. These procedures, and the extent to which they predict differences among experimental subjects in terms of their performance in tests of learning and memory, will be discussed in chapter 9.

When a psychologist attempts to specify various hypothetical constructs in developing a theory of cognitive processing, the usefulness of those constructs 'depends on the adequacy of the defining operations and the research procedures used to test the properties that have been theoretically attributed to them' (Paivio, 1971c, p. 6). The adequacy of the operational procedures defining a given theoretical construct is to be demonstrated in the course of empirical investigations. A minimal requirement is that each procedure should show meaningful correlations with performance in various psychological tasks. To anticipate the more detailed discussion in the later chapters of this book, it may be mentioned that the first two sorts of operational procedure (the use of imagery instructions and the study of stimulus attributes) have been generally successful in producing the desired relationships, whereas the third sort of procedure (the study of individual differences) has been much less successful.

However, satisfying this requirement of the adequacy of an operational definition will not guarantee that the various procedures are defining a single theoretical construct. Psychologists who work within this sort of operationalist framework usually require that the various logically independent operational procedures be demonstrated to 'converge' on the theoretical construct (Kosslyn and Pomerantz, 1977). This concept of convergence is typically never explained in any serious way, but for the present it is sufficient to say that it includes the idea that the various operational procedures show meaningful interactions in terms of their effects upon performance in psychological tasks (cf. Paivio, 1971c, p. 9; 1972). This can be illustrated by observing that concepts may be defined by means of several procedures in other sciences besides psychology. For example, a chemical substance may be defined in terms of its perceptual qualities (its colour or texture, for example), in terms of its melting point or its boiling point, and in terms of its atomic weight. But the adequacy of this definition depends upon the fact that the substance with the specified perceptual qualities is regularly found, on investigation, to have the appropriate melting point or boiling point, and the appropriate atomic weight. Thus, the various definitional properties are held together by purely empirical regularities (cf. Richardson, 1976c, pp. 123–4; Wittgenstein, 1953, §79; 1967, §§438–9). Similarly, the adequacy of a theoretical construct in cognitive psychology is supported by the demonstration of reliable and meaningful interactive relationships among the operational procedures defining the construct in terms of their effects upon performance in various experimental situations. Thus, the use of several procedures to define a theoretical construct need not indicate any inherent ambiguity or other unscientific quality in the concept. Indeed, Garner, Hake, and Eriksen (1956) argued that the use of a single operational procedure might mean that the theoretical construct would simply come to be identified with the instrument being used to measure the construct (cf. 'Intelligence tests merely measure the ability to do intelligence tests').

In contemporary psychological research, therefore, mental imagery is characterised as a theoretical, covert reaction which is to be defined by behavioural operations. I wish to emphasise that mental imagery is usually not characterised as a conscious experience, nor is it defined by reference to conscious introspection (Paivio, 1975*d*, 1978*b*). Whether mental imagery is a conscious psychological process or not is taken to be irrelevant to its importance and adequacy as a theoretical construct (Bugelski, 1977; Paivio, 1971*b*; 1971*c*, pp. 135–6). As Marks (1977) has mentioned, 'The mental image has been allowed to re-enter the arena of scientific psychology on condition that it be stripped of its mental and phenomenological aspects.' Some researchers do consider that the subjects' introspective reports may provide useful data to be encompassed by a satisfactory theory of mental imagery (for example, Kosslyn and Pomerantz, 1977; Lindauer, 1977; Paivio, 1975*d*). Doob (1972) suggested that psychologists might carry out experimental investigations of either *reported* images which are 'mentioned or described verbally by the subjects experiencing them', or *inferred* images which the investigator ascribes to the subjects on the basis of variations in the experimental procedure or in their objective performance. Nevertheless, most cognitive psychologists remain suspicious of introspective reports and sceptical of their value as empirical data. For example, Bower (1970*a*) claimed that 'people utter an awful lot of nonsense about their mental imagery . . . . The normal person's introspections are frequently neither very discriminating nor particularly valid . . . .' Again, Neisser (1972*b*) suggested that asking subjects for introspections was 'a little like asking them to describe the shifting cloud formations of a stormy sky'. There is also the problem of how the two sorts of investigation mentioned by Doob are to be related, and which should take precedence should they lead to contrary conclusions.

The position that mental imagery is a theoretical construct has implications for its epistemological and ontological status. When an ordinary empirical entity functions as a datum in a scientific investigation, its existence is not open to question; rather, it is part of the evidence on the basis of which the investigator arrives at various theoretical conclusions. However, a theoretical construct is a hypothetical entity whose existence cannot be assumed; it must be demonstrated by the procedures specified within a theoretical framework. Thus, we find that contemporary psychologists do not regard mental imagery as an interesting empirical phenomenon, but as a hypothetical entity whose existence must be proved in the course of experimental investigation (Hayes, 1973; Janssen, 1976, p. 16). Of course, this latter claim sounds distinctly odd, and some psychologists have tried to claim at the same time that the existence of mental imagery, at least as a phenomenal experience, is undeniable (Anderson, 1978; Kosslyn and Pomerantz, 1977; Paivio, 1975*d*; Pylyshyn, 1973). How the same term can be used to refer to an empirical phenomenon *and* a theoretical construct is never clearly explained (cf. Holt, 1972). More seriously, if a psychologist wishes to claim that the experience of imagery is undeniable, he must show how he knows of this experience, in the case of both himself and others, and why his claim is not subject to the standard behaviourist objections to the introspective reporting of mental experience.

Generally speaking, then, contemporary psychology has attempted to solve the problem of how to investigate mental imagery by identifying it as a theoretical construct with an operational definition. As was remarked previously, this is a standard and uncontroversial procedure within behaviourist methodology. Bugelski (1971) described the procedure as follows:

> The problem of defining images is not essentially different from the problems commonly faced by psychologists in defining many of their working concepts like *intelligence, habit, drive, personality,* or *cognitive dissonance.* The general approach to definition of such hypothetical constructs or concepts is that of operationism which, in the words of Hull, tries to 'anchor' such assumed mechanisms, devices, states, or processes at both ends of an S–R sequence—by spelling out the procedures and measurements applied to the independent and dependent variables under study. In practice, the operational procedure specifies certain conditions under which some alleged phenomenon, process, or state can be postulated to exist.

However, many psychologists feel that they have to go beyond the specification of operational procedures, because these identify the function of mental imagery, rather than its nature (cf. Neisser, 1972a). Many suggested definitions emphasise the relationship between mental imagery and perception. Thus, Neisser (1972b) claimed that 'a subject is imaging whenever he employs some of the same cognitive processes that he would use in perceiving, but when the stimulus input that would normally give rise to such perception is absent'. Unfortunately, this suggestion is not really helpful, since it does not distinguish between voluntary imagery and hallucinations. (It also seems to imply that after-images are not examples of mental imagery, since they are normally produced by a specifiable 'stimulus input'.) Moreover, what is meant by the phrase 'employs some of the same cognitive processes' is not explained, and so it is difficult to know how in principle one would verify, from this definition, that someone were imaging.

(The question of the precise relationship between mental imagery and perception is a difficult one, but not one which need cause undue concern here. At least three different sorts of suggestion have been made. First, that mental images are like perceptions. This stems from the classical position that both imaging and perceiving involve the apprehension of ideas, and that there are no intrinsic properties which distinguish the two sorts of idea. Second, that mental images are based upon perceptions. This occurs in the traditional empiricist theory that mental images are representations produced by perceptual experience: see Yuille and Catchpole, 1977. Clearly, it cannot explain the creative capacity of mental imagery. Third, that mental imagery and perception are functionally overlapping. This idea is contained in Neisser's 'definition' of mental imagery, and has produced much interesting research on the possibility of using one sort of process to interfere with the other: see chapters 4, 6, 7 and 8. Neisser's more recent writings have involved the more complex idea that mental images are anticipatory phases of perceptual activity: Neisser, 1976, pp. 130, 170–1. It does seem to be the case that the domain of possible objects of perception is coextensive with the domain of possible objects of mental imagery. Nevertheless, Neisser's 'definition' appears to be based upon the unwarranted conclusion that the processes of apprehending the two sorts of object are overlapping. The issue of the functional relationship between perception and mental imagery is to be resolved as much through conceptual analysis as through empirical investigation.)

It is important to ask whether it is legitimate to try to fill out a hypothetical construct by suggesting theoretical properties which are not clearly tied to operational procedures. Paivio (1975*d*) has claimed that it *is* legitimate, and that no one has really believed that the meaning of any theoretical concept is exhausted by defining operations: 'The investigator must have some kind of theoretical definition of a concept in mind or he would have no basis for selecting a particular indicator and no motivation to look for one. Pure operationism is accordingly impossible.' However, it is obvious that operational procedures constitute the only basis for carrying out an empirical investigation of a theoretical construct. Thus, any hypothesis which relates to properties of the theoretical construct which have not been 'unpacked' or translated into operational procedures will be untestable. It is therefore the duty of the theorist to ensure that his theoretical constructs are unpacked thoroughly, and are exhaustively specified by defining operations. This involves making unambiguous predictions concerning the empirical effects (both simple and interactive) of the various operational procedures upon performance. Paivio's own account of mental imagery appears to be inadequate in just this respect, since he conceded that he was unable to make specific predictions concerning possible interactions among the operational procedures in terms of their effects upon performance (for example, Paivio, 1971*c*, p. 502).

2.4 DUAL CODING THEORY

The theoretical framework proposed by Paivio (1971*c*) identified two sorts of coding or representation which might be used by subjects in a variety of psychological tasks. The theory was originally suggested on the basis of experimental research carried out during the 1960s, but Paivio's position on the role of mental imagery in human memory has remained essentially unchanged up to the present time (see, for example, Paivio, 1978*b*, 1979).

The basic theoretical approach is that 'images and verbal processes are viewed as alternative coding systems, or modes of symbolic representation' (Paivio, 1971c, p. 8). They are postulated as two basic 'cognitive modes' (Paivio, 1971b), as 'separate representational systems for nonverbal and verbal information' (Paivio, 1975b). A more detailed specification is the following (Paivio, 1979):

> The theory assumes that cognitive behavior is mediated by two independent but richly interconnected symbolic systems, which are specialized for encodirg, organizing, transforming, storing, and retrieving information. One (the *image* system) is specialized for dealing with perceptual information concerning nonverbal objects and events. The other (the *verbal* system) is specialized for dealing with linguistic information. The systems differ in the nature of the representational units, the way the units are organized into higher order structures, and the way the structures can be reorganized or transformed.

Elsewhere, Paivio (1975c) suggested that we 'distinguish the verbal system as an abstract, logical mode of thinking as compared to the concrete, analogical mode that apparently characterizes imagery'.

As these quotations suggest, there are several important respects in which the two hypothesised systems are assumed to differ. Paivio (1978b) has recently discussed these in some detail. The most important assumption is that of the 'independence-interconnectedness' of the two systems. They are intended to be functionally independent, so that either system may operate or be experimentally manipulated in isolation of the other system. However, they are also assumed to be richly interconnected, and it is more typical that the two systems interact continuously in a particular situation. Indeed, they are so closely related that 'whether these are regarded as distinct symbolic systems or as two kinds of sub-processes within a single system is probably irrelevant in a formal sense' (Paivio, 1975b).

Given a dichotomous system of this nature, it is possible logically to identify three levels at which information may be processed. The first is the *representational* level, where the sensory trace produced by a stimulus when it is perceived arouses the appropriate symbolic representation in long-term memory; thus, words activate verbal representations, and perceptual experiences activate imaginal representations. The second is the *referential* level, where symbolic representations in one system arouse corresponding representations in the other system; these interconnections are involved in naming objects or describing images, and in generating the image of an object when given its name. Finally, the *associative* level involves associative connections among imaginal or verbal representations, or both. Whether the processes at any of these three 'levels of processing' or 'levels of meaning' are involved in a given psychological task is assumed to depend upon particular characteristics of the task; this assumption gives rise to various empirical hypotheses concerning the effects of imaginal and linguistic variables in different experimental situations (Paivio, 1971c, 1972).

Another major assumption is that the two systems are taken to be different in the way in which their units are organised into higher-order structures. The imaginal system is assumed to represent information in a synchronous or spatially parallel manner, so that different components of a complex thing or scene are simultaneously available. On the other hand, the verbal system is taken to employ the sequential organisation which is characteristic of linguistic utterances. Similarly, the imaginal system is assumed to be capable of transformations along spatial dimensions, such as size, shape and orientation, whereas the verbal system is taken to allow transformations on a sequential frame, such as additions, deletions and changes in sequential ordering.

One of the major purposes of Paivio's research was to argue for the inherent inadequacy of theories of memory based upon the assumption of a single, verbal code. Such theories were popular up to the 1960s, but research on the role of mental imagery was generally taken to present grave difficulties for such accounts. Accordingly, dual coding theory was very successful, and was at first accepted by most psychologists investigating mental imagery as providing essentially the correct framework for subsequent research (for example, Bower, 1970a, 1972). However, in the last decade various theories have been put forward to try to handle the results of this research within a single hypothetical system, in a manner which was not subject to the limitations of the traditional verbal coding model.

2.5 COMMON CODING THEORY

This approach appears to stem from some ideas expressed by Bower (1972) at a conference in 1969. Although at that time he generally seems to have accepted the assumptions of dual coding theory, Bower specifically disagreed with Paivio over the organisational properties of the two hypothesised systems. On the basis of his own experiments on the effects of imagery instructions upon memory performance (see chapter 6), Bower argued that roughly the same general principles of relational organisation applied to imaginal and verbal representations. Indeed, he speculated that 'we may have a common generative grammar that underlies our verbal production of sentences and our imaginal production of visualized scenes or of hand-drawn pictures'. In a subsequent paper, Bower (1970b) made a more radical proposal. He suggested that this relational generating system 'may be a "conceptual deep structure" . . . into which sentences and perceptual experiences are translated for storage and out of which either surface sentences, imagery, or drawings may be generated, depending on the material and the task demands'.

This idea has become an important part of several theories of long-term memory which assume that information is represented in memory at an abstract level by networks of propositions (for example, Anderson and Bower, 1973; Pylyshyn, 1973; Rumelhart, Lindsay, and Norman, 1972; Yuille and Catchpole,

1977). These theories were originally devised to handle the results of experiments on the comprehension and retention of narrative by postulating abstract semantic representations (propositions) which were related in complex structures or networks (see chapter 9). However, it soon became obvious that it would be parsimonious to represent perceptual and linguistic information in a common propositional base which would be neutral with respect to the source of that information. That is, all cognitive and mnemonic processes should be explained by a single system of abstract propositional representations. Mental imagery should not therefore be regarded as implicating a qualitatively distinct form of mental representation. (Not all propositional theorists have made this step. In particular, Kintsch has assumed that mental images and propositions have underlying representations which are structurally distinct and functionally independent: see Jorgensen and Kintsch, 1973; Kintsch, 1974.)

Superficially, at least, dual coding theory and common coding theory appear to be quite different explanatory frameworks, and one might expect that it would be entirely possible to decide between them on purely empirical grounds. In fact, the situation is much more complicated, and a considerable amount of discussion has taken place concerning the appropriate experimental tests of the two positions. However, propositional theorists have also attempted to attack dual coding theory on conceptual grounds, by arguing that mental imagery is not a theoretically adequate form of mental representation. Before discussing the evidence for each of these theoretical positions, therefore, it is important to consider these arguments in some detail.

2.6 CONCEPTUAL CRITICISMS OF MENTAL IMAGERY

The most extensive critique of mental imagery as an explanatory construct has been given by Pylyshyn (1973). His ideas have been discussed in great detail by Kosslyn and Pomerantz (1977) and by Anderson (1978). Pylyshyn stated his position in the following way:

> It should be stressed that the existence of the experience of imagery cannot be questioned. Imagery is a pervasive form of experience and is clearly of utmost importance to humans. We cannot speak of consciousness without, at the same time, implicating the existence of images. Such experiences are not in question here. Nor, in fact, is the study of imagery either as object of study (i.e., as dependent variable) or as scientific evidence being challenged.

It is clear that Pylyshyn's approach is much less restricted than the standard behaviourist position: he accepts the existence and importance of mental imagery, and regards mental imagery both as a possible source of scientific evidence and as a possible object of scientific investigation. The main question which he wishes to consider is 'whether the concept of image can be used as a primitive explanatory construct (i.e., one not requiring further reduction) in psychological theories of cognition'.

Referring to the writings of Chomsky (1964), Pylyshyn claimed that an adequate theoretical description must possess 'explanatory adequacy'. However, Chomsky employed this expression in a very specific sense: a theoretical framework has explanatory adequacy when it specifies a general procedure for constructing a particular model (for instance, a grammar) for describing empirical data from a particular situation (for instance, a corpus of utterances from a natural language). This idea does not seem to be at all relevant to Pylyshyn's concern, and so one must conclude that his appeal to Chomsky's work was otiose. Nevertheless, it appears that an explanation is inadequate for Pylyshyn in the event that it fails 'to be mechanistic insofar as it may use terms such as "want", "guess", "notice", or "mind's eye", which, while they may faithfully reflect one's experience of doing the task, are inadequate as *primitive constructs* since they themselves cry out for a reduction to mechanistic terms'. This quotation indicates that Pylyshyn demands a reductionist definition of one's primitive constructs in terms of purely physical, mechanistic concepts, and a reductionist explanation of the phenomena which those constructs were intended to explain. It is by no means clear that reductionist explanations can always be produced. Putnam (1973) has given the example of explaining why a certain square peg will not fit into a certain round hole: an account of the peg's atomic structure would not make use of essential emergent properties such as rigidity and shape, and would thus be inadequate. Even if a reductionist explanation can be given, it may not be the sort of explanation required on a particular occasion. Finally, a reductionist explanation of concepts such as 'want', 'guess' and 'image' would imply a radical materialist theory of mind which many psychologists would find unacceptable.

Pylyshyn suggested further than an explanatory theory 'must be shown to be capable of providing a mechanistic explanation for the widest possible domain of empirical evidence in a manner which reveals the most general principles involved. An explanatory account must ultimately appeal to universal mechanistic principles'. Nevertheless, there seems to be no good reason to require that an adequate psychological explanation be based upon universal principles. However common such principles might be in other domains of scientific investigation, they seem to be exceedingly rare in psychology. Psychological facts are much more typically expressed in the form of qualified particular sentences. It might perhaps be of interest (even desirable) if one could specify general laws of human behaviour, but in the current state of the discipline it would be arbitrary to criticise theories of mental imagery as opposed to those in any other area of psychology for not having achieved a sufficient degree of generality.

One of the principal targets of Pylyshyn's article is the use of the picture metaphor in explaining and defining mental imagery (see also Anderson and Bower, 1973, pp. 453–4). Pylyshyn suggested that 'the whole vocabulary of imagery uses a language appropriate for describing pictures and the process of perceiving pictures. We speak of clarity and vividness of images, of scanning images, of seeing new patterns in images, and of naming objects or properties depicted in images.' He agreed that metaphors are important in developing scientific ideas, but he suggested that some metaphors might be inappropriate or positively misleading. In particular, the picture metaphor implies that what one receives from memory when one has a mental image has to be scanned and interpreted perceptually in order to obtain meaningful information about the presence of objects, properties, relations, and so on. On the contrary, Pylyshyn argued, mental images come already interpreted and organised; and when one forgets part of an image, what is missing is some integral object or attribute, not some arbitrary segment like a torn corner from a photograph.

There is no doubt that the picture metaphor is present in contemporary discussions of mental imagery. Thus, Segal (1971a) referred to 'one of the oldest of mental phenomena: the internal picture or mental image'. Neisser (1972b) suggested that the metaphor merely harked back to classical theories of perception and memory in which perceiving was like looking at pictures, and remembering was like looking at them a second time. Nevertheless, Paivio (1976c), Bugelski (1977) and Kosslyn and Pomerantz (1977) have all argued that the picture metaphor is not held by any serious study of mental imagery as a working hypothesis, and that the proponent of the picture theory attacked by Pylyshyn is merely a straw man. Janssen (1976, p. 19) has suggested that, if the picture metaphor *is* misleading, then one should look for better ways in which to conceptualise mental imagery, rather than abandon the concept altogether. Indeed, Anderson (1978) refused to accept Pylyshyn's arguments, and he concluded that it is still an open question whether the picture metaphor is misleading:

> It has not been shown that there is anything incoherent, contradictory, or impractical in using pictures as a representational format. Whether pictures are suitable depends on the processes that one assumes operate on them. To be sure, one can assume inadequate processes for a picture representation (e.g., a forgetting process that consisted of fading rather than loss of meaningful subparts) as did Anderson and Bower, Pylyshyn, and even some of the imagery theorists. But, then again, one need not.

Anderson's point concerning the distinction between process and representation will be discussed in more detail in a moment.

Pylyshyn went on to argue that the interpretation of mental images as representations of uninterpreted sensory information entailed 'an incredible burden on the storage capacity of the brain. In fact, since there is no limit to the variety of sensory patterns which are possible (since no two sensory events are objectively identical), it would require an unlimited storage capacity'. Kosslyn and Pomerantz (1977) gave three different objections to the force of this proposal as an argument against dual coding theory. First, most researchers in mental imagery agree with Pylyshyn that mental images come already interpreted and organised, and should not be assimilated to 'raw', uninterpreted patterns of sensory activity. If mental images are taken to be composed of relatively large, interpreted, perceptual 'chunks', then the amount of storage capacity required may be much reduced. Second, in any case we simply do not have any accurate idea of either the storage capacity of the brain or the amount of information contained in a mental image. There is thus no sound basis for claiming that the representation of mental images would make unreasonable demands upon the storage facilities of the human brain (see also Bugelski, 1977). Finally, the objection appears to apply with equal force to the major alternative theories of cognitive representation. It is difficult to make any clear comparison between dual coding theory and propositional theories, since there is no criterion for deciding which of an indefinite number of sets of propositions best represents the scene or event depicted by a given mental image. Nevertheless, as far as specific proposals by the proponents of common coding theory are concerned, vast numbers of propositions seem to be necessary to represent even relatively simple configurations of objects. As Anderson (1978) concluded: 'The simple fact may be that there is a great deal of information in an image and any representation of an image will have to acknowledge this fact.'

One of Pylyshyn's most important arguments is that dual coding theory is incoherent without the assumption of a third code or representation which is amodal and propositional in nature:

> But the need to postulate a more abstract representation—one which resembles neither pictures nor words and is not accessible to subjective experience—is unavoidable. As long as we recognize that people can go from mental pictures to mental words or vice versa, we are forced to conclude that there must be a representation (which is more abstract and not available to conscious experience) which encompasses both. There must, in other words, be some common format or interlingua.

Similar suggestions have been made by Anderson and Bower (1973, p. 453), Clark and Chase (1972) and Moscovitch (1973). However, Anderson (1978) pointed out that Pylyshyn's argument leads to an infinite regress, since it may be applied with equal force to the problem of translation between either of the two original representations and the postulated third code. Kosslyn and Pomerantz (1977) suggested that, however complex the transformation rules might be for carrying out translations between imaginal and verbal representations, it would be a mistake to suppose that such processes or routines constituted an additional, intermediate form of representation. Finally, Janssen (1976, p. 18) argued that, even if a propositional representation were necessary on *a priori* grounds, and even if it could be shown to be structurally isomorphic to any imaginal representation, this would not prove that the latter was redundant, since the two representations might have quite different functional properties.

Having considered Pylyshyn's arguments against the idea of mental imagery as a mnemonic representation, Kosslyn and Pomerantz (1977) reviewed empirical evidence which might be interpreted as supporting the functional utility of such a code. They considered two possible theoretical positions: one was the standard dual coding theory, which assumes that imaginal and verbal codes are adequate for the representation of information in memory; the other was a weaker position which accepts the necessity of propositions as a representational system, but which holds that mental imagery may also make a contribution, since mental images have emergent properties which propositions lack. Kosslyn and Pomerantz discussed the findings of a variety of experiments, and came to the following conclusion: 'We have found no reason to discard imagery as an explanatory construct in psychology, either on structural or functional grounds. There are no convincing arguments that images are not represented in a distinct format, nor can imagery phenomena be easily accounted for by appealing to propositional representations.' Nevertheless, they confessed themselves to be unable to discriminate between the 'weak' and 'strong' positions on the role of mental imagery, and they suggested that 'this question may be basically unanswerable'.

The most recent detailed discussion of these problems is that of Anderson (1978). He considered 'a representative subset' of the experimental evidence discussed by Kosslyn and Pomerantz, and concluded that in each case what had been taken as evidence for a particular representation was actually evidence for a possible process operating upon the representation, where there was no good reason to associate the process with that particular representation. The crux of Anderson's paper is that this is a general problem to be faced in deciding among different theoretical positions in any area of cognitive psychology:

It is not possible for behavioral data to decide uniquely issues of internal representation. The reason is that one cannot just test questions about a representation in the abstract. One must perform tests of the representation in combination with certain assumptions about the processes that use the representation. That is, one must test a representation-process pair. One can show that, given a set of assumptions about an image representation and a set of processes that operate upon it, one can construct an equivalent set of assumptions about a propositional representation and its processes. Or one can be given a propositional theory and construct an equivalent imagery theory. In fact, it is possible to establish a more general claim: Given any representation–process pair it is possible to construct other pairs with different representations whose behavior is equivalent to it. These pairs make up for differences in representation by assuming compensating differences in the processes.

Anderson's paper contains a formal proof of this latter assertion, and a concrete example of how one may generate a propositional model to mimic a plausible imaginal model of mental rotation (see chapter 4).

Thus, one has a rigorous and apparently general demonstration of the proposition that it is not possible to decide between imaginal and propositional representations strictly on the basis of behavioural data. Anderson considered various alternative, non-behavioural criteria for deciding among hypothesised representations. Most of these are formal criteria, concerning the logical structure of the proposed representations; these include parsimony, plausibility, efficiency and optimality. Such criteria have to do with the manner in which rival theories describe the findings which have actually been obtained. Only one set of criteria is substantive, in the sense that it is relevant to determining whether a theory correctly describes the operation of the causal mechanism underlying the behaviour to be explained. These criteria involve the use of physiological data and of neuropsychological experimentation to establish the cerebral localisation of the hypothesised functions.

Anderson considered that none of these alternative criteria was of much assistance in discriminating among different types of cognitive representation. He concluded that psychological theories of cognitive representation were in principle *non-identifiable*, such that no theory could give rise to a unique set of empirical predictions. Although this should dissuade researchers from attempting to discover the 'true' theory, Anderson suggested that one might proceed in a less ambitious direction:

> This is to formulate a more-or-less complete model without a commitment to discriminate it from all other possible models. Nonidentifiability results imply that there are other models which will generate the same predictions. However, the important fact is that many models will not generate the same predictions. One's nonunique model is perfectly capable of being tested and proven wrong. In proving it wrong one would also be proving wrong all of its equivalent models. It is no mean feat to come up with a model capable of accounting for the existing range of empirical facts. I think it is a fair statement that no current model handles the existing range of results on imagery. Producing such a model seems a more worthwhile endeavour than deciding among the grand contrasts such as imagery versus propositional.

Anderson seems to adopt a *fictionalist* or possibly a *sceptical* position on the epistemological status of theories of cognitive representation. A fictionalist believes that hypothetical entities have a status analogous to fictional characters: their names (the theoretical terms in a scientific explanation) may be used in the sorts of sentence-frame which are used to talk about real objects, but it does not make sense to ask whether they exist. A sceptic believes that they may exist, but that there is in principle no way of establishing whether they do or not (see Harré, 1972, chap. 3).

However, I believe that most psychologists would find this stance unpalatable, and that instead they would adopt a form of epistemological *realism*, according to which many hypothetical entities are believed to exist, and some may be shown to exist. The purpose of psychology is to investigate human faculties, and the role of psychological theories is to specify putative mechanisms which underlie those faculties. This will involve ascribing properties to those structures which are causally responsible for the behaviour being studied, in particular the structures of the human brain. Any adequate theory must therefore postulate hypothetical entities which must be considered at least as candidates for objective existence among the physiological structures of the central nervous system. This entails that physiological data and neuropsychological research will be of immense value in discriminating among alternative theories. Moreover, since these theories are offering putative descriptions of the real mechanisms responsible for behaviour, the truth or falsehood of those descriptions must in principle be demonstrable. (Further discussion of these points is contained in chapter 3.)

This approach is actually supported by Anderson's account of an experiment by Patterson and Bradshaw (1975) which he himself described as 'particularly interesting'. This study employed a face-recognition task to test the conventional idea that different representations are used in the two cerebral hemispheres (see chapter 9). Anderson interpreted the results to mean that the two hemispheres differ in their ability to perform certain types of operation upon a common representation of visual information. This is exactly the sort of conclusion which is necessary to specify the functions of the two cerebral hemispheres and the nature of cognitive representation, but it is the sort of conclusion which can only be made if neuropsychological evidence is relevant to deciding among different theories of cognitive representation.

2.7 CONCLUSIONS

Doubtless a great deal more could be said concerning the attempts of psychologists since the beginning of this century to carry through a systematic investigation of mental imagery. It will be sufficient, however, if I have managed to give some idea of the historical background to contemporary research, and to explain at least in rough terms the methodological framework in which that research is carried out. That framework is a thorough-going behaviourism of the traditional American variety, softened slightly by the addition of operationism. In contemporary cognitive psychology, then, concepts relating to mental states, events and processes may only be introduced as hypothetical constructs within an articulated theory, which specifies operational, behavioural procedures for investigating and defining those constructs. In particular, mental imagery is a theoretical construct whose existence is inferred from patterns of behaviour and performance in experimental tasks.

To some extent this account has oversimplified the true situation. Contemporary research encompasses a range of methodological positions, which vary in how closely they are tied to an operationist approach. At one end of the spectrum, there is the neobehaviourist position of Bugelski (1971, 1977) who adopts a rigorous operationism, and who defines mental imagery as a covert reaction which is 'at no time . . . equated with phenomenal or "mental" experience'. At the other end, there is the position of Alan Richardson (1969), who emphasises the phenomenal aspects of mental imagery, but who fails to specify an explicit, coherent methodology for experimental research (Bugelski, 1971). However, Neisser (1972a) has pointed out that Richardson's book is written in the classical, introspectionist mould, and does not reflect the current state of research into mental imagery. In between these two extremes, there is the neomentalism of Paivio (1971c, 1975d), which is claimed to combine the introspectionist and behaviourist traditions 'in that it embraces mental phenomena as its subject matter and behavioural approaches as the method of study'. (It should also be pointed out that this book is concerned almost entirely with research carried out in English-speaking countries. In European countries, psychologists have never departed to the same extent from the introspective method. However, although American and British psychologists are beginning to consider the implications of European phenomenological research, it has so far had little impact on the specific field of mental imagery.)

There are two further, related problems which should be mentioned briefly. In contemporary research, the theoretical construct of mental imagery is defined by reference to various operational procedures, of which the three most important were described earlier in this chapter. However, each of these procedures involves the use of the term 'imagery' in the instructions given to the experimental subjects. Investigations of mental imagery as a mnemonic aid include instructions to the subjects to use mental imagery in their learning; and research on both stimulus attributes and individual differences includes questionnaires in which the subjects judge the extent to which various stimuli evoke mental imagery. It is surely circular to offer an operational definition of a theoretical term if the specified operations involve the use of that term (cf. Bugelski, 1971). Even if the manoeuvre is not actually circular, it still begs the question of how the subjects know what the term means, and the question of whether their interpretation of this term corresponds to the psychologist's. Presumably, the subjects in an experiment have learned the meaning of the expression 'mental imagery' in everyday discourse with all its 'mental and phenomenological aspects'. But in that case the behaviourist's operational definition of mental imagery is still contaminated by a surreptitious reference to 'private' experience. This semantic point has certain psychological implications. Earlier in this chapter, it was mentioned that whether mental imagery is a conscious experience or not is usually taken to be irrelevant to its adequacy as a theoretical construct. In fact, as Marks (1977) has pointed out, the operational procedures which are taken to define that construct actually assume a conscious awareness on the part of the subjects of the mental imagery evoked by the stimulus material, and of the strategies employed in remembering that material.

The second problem concerns the psychologist's motivation for using the term 'mental imagery' in the first place. If a term is rigorously defined by certain operations, and if it is introduced to refer to a hypothetical construct within a scientific theory, it is not clear why one should employ a term which is already in common currency with an informal, unscientific meaning. On the contrary, one might expect this to be a rich source of confusion. Since the operations already refer to mental imagery, it might have been thought reasonable to use the term in theorising ('Mental imagery is what people use when told to use mental imagery'). However, it is more likely that an individual psychologist considered 'mental imagery' to be an appropriate label for his theoretical construct before he had determined particular operational indicators for that construct (cf. Paivio, 1975*d*). Presumably, the label was appropriate because the theoretical construct bore certain similarities to the everyday concept of mental imagery. In this case, it is important to ask how the two concepts differ, and whether an ordinary-language concept can function as a hypothetical construct within a psychological theory. In order to answer these questions, it is necessary to attain a clear idea of the concept of mental imagery in ordinary language.

3

A Conceptual Analysis of Mental Imagery

The philosopher Ludwig Wittgenstein (1953, p. 232) once made the following remarks concerning the state of psychology in the 1940s:

> The confusion and barrenness of psychology is not to be explained by calling it a 'young science'; its state is not comparable with that of physics, for instance, in its beginnings . . . . For in psychology there are experimental methods and *conceptual confusion* . . . .
>
> The existence of the experimental method makes us think we have the means of solving the problems which trouble us; though problem and method pass one another by.

These remarks were addressed to the experimental methodology being propounded by behaviourist psychologists. In the previous chapter, I suggested that their attitudes have continued to be responsible for the nature of much research, especially in the area of cognitive psychology. The reservations which the behaviourists expressed concerning the concepts of mind and of mental states have had a very real effect in restricting the sorts of explanations which psychologists have considered themselves able to put forward. Nevertheless, like Wittgenstein, I consider that these attitudes do not stand up to any serious conceptual analysis. It follows that the restrictions which psychologists have placed upon their own theorising have been needless and counterproductive.

In order to substantiate this conclusion, it will be necessary to consider the behaviourists' methodology in more detail, and to demonstrate conceptual confusion in their own criticisms of the earlier introspectionist approach. Insofar as contemporary experimental research on mental imagery is heavily influenced by the behaviourist tradition, it will then be necessary to give an alternative conceptual analysis of mental imagery, and to determine the extent to which the experimental methods employed in current psychological research are adequate for investigating that concept.

3.1 THE BEHAVIOURIST CRITIQUE OF INTROSPECTIONISM

One of the most common epithets used by behaviourist psychologists in disparaging the efforts of their introspectionist predecessors was 'mentalistic'. But what does it mean to decry concepts such as imagery and attention as mentalistic (Holt, 1972)? Presumably, it means, among other things, 'appertaining to the mind', but this is tautological and in no way legitimates a critical rejection of such concepts. Can the epithet be related to a coherent philosophical position of *mentalism*, which might have been the target of the behaviourist movement? Holt (1972) attempted to argue that the behaviourist critique was directed against a metaphysical *dualism*, a philosophical analysis which assigned a separate metaphysical reality to mental events. It is clear that the introspectionist approach typically assumed that mind and body were ontologically separate and independent, and thus it involved an implicit form of metaphysical dualism. It is also clear that this sort of philosophical theory is inconsistent with metaphysical *materialism*, a position which reduces mind to body or to some property of body (Armstrong, 1968, p. 5), and which is implicit in a behaviourist approach to the study of mind. However, to regard the behaviourist critique of introspectionism as a philosophical attack upon metaphysical dualism is probably to assume a degree of philosophical sophistication among behaviourist psychologists which has typically been lacking. In any case, dualism is also inconsistent with metaphysical mentalism, at least in the way in which this latter position is usually understood, as a theory which reduces body to mind or some property of mind. This approach has not been seriously proposed by any philosopher of status in modern times, as Armstrong (1968, p. 6) has pointed out, and it certainly was not implicit in the ideas of the introspectionist movement. One can only conclude that the use of the term 'mentalistic' by behaviourist psychologists merely constituted a pejorative expression for deriding the earlier methodology in the absence of any serious analysis of the underlying conceptual issues.

Another term which is commonly used in describing personal experience in general and mental imagery in particular is the adjective 'private'. The concept of the privacy of introspection has been expressed in the following manner: 'We cannot observe any sensations or images but our own' (Knight and Knight, 1959, p. 3). This notion of privacy crops up frequently in all kinds of discussions, scientific or informal, philosophical or empirical, and the idea that mental events are inherently private is generally accepted as a truism. However, this acceptance is usually uncritical, and if one attempts to clarify what is meant by the word 'private', it too begins to lose its pejorative capacity. Wittgenstein (1953, §§246–53) pointed out that there are at least two different senses in which the word 'private' is used to talk about personal experience.

1. One sense has to do with the question of ownership: in this sense, it might be suggested that personal experiences are inalienable or unsharable, that only I can have my mental images, whereas another person cannot have them (Kenny, 1971). This might be accepted as a truism, even as tautological (although Wittgenstein commented that one still has to specify a criterion of identity, to explain what is meant by *my* mental images: §253). However, Kenny (1971)

pointed out that, if the inalienability of personal experience is a matter of definition, it is also comparatively uninformative about the nature of that experience. The definition serves to distinguish mental states and events from sharable entities like offices and bank accounts, but not from certain inalienable, yet purely behavioural entities, like coughs, blushes and sneezes, about which there is nothing especially mysterious, occult or unscientific. As Kenny concluded, one may allow that sensations, thoughts and images are inalienable, but this will not make them any more private than behaviour.

2. The second concept of privacy which was identified by Wittgenstein (1953, §246) and explained by Kenny (1971) has to do with the question of knowledge: in this sense, it might be suggested that personal experiences are incommunicable or undisclosable, that only I can know whether I have a mental image, whereas another person cannot know this. Of course, one need not seriously consider this idea: if the word 'know' is taken to have its normal meaning, it is clearly false, since other people sometimes do know whether a person has a mental image or not. Nevertheless, it is a position which constituted an important plank of the behaviourist attack upon introspectionism, and which is often taken for granted today. Thus, Doob (1972) asserted that mental events 'quite obviously are private and solipsistic and hence cannot be utilized scientifically . . . '. (The use of 'solipsistic' in this connection is rather puzzling. Solipsism is a particular form of mentalism which attempts to reduce body to *my* mind or some property of my mind. It is hard to see what point there would have been to the introspective method if its practitioners had held this philosophical position.) The undisclosable nature of personal experience is often characterised by the metaphor of the 'inner world', but this is typically even more obscure than the concept of privacy.

(Kenny identified a slightly different epistemological sense of privacy which has to do with the idea of secrecy, the idea that mental images *can be* kept secret without being publicly manifested in any way. One might wish to call undisclosed experiences private, but again this would be comparatively uninformative about the nature of those experiences. Moreover, a person might not wish to disclose the existence of an unslightly mole located somewhere on his body, or the size of his personal fortune, but undisclosed moles and fortunes are not in any way subjective or occult.)

If the claim that personal experience is incommunicable is so obviously false, why should anyone put it forward? As Kenny pointed out, one reason is a failure to distinguish between having and knowing, between inalienability and incommunicability. It is assumed that to know a sensation is to have a sensation, and because it is believed that one person cannot *have* another's sensations, it is concluded that one person cannot *know* another's sensations. The error is evident in Bower's (1972) assertion that 'by definition, I am not aware of my son's private mental event'; in this example, 'I am not aware of' is ambiguous between 'I cannot experience' and 'I cannot know'. It should be obvious that the concepts of inalienability and incommunicability are quite different, and should be rigorously separated in discussing the nature of personal experience.

Another reason for claiming that personal experience is incommunicable is that one's beliefs about another person's experience seem to be much less well founded than those about one's own experience. It might be argued that *I* can know whether I have a mental image, whereas another person can only surmise this (cf. Wittgenstein, 1953, §246); that the experiences of others are only inferred or conjectured, whereas one's own experiences are known with certainty. On this account, introspection provides the only conclusive evidence for statements describing personal experience, and this evidence is only available to the person who has that experience. It follows that introspective evidence cannot form the empirical basis of an objective, interpersonal, scientific discipline. It is not surprising therefore that, even though introspective evidence has always been available to behaviourist psychologists for consideration in their research, it has been continually ignored and regarded as quite inadequate. But in what sense might introspection provide evidence for the person who has a particular personal experience? A person who has a mental image and who introspects (whatever that might mean) does not acquire a particular set of evidence, on the basis of which he infers that he has a mental image; he merely apprehends that he has a mental image. It simply is not coherent to think of a person looking for evidence to find out whether he is having a mental image, unless the expression 'having a mental image' is being used in a manner (yet to be explained) which is systematically different from its ordinary, everyday usage. Thus, it is difficult to see how statements ascribing personal experiences to oneself can be based upon any sort of evidence, introspective or otherwise. (The question of the epistemological status of self-ascriptions of psychological states is actually a serious and difficult problem in the philosophy of mind.)

Nevertheless, a corollary of the position described in the previous paragraph is that any scientific investigation of a person's mental imagery must be restricted to the sort of fallible, inferential evidence which is available to others. The early behaviourists took this to mean that no *conclusive* evidence was available concerning another person's mental states, and that therefore there was no legitimate basis for even assuming the existence of those states. Watson (1928, p. 75) expressed this scepticism in the following way:

> The behaviorist, having made a clean sweep of all the rubbish called consciousness, comes back to you: 'Prove to me,' he says, 'that you have auditory images, visual images, or any other kinds of disembodied processes. So far I have only your unverified and unsupported word that you have them.' Science must have objective evidence to base its theories upon.

But is it really the case that the sort of evidence available to other people concerning a person's mental states is not conclusive? Baker (1974) has pointed out that the notion of conclusive evidence is typically ambiguous:

1. In one sense, one might say that evidence is conclusive if it is not logically

possible that it can be overturned. Clearly, the evidence available concerning another person's personal experience is not conclusive in this sense: he might be pretending to have an experience which he does not in fact have, or he might be withholding an experience which he does in fact have. But is this true of all sentient creatures? Is the supposition of either pretence or concealment sensible in the case of infants or animals, for instance (Kenny, 1971; Wittgenstein, 1953, §§249–50)? If not, then the behaviourist appears to be in the odd situation of having a legitimate basis for studying the mental states of infants and animals, but not for studying those of adult human beings. In any case, it should be pointed out that conclusive evidence (in this sense) is extremely rare in the knowledge-systems which we employ. It is characteristic of virtually any interesting knowledge-claim that it may in principle be overturned by subsequent counterevidence; for example, claims about ordinary physical objects may subsequently be found to be based upon hallucinations.

2. In another sense, one might say that evidence is conclusive if it is not logically possible that it could be improved. It is true that what one knows of another person's mental states is based upon what he says and does, and any knowledge-claim which one makes on this basis may in principle be overturned. But there is no other sort of evidence which could provide a sounder basis for such a claim. Our knowledge of other people's personal experience is not indirect or inferential: the evidence for knowledge-claims relating to that experience could in principle be overturned, but it could not in principle be bettered.

To sum up, therefore: on the first interpretation of the notion of conclusive evidence, there is no conclusive evidence for claims about another person's mental states, but there is no conclusive evidence for any other interesting class of knowledge-claim, either; on the second interpretation of the notion of conclusive evidence, what a person says and does provides just this sort of evidence and could constitute the basis of a scientific investigation of mental imagery.

3.2 THE NOTION OF A CRITERION

I shall now try to spell out a more positive argument for this latter conclusion by giving a conceptual analysis of mental imagery which is based upon the theory of criteria to be found in Wittgenstein's (1953, 1958, 1967) later philosophical writings. The idea of a criterion is an important device in his philosophy of language (Baker, 1974; Richardson, 1976c), and is central to his philosophy of mind (Hacker, 1972). It is a difficult concept, over which there has been much philosophical controversy, but it is important to get to grips with the concept of a criterion if one is to achieve a proper appreciation of the status of mental imagery.

Wittgenstein (1958, p. 24) suggested that, to obtain a systematic explanation of a concept, one must be able to specify what must be the case if that concept is correctly applied. The basis on which such an ascription is made he called a *criterion*. The criteria for the use of a word or phrase determine its meaning or sense. (They also specify what are to count as legitimate knowledge-claims: one can claim to know that a concept applies to a given object only if the criteria of that concept are satisfied.) Wittgenstein explained what kind of thing he had in mind in the following way:

> When we learnt the use of the phrase 'so-and-so has toothache' we were pointed out certain kinds of behaviour of those who were said to have toothache. As an instance of these kinds of behaviour let us take holding your cheek. Suppose that by observation I found that in certain instances whenever these first criteria told me a person had toothache, a red patch appeared on the person's cheek. Supposing I now said to someone 'I see A has toothache, he's got a red patch on his cheek'. He may ask me 'How do you know A has toothache when you see a red patch?' I shall then point out that certain phenomena had always coincided with the appearance of the red patch.
>
> Now one may go on and ask: 'How do you know that he has got toothache when he holds his cheek?' The answer to this might be, 'I say, *he* has toothache when he holds his cheek because I hold my cheek when I have toothache'. But what if we went on asking:—'And why do you suppose that toothache corresponds to his holding his cheek just because your toothache corresponds to your holding your cheek?' You will be at a loss to answer this question, and find that here we strike rock bottom, that is we have come down to conventions.

Thus, there are two kinds of evidence which might be used to justify the ascription of toothache to another person. The evidential value of criteria is guaranteed by linguistic convention: they are specified as the defining properties of a concept when it is taught. However, the evidential value of the other kinds of evidence which might support the application of a concept is guaranteed merely by their empirical correlation with its criteria. (Wittgenstein referred to this latter sort of evidence as the *symptoms* of the concept.)

It is characteristic of many concepts, according to Wittgenstein (1958, pp. 51, 143–4), that there are many different criteria for their application which might be employed under different circumstances. It follows that there is not necessarily one thing in common to all the objects to which the concept may be ascribed; rather, they may be related to one another in many different ways, just like the members of a family (Wittgenstein, 1953, §§66–7, 164). Thus, he rejected the philosophical position known as *essentialism* (Richardson, 1976c, pp. 85–7), which holds that the meaning of an expression is given by what is common to all of the things to which it applies, their essence. He also rejected the idea that a criterion for ascribing a concept to an object must constitute a logically *necessary* condition for the truth of the proposition that the object falls under the concept.

It is perhaps more important that the notion of a criterion is also used to show that an item of evidence need not constitute a logically *sufficient* condition for the truth of this proposition. Knowledge-claims which are based upon criterial evidence may nevertheless be overturned and contradicted by further evidence (Wittgenstein, 1958, pp. 145–6). Philosophers express this point in various ways, by saying that criteria are not *logically decisive* (see above), that their employment is *defeasible* or *corrigible*. To clarify these notions, Pollock (1970) gave an excellent account of the various types of reasons or grounds for beliefs or knowledge-claims. In his terminology, a *good* reason is one which is adequate or sufficient to justify the belief for which it is a reason, a *logical* reason is a statement that constitutes a reason simply by virtue of its meaning or logical nature, and a *non-conclusive* reason is a logical reason which does not deductively guarantee the truth of what is believed. Wittgenstein's notion of a criterion is very similar to what Pollock called a *prima facie* reason; this is a non-conclusive logical reason which by itself would be a good reason for believing something, but which might cease to be a good reason when taken together with some other beliefs. These various properties of the concept of a criterion must be remembered in considering how one can carry out a scientific investigation of other people's personal experience.

3.3 THE CRITERIA FOR PSYCHOLOGICAL STATES

If one wishes to give a philosophical analysis of some interesting class of concept, then, one should attempt to determine the sorts of ground on the basis of which the relevant concepts are ascribed. It is fairly uncontroversial that concepts relating to psychological states are ascribed on the basis of behavioural criteria. (For example, one supports one's claim that another person has toothache by pointing out that he is holding his cheek.) Indeed, the epistemological 'Problem of Other Minds' and the methodological problem for behaviourist psychologists is that of explaining *how* legitimate knowledge-claims about another person's psychological states may be made on the basis of (purely) behavioural evidence.

Nevertheless, it may be argued that psychological concepts *could only* be ascribed on the basis of behavioural criteria. Wittgenstein (1953, §202) suggested that the possibility of the *correct* ascription of a psychological concept depends upon its application being open to evaluation and correction by other speakers of the language. Thus, the grounds on the basis of which that ascription is made must be open to public inspection. On the other hand, he produced a famous, extended argument to show the impossibility of a 'private' language, in which psychological concepts are ascribed purely on the basis of descriptions of subjective experience (Wittgenstein, 1953, §§243–71; for discussion see Kenny, 1971, 1973, chap. 10). It may therefore be concluded that psychological concepts are to be ascribed on the basis of a characteristic behavioural manifestation, or, as Wittgenstein (1953, §580) expressed this point: 'An "inner process" stands in need of outward criteria.' Since psychological concepts may *only* be ascribed on the basis of behavioural criteria, there can be no better source of evidence about another person's personal experience, as was mentioned above.

The behavioural criteria which are employed to ascribe psychological concepts include both non-verbal behaviour and verbal utterances. A person's psychological state may be evidenced as much by what he says as by what he does. Wittgenstein (1958, p. 68) suggested that ascribing a psychological state to oneself (for instance, saying, 'I am in pain') might replace the natural behavioural expression of that state. So, the expression 'characteristic behavioural manifestation' is not intended to oppose the natural behavioural expression of a psychological state to what a person says. Rather, the characteristic behavioural manifestation is taken to include characteristic verbal utterances. (Wittgenstein went further to argue that the self-ascription of a psychological state had the same logical status as the natural behavioural expression of that state. This is part of his theory of avowals, which is a difficult and highly problematic topic in his later philosophy; see, for example, Hacker, 1972, chapter 9.)

The criteria for the application of a psychological concept are prima facie reasons for justifying its ascription. Such a concept is defeasible in the usual sense, in that it allows a variety of criteria and sometimes these criteria may conflict. On the other hand, as was mentioned earlier in this chapter, psychological concepts admit an additional dimension of defeasibility because of the possibility of pretence. A knowledge-claim which ascribes a psychological state to a person may be incorrect because he is pretending to be in that state. There is a converse situation whereby the characteristic behaviour may not be necessary for ascribing the psychological state. In this case, the person may be concealing his psychological state. Wittgenstein (1968) argued that there are behavioural criteria both for saying that someone is in a psychological state and expressing it, and for saying that he is in a psychological state and concealing it. These are possibilities which are encompassed in ordinary language and which have to be encompassed by any adequate conceptual analysis of psychological concepts.

However, some psychological concepts have the vitally important property that a particular sort of use does *not* seem to be defeasible, at least in the following respect. While I can say truthfully that I am in pain, or I can lie about my pains, I cannot be *mistaken* about whether I am in pain, in the same sort of way that I *can* be mistaken about whether someone else is in pain (Wittgenstein, 1953, §246). Thus, there is an epistemological asymmetry between the first-person present-tense use and the third-person present-tense use of an important class of psychological concepts. These are often referred to as 'mental states' or 'psychological states' (cf. Malcolm, 1977, p. 256), and the epistemological property which has just been described is that of the *incorrigibility* of the self-ascription of psychological states. However, relating to the discussion earlier in this chapter, these concepts are also identified in terms of the grounds on the basis of which they are ascribed. When I say of myself that I am in pain, I do not do so on the basis of any observation of my behaviour; whereas to ascribe pains to other people, I must be prepared to justify my ascriptions on the basis of behavioural criteria. This characterises the phenomenon as the *criterionless* self-ascription of psychological states (Wittgenstein, 1953, §377; 1967, §472). It is sometimes referred to as the phenomenon of 'privileged access', according to which the person who has a particular psychological state knows of its occurrence without having to make the defeasible observations or inferences which others must make to know of its occurrence.

Not all psychological concepts manifest this asymmetry between their first-person present-tense use and their third-person present-tense use. One may make a rough distinction between 'psychological states', which do possess this property, and 'dispositions', which do not. By 'disposition' is meant the tendency of a person to behave in a particular sort of way. An important class of dispositions is that of human capacities, that is, the tendency of a person to behave according to a certain standard or rule. These include knowing how to do certain things, being able to do certain things, and understanding certain things. The self-ascription of a disposition (such as being intelligent) or a capacity (such as knowing how to ride a bicycle) is corrigible, and is made on the basis of public, behavioural evidence. This evidence is the same as that which another person would use in order to ascribe the same disposition or capacity. For example, I could be mistaken in thinking that I still know how to ride a bicycle, and I would support my belief in the same way that any other person would: by testing that ability out (Wittgenstein, 1958, pp. 100–4).

Moreover, the sorts of criteria relevant to the two cases are different. A psychological state possesses a genuine duration, during which it is evidenced by a characteristic form of behaviour. However, one can distinguish between a disposition or capacity and its *exercise* (Kenny, 1972; 1975, pp. 9–10). One ascribes a human disposition on the basis of appropriate or adequate behaviour in relevant circumstances, but the person one is talking about continues to have that disposition in the periods when the circumstances are no longer appropriate. Similarly, one may verify that a person continues to have a particular capacity by carrying out spot checks to see if he can produce an adequate level of performance.

3.4 IMAGERY AND MEMORY

After the more general philosophical preliminaries of the two previous sections, I shall now apply the framework of criterial semantics to the concepts of mental imagery and of memory. In each case the appropriate strategy will be to locate the concept within a class of similar concepts, and then to consider in a very schematic way the criteria which operate in the ascription of the particular concept of interest. It should perhaps be mentioned that an extended discussion of both mental imagery and memory is to be found in Wittgenstein's (1967) *Zettel* (the former in sections 621–49, and the latter in sections 650–69). Unfortunately, his discussion consists of a great many disjointed remarks, with no obvious coherent or systematic analysis of those concepts.

Nevertheless, it is possible to locate the concept of mental imagery within the category of psychological states which I defined in the previous section. Like both sensations and emotions, mental images are conscious mental episodes of a definite temporal duration. Unlike emotions, mental images do not seem to have a characteristic, natural (that is, non-verbal), behavioural manifestation. (I shall expand on this comment below.) Unlike sensations, mental images do not yield information about the world, and the formation of images may be a voluntary activity (though one also talks of mental images being evoked involuntarily). Like sensations, emotions, and thoughts, mental imagery manifests an epistemological asymmetry between its ascription to oneself and its ascription to others: the ascription of mental imagery to oneself is incorrigible, in that one cannot be mistaken about whether one has a mental image, and it is criterionless, in that it is not based upon any process of observation. (Cf. Wittgenstein, 1967, §§472, 478, 488, 627, 632.) Moreover, it seems central to all psychological states that, if a person is in a particular state, then he knows that he is in that state; so the notions of consciousness and self-consciousness are crucial in discussing mental imagery (cf. Marks, 1977).

But what are the criteria of mental imagery? A psychological state is ascribed on the basis of a characteristic behavioural manifestation, and the non-verbal criteria typically refer to the natural, primitive, prelinguistic expression of that state. However, in the case of some psychological concepts, a person's verbal utterances may be the sole criteria for describing his state. For example, there seems to be no obvious primitive behavioural manifestation of a person's thoughts, hopes or wishes. Quinton (1973, p. 328) has argued specifically that there is no natural primitive behaviour characteristic of having a particular mental image. He observed: 'There is no natural expression of having an image of Salisbury cathedral for "I am having an image of Salisbury cathedral" to be a conventionalized extension of.' Quinton's point concerns the criteria for a person's having a particular mental image, but the same conclusion seems to apply to the more general notion of a person's having any mental image. There are certain behavioural signs which might be observed, such as the subject's having a pensive expression and gazing towards an indeterminate and intrinsically unimportant area of space, but these signs would not distinguish between thinking and imaging, nor are they intimately involved in teaching or justifying the employment of the concept of mental imagery. In personal discussion, Peter Hacker has observed that one could devise a situation in which a subject indicated whether he had a mental image or even which mental image he had by making arbitrary pointing responses (towards different pictures, for example); but this would merely constitute a conventional extension of the normal method of describing one's mental images, and could only be taught and explained by reference to the usual verbal criteria.

This conclusion has important implications for the suggestion of Doob (1972) that a scientific investigation of mental imagery might be based upon both reported images and inferred images. If there are no non-verbal criteria for the ascription of mental imagery, then the subjects' verbal reports constitute the only logically adequate source of information concerning their mental imagery. Thus, any scientific investigation of mental imagery which pays any regard at all to the considerations of ordinary usage will place primary emphasis upon these reports, and will attempt to formalise them in a system of protocol question- naires. On the other hand, any other behavioural manifestations of mental imagery which might be correlated with these reports are at best *symptoms* of mental imagery: their evidential value is based not upon the conventions of ordinary language, but upon their empirical correlation with the criteria of mental imagery. These 'indicants', as Bower (1972) called them, will not constitute logically adequate evidence for the ascription of mental imagery. The general form of a problem to be investigated following this psychological methodology will be: How does the performance of subjects in cognitive tasks vary with their use of mental imagery (where the latter is indexed by the subjects' reports)?

This methodological approach is of course exactly the reverse of that which is generally employed in psychological research on mental imagery, as described in the previous chapter. In this research, variations in performance in response to specific operational procedures are taken to be the best source of information on the subjects' use of mental imagery. The subjects' own 'introspective' reports are regarded with considerable suspicion, and are taken at best to be a secondary source of information. The general form of a problem to be investigated following this prevailing methodology is: How does the performance of subjects in cognitive tasks vary with the operational procedures defining mental imagery, and how might the use of mental imagery thus be inferred? A conceptual analysis of mental imagery therefore leads to the conclusion that cognitive psychology has turned the everyday concept of imagery inside out, and taken as the defining criteria of that concept properties which in the ordinary use are merely symptoms of the concept. This substitution of criteria and symptoms was motivated by superficial and erroneous arguments concerning the supposed 'privacy' of personal experience. If one rejects those arguments, there is no motivation for adopting the somewhat bizarre concept of mental imagery to be found in contemporary psychology, and every reason for reinstating personal reports of mental imagery in their appropriate place as defining criteria. The primary task for the scientist and theoretician who adopts this latter course is to rework and to rewrite research on the function of mental imagery in this light. I shall attempt to make some progress in this direction in the remaining chapters of this book.

The correct philosophical account of the faculty of memory is extremely complex, but a central part of this concept is the ability to recollect or to recognise information on the basis of prior experience. Like all capacities, the ability to remember is only manifest when it is being exercised, but a person may (and typically does) continue to have that ability even when it is not being exercised. At any time, under suitable circumstances, one may verify that the person continues to have that ability by a spot check. Moreover, like all capacities and dispositions, the ability to remember does not exhibit an epistemological asymmetry between its first-person present-tense use and its third-person present-tense use, and the self-ascription of this ability is corrigible. Consciousness and self-consciousness are not defining characteristics of the ability to remember: a person may manifest that ability without realising or otherwise being aware of doing so, and, on the other hand, he may falsely believe that he can remember something.

The faculty of memory is a capacity of a certain kind of object: namely, a conscious, living body, or what one would ordinarily refer to as a person. That body exhibits or embodies the capacity by virtue of certain properties of its physical structure. This distinction between a capacity and its *vehicle* is a perfectly general one, applying equally to human beings and to inanimate objects or systems. (It can be argued that there are no major logical differences between the two sorts of capacity; cf. Wittgenstein, 1953, §182.) For example, Kenny (1972) gave the example of the ability of a thermostat to regulate a room's temperature and the structure by virtue of which the thermostat has that ability. Elsewhere, he gave the example of the capacity of whisky to intoxicate and the ingredient of alcohol which is responsible for that capacity (Kenny, 1975, p. 10). These examples indicate that one explains the possession of a capacity by specifying the physical properties of its vehicle which are causally responsible for that capacity. Naturally, limitations in one's knowledge may mean that one can give only a putative, sketchy and functional account of the physical structure of interest, in other words a theoretical account rather than a definitive description. For example, one might explain apparent constraints upon the forms of human natural languages by the theoretical assertion that the brain is 'pre-programmed' in some way (cf. Kenny, 1972). However, it is important to realise that the hypothetical states and processes which are ascribed to the vehicle which underlies a human capacity are the putative physical states and processes of a physical structure (the central nervous system), and not the mental states and processes of the person who possesses that capacity.

More generally, one must bear in mind two important distinctions. The first is that between psychological states and human dispositions, which was mentioned earlier. The second is that between a capacity and its vehicle, which has just been explained. Both distinctions reflect differences of conceptual category; to violate or to ignore these categorial differences will lead to profound conceptual confusion (Kenny, 1972; 1975, pp. 10–1; Wittgenstein, 1953, p. 181). Nevertheless, contemporary research in cognitive psychology commits exactly this error. The source of the error lies in taking expressions which have an established employment as the names of mental states, and using them in theoretical descriptions of the vehicles underlying human dispositions. This move is especially obvious in research on mental imagery, which employs a term referring to a conscious mental episode to refer to a hypothetical form of coding or representation within an articulated theory of human memory (Kosslyn and Pomerantz, 1977; Marks, 1977; Paivio, 1975*b*). (In this case, there is some superficial justification, insofar as the voluntary arousal of the mental state is regarded as a strategy which has causal implications for the mnemonic representation employed.)

The confusion is encouraged by and is reflected in an uncritical use of the term 'representation'. This expression is widely used in contemporary discussions of human memory to refer to theoretical conceptualisations of the knowledge which is ascribed to human subjects (Anderson and Bower, 1973, p. 151). However, neither the meaning of this term nor its epistemological status is ever clearly explained. Malcolm (1977) has recently given an extensive analysis and criticism of the concept of a memory representation, both in traditional philosophy and in contemporary psychological theories concerning the neural basis of memory, but his remarks apply equally to theoretical discussions in human experimental psychology. A representation is a spatial or temporal configuration of symbols which is conventionally regarded as standing in a certain relationship to something else. Representations are created, used, and interpreted by human beings in order to think or to communicate more easily about concepts and ideas which would otherwise be less tractable. Representations are only rarely used in recollecting past experiences (Malcolm, 1977, pp. 128–9). Mental images are representations in just this sense.

However, theories of memory (both philosophical and psychological) typically postulate the existence of a representation as a hypothetical cause in all cases of remembering. Representations are created, stored and retrieved by the mechanism which is responsible for the faculty of memory (namely, the brain). If the expression is being used in its ordinary sense, this would be incoherent: 'It is a conceptual absurdity to attribute to the brain the employment of symbols, rules, descriptions, codes' (Malcolm, 1977, p. 221). Clearly, 'representation' is being used in a different (and unspecified) sense in these cases (Malcolm, 1977, p. 132). In cognitive psychology, and especially in the theories discussed in the previous chapter, it is intended to pick out certain structural properties of the mechanism which is postulated to explain the faculty of memory. In this sense it has no conceptual connection with the conscious manipulation of symbols (nor, *a fortiori*, with the use of mental imagery). Indeed, it may be questioned whether 'representation' is an appropriate term to use in this case. Nevertheless, this usage is so entrenched in psychological discussions that it is extremely difficult to avoid. Accordingly, both senses of 'representation' will be used in this book, but the context should permit the reader to distinguish between the concept of an intentional object of thought and that of a structural property of the brain.

At least three sorts of confusion or uncertainty can be identified as being clearly engendered by the conceptual error of using the same term to refer to a conscious mental episode and the vehicle of a human faculty. First, is the existence of mental imagery obvious or to be proved? Second, are mental images conscious episodes? Third, does mental imagery have an explanatory function? The existence of a hypothetical construct would need to be proved by experimental research, but the ordinary use of the term 'mental imagery' makes this idea seem distinctly odd. The latter suggests an empirical phenomenon which might be correlated with the exercise of the faculty of memory, but which would not be regarded as providing a scientific explanation of the ability to remember. Thus, Anderson and Bower's (1973, p. 450) conclusion that subjective reports of mental imagery do not explain variations in objective performance 'in any acceptable sense' is probably correct. Conversely, how can a hypothetical construct be amenable to conscious introspection? The typical answer is to suggest that such a construct is a mental content which is not necessarily available to consciousness (Fodor, Bever and Garrett, 1974, pp. xii, 3–4; Paivio, 1975*d*; Pylyshyn, 1973; cf. Wittgenstein, 1958, pp. 1–10), which leads down a slippery path to the idea of 'unconscious mental images'.

This sort of confusion can be avoided by disinguishing in a rigorous fashion between the empirical phenomenon of mental imagery and a hypothetical construct postulated to explain the faculty of memory. The postulated 'unconscious mental states' are physiological states of the brain which are intended to explain the faculty and its exercise, not states of consciousness of the person who has that faculty. They are 'mental' only in the tenuous sense that they are intended to explain a capacity of a conscious being (cf. Kenny, 1972). They are 'unconscious' only in the sense that the person who has that capacity may be totally unaware of their existence; but this is merely to point out that one finds out about such a mechanism in a different way from how one 'finds out' about one's mental states, and there is no more justification for calling states of that mechanism 'unconscious', than there is for calling the states of the digestive or vascular systems unconscious.

These remarks have been primarily intended to apply to the faculty of memory, but they may be taken to apply equally to the faculty of mental imagery. In this case, one must distinguish between the experience of a specific mental image and the physiological states of the mechanism which is causally responsible for that experience. Once again, our knowledge of neurophysiology is so limited that it is not possible to specify the properties of this mechanism in any detail (Bugelski, 1971). In such a case, as Kenny (1972) pointed out, the theorist will

> only be able to define the parts of the structure in terms of their function, without having any understanding of the nature of the material embodiment of the structure; just as one might well know that the body, since it regulates its own temperature, must contain a thermostat, and yet have no idea of the material structure of the thermostat.

Nevertheless, it is clear that experimental psychology is ultimately concerned with understanding the properties of the neurophysiological systems which are causally responsible for human faculties, and the research by Whitaker (1971) on the neurological basis of language skills has indicated the general strategy which might be followed in future research. First, one must establish the most important empirical relationships between mental imagery and human memory (for example, constructing mental images of the material to be remembered leads to improved recall). Second, one must offer an articulated psychological analysis of the faculties under investigation, which will postulate functional components of the vehicles of those faculties. Dual coding theory and common coding theory are obviously rival accounts in this phase of the inquiry. Third, the neuropsychological evidence relevant to these components must be critically evaluated, so that empirical hypotheses may be set up concerning the cerebral locus of each component. Some discussion along these lines will be given in chapter 9. This permits one to derive theoretical predictions concerning the functional connections between these anatomically localised components. Finally, these predictions should be supported by demonstrating major neuroanatomical connections among the relevant cerebral loci.

3.5 THE INTENTIONALITY OF MENTAL IMAGERY

In the previous section, it was mentioned that mental images are representations (in the usual sense of that word). An important logical feature of all representations is their *intentionality*: the *object* of a representation (what it is a representation of) is determined by how it is intended, not by what it resembles. This point, and its implications for understanding mental imagery have been discussed by Fodor (1975, chap. 4). On the one hand, an image does not have to resemble what it represents. Malcolm (1977, p. 216) has given the examples of a cartoon caricature and a piece of modern sculpture. Of course, if an image *did* have to resemble what it represented, one would have to inspect one's images to find out what they represented (cf. Wittgenstein, 1967, §621). On the other hand, even if an image does resemble what it represents, any pictorial representation can be interpreted in various ways. Fodor (1975, pp. 182–3) gave the example of a hexagon with its major diagonals, which can be seen as either a plane figure or a three-dimensional cube viewed from one of its corners (see also Malcolm, 1977, pp. 147–53; Wittgenstein, 1953, p. 139). In general, two pictures can represent the same thing (for example, an isosceles triangle and a scalene triangle can both represent the notion of triangularity), while one picture can represent two things (for example, an ambiguous figure can be interpreted as a duck or as a rabbit) (Fodor, 1975, p. 192).

Thus, the object of a mental image is not defined by any of the pictorial properties of the image itself, but is carried by the description under which the image is intended. This is similar to the idea expressed by Pylyshyn (1973) that mental images come to mind already interpreted. It has already been mentioned that whether another person has a mental image and which image he has is determined by his verbal utterances. This last point means that, for the imager himself, the identity of his image is determined by the description which he attaches to it. Fodor (1975, p. 191) explained this as follows:

> Suppose that what one visualizes in imaging a tiger might be anything from a full-scale tiger portrait (in the case of the ideticist) to a sort of transient stick figure (in the case of poor imagers like me). What makes my stick figure an image of a tiger is not that it looks much like one (my drawings of tigers don't look much like tigers either) but rather that it's *my* image, so I'm the one who gets to say what it's an image of. My images (and my drawings) connect with my intentions in a certain way; I *take* them as tiger-pictures for purposes of whatever task I happen to have in hand.

This suggests that the functional origin of mental imagery lies in the descriptions in accordance with which images are constructed. Of course, there may be an indefinite number of equivalent descriptions of one and the same state of affairs, and any one of these possible descriptions would be accepted by the imager as a true account of his intended representation. Thus, one must regard the identity of a mental image as consisting not in any particular verbal statement, but in the abstract proposition which underlies the set of equivalent descriptions. In other words, the functional origin of mental imagery lies in a system of knowledge which is 'essentially *conceptual* and *propositional*, rather than sensory or pictorial, in nature' (Pylyshyn, 1973; see also Yuille and Catchpole, 1977). It should be added that exactly the same argument can be carried through even when it is difficult or impossible for the imager to give a verbal account of his mental image (for example, in contemplating the look or smell of a thing). In such cases the image will allow the same ambiguity or indeterminacy without the interpretation or intention of the imager (cf. Fodor, 1975, pp. 193–4).

This is not to say that mental imagery is without functional utility. This must be established on the basis of experimental investigation, but *a priori* one can point out two respects in which the construction of mental images might be helpful (Fodor, 1975, p. 191). First, if mental images represent spatial properties and relationships in a quasi-pictorial form, then they may be more efficient for carrying out certain tasks than discursive, verbal representations. An example of such a task would be successive crossmodal similarity judgements (Posner, Boies, Eichelman and Taylor, 1969). Second, a mental image may be determinate under several different descriptions other than that on the basis of which it was constructed. The image might therefore manifest emergent properties which could not be readily computed from the original description (Kosslyn and Pomerantz, 1977). An example of this would be counting the number of windows in one's house by 'reading off' the information from a mental image (Shepard, 1966).

This last point would seem to block a fundamental and otherwise devastating criticism of dual coding theory which might be taken to follow from the previous discussion. The intentionality of mental imagery appears to imply that an image cannot contain any new information which was not already available when the image was constructed; for, otherwise, the imager would have to inspect the image to determine whether it was in accordance with his intentions (cf. Wittgenstein, 1953, §389, p. 177). Consequently, mental imagery would be merely an epiphenomenon, and could not be used as a means to recalling information. (In personal discussion, Peter Hacker has suggested that mental imagery might be seen rather as a manifestation of the ability to recall that information, of the same logical status as producing a spoken or written response. Cf. Wittgenstein (1967, §650): 'My memory-image is not evidence for that past situation, like a photograph which was taken then and convinces me now that this was how things were then. The memory-image and the memory-words stand on the *same* level.') Nevertheless, the intentional description according to which an image is produced does not exhaustively specify all of the properties of the image; on the contrary, any mental image will have emergent properties which are not included in that description (though they might be deductively entailed by the properties which *are* contained in the description). In those situations which make use of the emergent properties of images, therefore, mental imagery will deserve a role in psychological investigation as a distinctive mode of thinking (cf. Kosslyn and Pomerantz, 1977). In the following chapters, special attention will be paid to whether the functional elements in cognition and memory are the emergent properties of a mental image, or properties contained within the propositional description under which the mental image is interpreted.

3.6 CONCLUSIONS

The principal task of modern cognitive psychology is to offer a scientific explanation of cognitive capacities, including human memory. This goal is to be attained by devising satisfactory theories of the vehicles of those capacities. Previous research in human experimental psychology has attempted to label the hypothetical states and processes of these vehicles with the terms which are employed in ordinary language to refer to mental states and processes. In particular, mental imagery has been introduced as a theoretical construct to explain the capacity of memory, and the personal reports of experimental subjects concerning their use of mental imagery are regarded as incidental to this exercise. Adopting the arguments given by traditional behaviourists against the ordinary-language use of such concepts, cognitive psychologists define their theoretical constructs in terms of non-verbal behaviour, and especially in terms of observed variations in performance in psychological taks. In so doing, they take as the defining criteria of such concepts phenomena which in the ordinary use are mere symptoms. This step, in particular, is guaranteed to ensure that 'problem and method pass one another by'.

The arguments of the behaviourists against so-called 'mentalistic' concepts may be dismissed as erroneous. There is no reason why a scientific investigation of cognitive capacities cannot be carried out with the appropriate ordinary-language concepts. This will remove the conceptual confusion created by interchanging the criteria and the symptoms of such concepts. A second source of confusion will be removed by appreciating that psychological theories of cognitive capacities offer putative descriptions of the physical structures underlying those capacities, and not of the mental states which might accompany a person's exercise of those capacities. The feature of the intentionality of mental imagery implies that the functional origin of imagery lies not in any pictorial properties of mental images themselves, but in the abstract propositional descriptions under which they are intended and in accordance with which they are constructed. On the other hand, mental images possess emergent properties which are not contained within those descriptions, and constitute cognitive representations which may play a significant role in psychological tasks.

The conceptual analysis which I have given in this chapter identifies mental imagery as an empirical phenomenon which is open to scientific investigation, and which is manifested primarily in personal reports. There are various questions which may be asked of this phenomenon and which may be approached experimentally, such as 'How long does it take to produce a mental image?' (Beech, in press; Beech and Allport, 1978), and 'What is the visual angle of a mental image?' (Kosslyn, 1978). However, I do not consider that these investigations have any general theoretical significance, and I shall not discuss them in this book. The more interesting questions for cognitive psychology concern the possibility of correlations between the phenomenal experience of mental imagery and performance in cognitive tasks, and the identification of the physiological structures which are responsible for the two sorts of empirical phenomena. As Marks (1977) has pointed out:

Self-reports of imagery obtained from conscious inspection of ongoing processing provides systematic data, lawfully and reliably linked to performance data of an entirely objective nature. While correlation is not causation, it is a useful technique in the development of new theories.

4

Mental Imagery in Immediate Memory

In the previous chapter, I gave a conceptual analysis which implied that one should distinguish carefully between the phenomenal experience of mental imagery and a form of mnemonic representation which might be produced by the use of mental imagery in learning. I would now like to extend this idea by proposing a theoretical distinction between what may be called the *constructive* and the *elaborative* uses of mental imagery. First, mental images are symbolic representations which may be maintained over a definite period of time and which may be manipulated in various ways. It is therefore reasonable to suggest that mental imagery constitutes a non-verbal, short-term, working memory in which information may be pictorially represented and spatially transformed. Second, mental images are symbolic representations which may be evoked by the presentation of verbal information to be remembered over an indefinite period of time. In this case, the use of mental imagery may be regarded as a way of elaborating or qualitatively transforming the material to be learned, and it is therefore reasonable to suggest that mental imagery constitutes an elaborative form of coding in long-term memory. Most of the original research on the nature and function of mental imagery was concerned with its elaborative role in long-term memory, but more recently a 'second generation' of experimental research has been concerned with operations on mental images in immediate memory (Anderson, 1978).

Other researchers have made similar distinctions. For example, Marks (1972) observed that experiments on mental imagery could be divided into two groups. One group, concerned with the *literal* function of mental imagery, considers the performance of subjects who are asked to form an exact mental image of a stimulus pattern. The other group, concerned with the *associative* function of mental imagery, considers the performance of subjects who are asked to form an association between two different stimuli by the use of mental imagery. Similarly, Janssen (1976) argued for the existence of two components in visual imagery: a spatial component, relating to the location and orientation of a mental image; and a non-spatial component, relating to the identity and internal properties of the mental image (cf. Baddeley, 1976, p. 229). Other writers have suggested a functional distinction between 'dynamic' or 'kinetic' imagery and 'static' imagery (Janssen, 1976, chap. 6; White and Ashton, 1977). Paivio (1971c, p. 509) made a rather different distinction between the use of mental imagery as a form of short-term memory for concrete events, and the use of mental imagery as a non-verbal representation in long-term memory. Finally, a distinction between 'maintaining' and 'elaborative' activities has been made in considering the nature of the verbal rehearsal of stimulus material (Craik and Watkins, 1973).

In this chapter, I shall discuss the constructive or manipulative use of mental imagery in immediate memory. In subsequent chapters, I shall discuss the elaborative use of mental imagery in long-term memory.

4.1   THE REPRESENTATION OF SPATIAL INFORMATION

One might suppose that mental imagery offers an efficient means of representing, maintaining and manipulating information under many different circumstances. Paivio (1975*b*) suggested that it should be especially helpful in tasks that involve the spatial organisation of informational units or the retrieval of spatial information from long-term memory. Pinker and Kosslyn (1978) have made more detailed proposals:

> One desirable property of imagery would be that one could 'move' one part or portion [of a pattern] and all of the spatial relations between that part and the others would 'emerge', that is, would become evident to the mind's eye without specifically being calculated . . . . Such a property of images would be especially useful if images occurred in a three-dimensional structure, a kind of 'work-space'. The space which we perceive and in which we move about is three-dimensional, and it surely would be useful to have an internal three-dimensional 'model' of space that we can manipulate mentally and in which the consequences of various contemplated actions can be visualized . . . .

Does a mental image constitute a relatively faithful model of an objective situation? In particular, is it the case that the information in a mental image concerning external objects and events 'bears a rather direct, isomorphic relation to the perceptual information given by those objects and events' (Paivio, 1975*b*)? Preliminary research on these questions was carried out by Kosslyn (1973; Kosslyn, Ball and Reiser, 1978), but a more systematic investigation was carried out by Pinker and Kosslyn (1978). They asked their subjects to form a mental image of a specific three-dimensional scene, and to 'move' objects mentally within the scene. It was found that the time taken to scan between two objects in the scene increased in a linear fashion with the distance in three dimensions between those objects; and that, after an imagined displacement of an object, the time to scan to and from that object reflected the new distances in the mental image between that object and others (but cf. Lea, 1975). An informal situation which bears certain similarities to this task is where a person is asked how many windows there are in his house (Shepard, 1966). Most people who are asked this question report that they have to imagine moving around the house, visualising and counting the windows (Janssen, 1976, p. 59). Meudell (1971) found that the time taken to answer the question varied in a linear fashion with the number of windows counted. Another task which has been studied is one where the subjects are asked to name the states, counties, or cities of a particular country. This is a form of *category generation*, which typically shows a negatively accelerated function between the cumulative number of items named and the time spent in naming them (Bousfield and Sedgewick, 1944). However, if the subjects are asked to name the items by working in a given direction (from north to south, say), they produce a linear function comparable to that obtained by reading the items from an actual map (Indow and Togano, 1970; cf. Berlyne, 1965, p. 142).

Naturally, mental imagery should be especially useful in tasks which require the short-term retention of spatial-order information. Milner (1971) described a task devised by P. Corsi, in which the subject has to recall a sequence of spatial locations on a display. The 'spatial memory span' measured by this test is quite independent of a subject's verbal digit span (J. T. E. Richardson, 1977a). Another task is one devised by Bower (1972), in which the subject memorises a sequence of compass directions by imagining a sequence of steps taken in the appropriate directions. Healy (1975, 1978) carried out an extensive investigation of the memory codes used in the short-term recall of sequences of letters. When the spatial order in which items occur is completely correlated with their temporal order, it appears that spatial-order information is not retained (Hitch and Morton, 1975). However, when the two orders are varied independently, Healy found that the recall of the spatial ordering was based upon a complex encoding of the temporal–spatial pattern which had been presented. Similarly, Anderson (1976) found evidence for the independent coding of spatial and temporal information in short-term memory. She found that pictorial displays tended to be recalled better in terms of their spatial structure, whereas verbal presentation emphasised their temporal structure (cf. Fodor, 1975, pp. 186–7). Finally, a rather different situation in which mental imagery seems to be important is the short-term recognition of faces (Nielsen and Smith, 1973) and of random visual patterns (Phillips and Christie, 1977a).

4.2 THE MANIPULATION OF SPATIAL INFORMATION

The experiments which have been described thus far have provided some support for the idea that mental imagery is a literal representation of spatial information. That is, the spatial relationships between the objects in an imaged array appear to correspond to the relationships which would hold between the same objects in an actual array. A further question is whether the way in which imaged objects are manipulated corresponds to the way in which actual objects might be manipulated (Shepard and Podgorny, 1979).

Most of the experimental research in this area has been carried out by Shepard and his collaborators. The original study by Shepard and Metzler (1971) showed that the time taken to match two different views of the same three-dimensional object was linearly related to the angle between the two views. This indicated that the subjects were mentally rotating one or both of the objects at a constant rate until they had the same orientation. All of their subjects reported using mental imagery in order to carry out this process of mental rotation. The question arises whether similar patterns of performance will be obtained when subjects have to carry out a whole sequence of distinct manipulations. Shepard and Feng (1972) investigated this possibility by presenting patterns of six connected squares which result when the faces of a cube are unfolded onto a flat surface. The subjects were asked to decide whether two arrows marked on edges of different squares would meet if the squares were folded back up into the cube. The results indicated that reaction time varied in a linear fashion with the sum of the number of squares that would be involved in each fold, if the folds were actually performed physically. Once again, all of the subjects reported using mental imagery to carry out the task: 'Some Ss described this imagery process as being primarily visual; others spoke, as well, of a strong kinesthetic component in which they imagined folding up the cube with their own hands . . . .'

A more complex task was devised by Cooper and Shepard (1973), in which the subjects were required to judge whether common alphanumeric characters were presented in their normal form or as mirror-image reversals. On each trial, the subject was instructed to construct a mental image of the appropriate character in one of six different orientations; the stimulus was then presented in that orientation or in one of the other five. The results showed that reaction time increased in a linear fashion with the angular discrepancy between the anticipated orientation and the actual orientation of the stimulus. On the basis of this relationship, it was suggested that the subjects rotated their visual images at a constant rate until they were at the same orientation as the test stimulus. This interpretation of the results was borne out by the subjects' own reports concerning their use of mental imagery; however, as Sheehan (1978) has pointed out, some subjects indicated that what they were mentally rotating was very schematic and that their phenomenal experience was as much kinaesthetic as visual. Essentially the same findings were obtained by Cooper (1975) using nonsense patterns as stimuli, and further discussion of these experiments is contained in papers by Metzler and Shepard (1974) and by Cooper and Shepard (1979).

4.3 MENTAL COMPARISONS

An experimental paradigm which has been extensively used in recent years involves the comparison of pairs of objects along some dimension when the objects are presented in a symbolic form (for example, as their names or as pictures). A considerable amount of research has consistently demonstrated a number of basic findings, and these results have been taken to have implications for the nature of the cognitive representation which is employed in such comparisons.

When subjects compare two actual objects on some physical dimension, such as size or area, their reaction times obey a reliable psychophysical function, such that responses are given more quickly, the greater the absolute difference between the two objects along the relevant dimension (Curtis, Paulos and Rule, 1973; Johnson, 1939; Moyer and Bayer, 1976). Moyer (1973) considered whether a similar function would be found when subjects were comparing visual symbols which represent physical objects. Specifically, he presented his subjects with the names of two animals, such as *frog–wolf*, and asked them to indicate which was the name of the larger animal. He found that their reaction times decreased as the difference between the actual sizes of the animals increased. Moyer suggested that subjects compare named animals by making an 'internal psychophysical judgement' after converting the names to some analogue representation which preserves actual physical size.

To the extent that similar results are obtained from perceptual comparisons and from symbolic, mental comparisons, it might be suggested that the cognitive representation employed in mental comparisons is structurally isomorphic to perceptual experience (Shepard and Podgorny, 1979). Paivio (1975e) made a more specific proposal that mental comparisons were carried out on the basis of mental images of exemplars of the two concepts to be compared. His preliminary investigations included the use of questionnaires in which subjects reported the sorts of strategies employed in considering the physical sizes of named objects, and the results 'indicated an overwhelming reliance on visual imagery'. However, as was mentioned in earlier chapters, 'introspective' reports are generally regarded as being of only minor importance in devising and testing theories of psychological function. As Paivio (1975e) himself remarked with specific reference to the study of mental comparisons: 'The important point here is that consciousness is not viewed as a necessary defining attribute of the imagistic representations presumably involved in size comparisons and other tasks, although it often provides supplementary evidence that such a process is functionally activated.' Accordingly, most of the research in this area has neglected to obtain subjects' reports, and has concentrated instead upon exploring the generality of the original experimental findings.

The regular empirical function which was obtained by Moyer (1973) between reaction time and the magnitude of the difference between two named objects has been called the *symbolic distance effect* (Banks, 1977; Moyer and Bayer, 1976; Moyer and Dumais, 1978). Moyer's original results obtained with judgements of physical size were replicated by Paivio (1975e) and by Kerst and Howard (1977). Similar functions were obtained by Paivio (1976b) when subjects were asked to judge which of two named objects was more round or more angular, or which of two named objects was brighter or darker in colour. A further experiment by te Linde (Paivio, 1978c) produced comparable results when subjects were asked to judge which of two colour chips was closer in hue to a named colour. Finally, an interesting variant of the mental comparison task was devised by Paivio (1978a), who asked his subjects to compare clock times in terms of the angles between the hour and the minute hands. For example, at which of the following times do the hour and minute hands form the smaller angle: 3.25 and 7.55? Most subjects reported the use of mental imagery (that is, they compared the angles formed by the hands on visualised clock faces), and once again there was reliable symbolic distance effect, so that the reaction times were longer with smaller angular differences.

Not surprisingly, mental comparisons on abstract dimensions appear to take longer than those on concrete dimensions (Kerst and Howard, 1977). What is perhaps more surprising is that mental comparisons on abstract, semantic dimensions reliably produce symbolic distance effects. Indeed, the earliest studies of mental comparisons involved judgements of numerical magnitude when subjects were presented with pairs of single digits (Buckley and Gillman, 1974; Moyer and Landauer, 1967; Parkman, 1971; Restle, 1970; Sekuler, Rubin and Armstrong, 1971). Similar effects of symbolic distance have been found in judgements of the alphabetic ordering of pairs of letters (Lovelace and Snodgrass, 1971; Parkman, 1971). However, several recent experiments have produced similar findings with a wide variety of semantic dimensions. For example, Holyoak and Walker (1976) demonstrated a symbolic distance effect with the dimensions of time (longer versus shorter), quality (better versus worse), and temperature (warmer versus colder). Banks and Flora (1977) found symbolic distance effects of similar magnitude when subjects compared pairs of named animals either on their physical size or on their intelligence ('smarter' versus 'dumber'). Kerst and Howard (1977) also found comparable effects with judgements of the ferocity of animals, the military power of countries, the monetary cost of cars, and the physical size of all three categories of item. Paivio (1978d) demonstrated symbolic distance effects with judgements of both pleasantness and monetary value. Finally, Friedman (1978) produced a clear symbolic distance effect when non-imageable materials were compared along a non-perceptible dimension. She presented pairs of abstract words, and asked her subjects to judge which word in a pair made them feel better or worse, in the sense defined by the Evaluative Dimension of the Semantic Differential (Osgood, Suci and Tannenbaum, 1958).

However, the theoretical relevance of the symbolic distance effect is even more questionable when it is appreciated that it may be demonstrated with non-semantic properties of words. Paivio (1978b) obtained such an effect both with judgements of the relative frequency with which words occur in everyday language, and with judgements of the relative ease with which words may be pronounced. The symbolic distance effect has also been found when subjects make mental comparisons among items which they have learned in an arbitrary linear ordering along some dimension (Moyer and Bayer, 1976; Potts, 1972,

1974). Since the effect appears to result from mental comparisons made along any ordered dimension whatsoever, it will not be informative as to the specific strategy or process used by subjects in order to carry out certain particular sorts of mental comparison.

Perhaps I should spell out this latter point more clearly. Most researchers are agreed that the finding of a symbolic distance effect in mental comparisons entails that the relevant information is represented in a continuous, analogue form (Kerst and Howard, 1977; Moyer, 1973; Paivio, 1975*b*, 1975*e*, 1976*b*, 1978*d*). Paivio (1975*b*, 1975*e*) went further to argue that the symbolic distance effect was consistent with his account in terms of mental imagery, but inconsistent with 'any model which assumes that the size attribute of animal names is represented in the form of discrete semantic features of propositions'. The finding of a symbolic distance effect with abstract properties of concrete things (Banks and Flora, 1977; Kerst and Howard, 1977) creates some difficulty for this view, but Paivio (1978*b*) argued that, insofar as these properties were attributes of *things*, it was reasonable to suppose that mental images of those things might be involved. Nevertheless, this does not resolve the problem caused by Friedman's (1978) finding of a symbolic distance effect with abstract properties of abstract concepts.

Paivio's arguments were well-motivated and accurate so far as specific proposals by propositional theorists went at the time (see, for example, Anderson and Bower, 1973, p. 461). However, Friedman (1978) has recently pointed out that the assumption that propositional structures can only represent discrete information rests on a confusion between structure and content. Thus, the symbolic distance effect does not even count as evidence against propositional theories (see also Anderson, 1978). Indeed, in his most recent papers, Paivio (1978*b*, 1978*d*) has accepted that other analogical representations might be conceptualised beyond mental imagery. As Kerst and Howard (1977) concluded in their investigation:

> The symbolic distance effect . . . cannot be taken as a unique property of the imagery system which sets it apart from the verbal system. Rather the case for the role of visual imagery in the comparison process must rest on evidence other than the symbolic distance effect.

(A finding which does seem to create difficulty for propositional theories is that reaction times are similar when comparisons are made between conceptual categories to when comparisons are made within a conceptual category: see Paivio, 1975*e*.)

A major alternative source of evidence concerning the nature of the representation used in mental comparisons has been the investigation of performance with pictures and words as stimuli. A basic assumption of Paivio's (1971*c*) theoretical position is that mental imagery should be evoked more readily by pictures of objects than by the names of those objects. If mental comparisons are based upon the use of mental imagery, it follows that such comparisons should be faster with pictures than with words as stimuli (even if the pictures do not faithfully represent size information). The first investigation of this idea was carried out by Paivio (1975*e*), with concrete objects being compared in terms of their physical size. Both pictures and words produced a symbolic distance effect, and, as predicted, reaction times were substantially faster with pictures than with words. Similar results were obtained by Paivio (1978*a*) with comparisons of mental clocks, but in this case the pictorial stimuli directly represented the relevant information (the angular separation of the hands), and so the pictorial comparison was reduced to a perceptual comparison.

Paivio (1975*e*) also investigated performance with pictorial presentation when the pictured sizes of the two objects were incongruent with their actual size. Thus, the subjects had to respond 'larger' to the physically smaller picture. Under these circumstances, reaction times were slower than with congruent pictorial representations. Moreover, pairs which are incongruent with respect to size are congruent with respect to apparent distance. In accordance with this idea, such pairs produced faster reaction times when the subjects made judgements of apparent distance. However, although these experiments show that mental comparisons may be speeded or slowed by congruent or incongruent perceptual information, they do not show that such comparisons are made on the basis of representations which preserve such information in an analogical fashion.

The superiority of pictorial presentation over verbal presentation is consistent with the idea that mental imagery is involved in mental comparisons between concrete objects on the basis of physical attributes. However, Banks and Flora (1977) considered performance on words and pictures in their study of comparisons between animals in terms of their intelligence. They also found that the comparison time was faster with pictures than with words; since the relevant dimension was abstract rather than concrete, they took the result to be evidence against Paivio's (1975*e*) position. Paivio (1978*d*) himself compared pictorial and verbal presentation in judgements of pleasantness and monetary value. In both cases, mental comparisons were faster with pictures than with words, and for judgements of pleasantness mental comparisons were faster with concrete nouns than with abstract nouns. Paivio suggested that properties such as intelligence, pleasantness and value should be regarded as attributes of things rather than words, and that it is necessary to produce mental images of such things in order to make comparisons with respect to these properties (see also Paivio, 1978*b*).

Support for this idea has been provided by comparing performance on pictures and words in judgements of non-semantic properties of words. For example, Paivio (1975*e*) showed that mental comparisons of the pronounce-ability of object names were slower when the objects were pictured than when their names were visually presented. Similar results were obtained by Paivio (1978*b*) when subjects compared the relative frequency with which object names occur in everyday language. Paivio concluded that these sorts of mental comparison are not made with the help of mental imagery. However, two other dimensions have failed to produce the expected pattern of results. These are the properties of brightness and hue, which were investigated in experiments by Paivio (1978*b*) mentioned above. In neither case was the difference between pictorial and verbal presentation significant, and the brightness judgements actually tended to be faster with words when the differences in brightness were small. Nevertheless, with these two exceptions, the evidence on mental comparisons with pictures and words is reasonably in accordance with Paivio's (1975*e*) proposal that such comparisons are carried out on the basis of mental images. It is certainly true that significant picture-word differences can only be accommodated by alternative accounts with the help of *post hoc* modifications (Paivio, 1978*d*). However, if one wishes to claim that mental comparisons employ images as symbolic representations even in the case of abstract properties, some additional source of evidence is needed.

The third category of evidence concerning the nature of the representation used in mental comparisons is the investigation of individual differences in the use of mental imagery. This general topic is the subject of chapter 9, and will be discussed in much more detail then. However, it will be sufficient for the present to note that this line of investigation in the study of mental comparisons has employed tests of spatial thinking similar to the manipulative tasks investigated by Shepard and his colleagues which were discussed earlier in this chapter. (I have elsewhere characterised these tests as measures of objective imagery ability: Richardson, 1978*c*.) It is reasonable to regard these tests as indices of a subject's ability to employ mental imagery as a form of short-term, non-verbal, working memory. To the extent that mental comparisons employ mental imagery in a similar manner, one would expect performance in the two sorts of task to be correlated. Conversely, a positive correlation between spatial thinking ability and speed in a mental comparison task would be evidence that mental imagery is employed in that task (Paivio, 1978*d*).

Published results are not available concerning the effects of imagery ability upon mental comparisons of physical size or angularity. However, Paivio (1976*b*, 1976*d*) reported that unpublished investigations had obtained the anticipated correlations. That is, subjects of high spatial ability carried out mental comparisons of physical objects in terms of their size or shape faster than subjects of low spatial ability. Verbal ability, as measured by a test of verbal associative fluency, was unrelated to performance in these tasks. The published investigation concerning mental clocks (Paivio, 1978*a*) produced similar findings; in particular, subjects of high spatial ability produced faster responses than subjects of low spatial ability in comparing the angular separation of the hands of imagined clocks at times expressed in a digital form, whereas verbal ability did not predict performance. Throughout these experiments, subjects of high and low spatial ability produced similar symbolic distance effects, but they differed in terms of their overall reaction times. The results suggested that the mental comparisons were based on mental images, and that these were more readily produced by subjects of high spatial ability (Paivio, 1978b).

Evidence on individual differences for mental comparisons involving abstract attributes was provided by Paivio (1978d). For comparisons of both pleasantness and monetary value, the reaction times of subjects of high spatial ability were significantly faster than those of subjects of low spatial ability. In neither case was the effect of verbal ability significant. These results support Paivio's idea that properties such as intelligence, pleasantness and value are attributes of things rather than words, and that even mental comparisons on abstract dimensions such as these are made on the basis of mental images of the named objects. Finally, Paivio (1976b, 1978d) referred to an unpublished study which found no sign of an effect of spatial ability upon mental comparisons with respect to word familiarity. This supports the converse suggestion that mental comparisons on non-semantic dimensions of words are not made with the help of mental imagery.

In order to check on the compatibility of these conclusions with the subjects' phenomenal experience, unpublished experiments on mental comparisons carried out at Brunel University have included questionnaires on the strategies employed to carry out these tasks. One study employed pairs of animal names, as in the original experiment by Moyer (1973); the subjects reported using mental imagery 73% of the time in making judgements along concrete dimensions (size and angularity), 79% of the time in making judgements along abstract dimensions (ferocity and intelligence), and 13% of the time in making judgements along non-semantic dimensions (frequency and pronounceability). A further study employed homogeneous pairs of concrete and abstract nouns with judgements along the Evaluative and Potency Dimensions of the Semantic Differential (Osgood et al., 1958); the subjects reported using mental imagery 68% of the time with concrete pairs, but only 24% of the time with abstract pairs.

These results are quite consistent with Paivio's account of mental comparisons, according to which concrete objects are judged along both concrete and abstract dimensions by a comparison of mental images. However, there is a crucial conceptual difficulty with this account which has been pointed out by Banks (1977):

> If images are to be compared to compute the correct response in, say, a size judgement, it is necessary to make the images the right size to begin with. Kosslyn's (1975) research shows that mental images are flexible as to relative size, and it would seem necessary to retrieve size information along with shape information in constructing the images. (Our long-term memory for imageable things cannot be little snapshots that are all just the right size.) Thus, size information must be available, and used, before the image is constructed, and the imagery process itself hardly seems to be necessary.

This point is connected with the property of intentionality which was discussed in the previous chapter. Not only is the identity of a mental image determined by the description under which the image is intended; the apparent or relative size of the imaged object is also carried by the intentional description. To the extent that the words to be compared evoke a mental image in which the appropriate objects are represented with the correct relative sizes, that image only serves to manifest knowledge which must have been independently available.

Banks' conceptual argument was supported empirically by the results of a study by Holyoak (1977). The subjects in these experiments made judgements of relative magnitude of pairs of objects whose names were presented successively. The subjects were instructed to prepare themselves with an image of the first object in each pair at its normal size, with an image that was abnormally big or small, or with no image at all. Independent of this, the subjects either were specifically instructed to use mental imagery to make the comparison of the two objects, or were not so instructed. The different preparatory instructions only influenced the reaction times when the subjects were specifically instructed to use mental imagery in the comparison itself. In addition, when the subjects were asked to maintain irrelevant images of digits at the same time as making the mental comparison, this had a greater effect upon performance when the subjects were told to use mental imagery in the comparison itself. These results suggested that subjects normally compare the sizes of named objects not using mental imagery, but using more abstract information. Moreover, they do not even show that subjects can use mental imagery to make such comparisons when specifically instructed to do so. Holyoak's results indicate merely that mental comparisons are slowed by maintaining two mental images (either a congruent image and an incongruent image, or a relevant image and an irrelevant image) instead of one.

Banks (1977) interpreted his conceptual criticism and Holyoak's results to mean that 'imagery is not frequently or importantly involved in symbolic comparative judgements'. Nevertheless, it is unlikely that his point applies to all or even to most of the dimensions that have been used in mental comparison studies. It is apposite precisely because the apparent size of an imaged object is an intentional property which is incorporated into the description under which the image is constructed. However, most of the other attributes of concrete objects which have been employed (angularity, intelligence, ferocity, angular separation of the hands of a clock, pleasantness, monetary value, and so on) are not intentional properties, and could only be computed from the intentional properties with the utmost difficulty, if at all. Rather, they are emergent properties which are only manifest in mental images of the relevant objects. So, although there are good conceptual reasons for rejecting Paivio's account in the case of judgements of relative size, and although the various sorts of evidence on mental comparisons might individually be open to alternative interpretations, the explanation which is most in accord with the findings to date is that which identifies mental imagery as the cognitive representation employed in making judgements among pictured and named concrete objects along physical and semantic dimensions. As Paivio (1978d) remarked: 'The combined influence of symbolic distance, picture superiority, and imagery ability in the present tasks strongly suggest that the comparison is based on information that is analog and continuous, as well as specifically nonverbal and imagistic in nature.'

Other researchers have used somewhat different psychophysical techniques to argue for an isomorphism between perceptual and cognitive representations. Shepard and Chipman (1970) used multidimensional scaling to analyse judgements of shape similarity between pairs of states of the U.S.A., presented either as cut-out maps or as their names. Fillenbaum and Rapoport (1971) used similar methods to compare the memory structures underlying colour names and the perceptual structures of the colours themselves. Kerst and Howard (1978) demonstrated that similar psychophysical functions were produced from estimates of geographical areas or distances whether these were made from studying a map or from memory of a map. The latter experiment produced intriguing evidence on the question of the functional similarity between judgements based upon perception and 'internal psychophysical judgements' based upon memory representations. The psychophysical function obtained in perceptual estimation is typically a power function whose exponent may deviate from unity in either direction. Kerst and Howard found that estimates made from memory were also well fitted by power functions, and that the exponent of such a function was close to the square of that produced in perceptual estimation. They argued that this is exactly the relationship which would be expected if memory judgements of perceptual continua result from a 're-perceptual' process that operates upon stored perceptual representations (see also Moyer and Dumais, 1978).

4.4   SELECTIVE INTERFERENCE

A rather different sequence of experimental research has been concerned with the possibility of finding specific sorts of experimental task which might selectively interfere with a subject's ability to create and use mental images. This research is based upon the general idea that the psychological mechanisms underlying perception and mental imagery are functionally overlapping. In chapter 2, it was suggested that there were no adequate grounds for this proposal. Nevertheless, one has the intuitive idea that 'looking at one thing and visualizing another at the same time is as difficult as trying to look at two things at once' (Marks, 1977; see also Neisser, 1976, p. 146), and this indicates the possibility of using perceptual tasks to disrupt the use of mental imagery. Indeed, Neisser (1972b) argued that this sort of experimental paradigm could provide an 'operational interpretation' of his 'perceptual definition' of mental imagery as the use of the cognitive processes involved in perception in the absence of adequate stimulus input. Stronger forms of the assumption that perception and mental imagery are functionally overlapping appear to lead to the prediction that the two sorts of activity will disrupt each other to a greater extent when they are in the same sensory or quasi-sensory modality than when they are in different modalities (for example, Janssen, 1976, p. 29). That is, the effect of perceptual tasks upon mental imagery should not only be *selective*, in the sense that such tasks disrupt mental imagery disproportionately more than other faculties, but it should also be *modality-specific*, in the sense that visual tasks disrupt visual imagery more than auditory imagery.

The original experiments along these lines were carried out by Brooks (1967). His initial research was concerned with investigating the extent of competition or functional overlap between reading, listening and imaging. In a typical experiment, Brooks asked his subjects to listen to messages describing the spatial relationships among digits in an imaginary matrix array. An example would be: 'In the starting square put a 1. In the next square to the *right* put a 2. In the next square *up* put a 3,' and so on. Some of the messages were also presented visually as a typewritten display. For comparison, control messages of the same form and length were presented in which the words *quick, slow, good* and *bad* were substituted for the words *right, left, up* and *down*. In each condition, the subjects were asked to recall the message verbatim immediately after it had been read out. For the control messages, simultaneous auditory and visual presentation produced better performance than auditory presentation alone. However, the reverse was true for the spatial messages, with visual presentation producing more errors in recall. Brooks concluded that reading interfered with the visualisation of spatial relationships.

In arriving at this conclusion that reading disrupted the creation of mental images, Brooks was inferring the use of mental imagery from the comparison of spatial and non-spatial messages, and he was inferring the effectiveness of mental imagery from performance in the recall of such messages. However, in chapter 3 it was suggested that such 'operational procedures' were only indirect indicators of the use of mental imagery, and that primary emphasis should be given to subjects' reports of the use of imagery. A relevant and more recent investigation in this respect was that of Beech (1977). If subjects are presented with a description of an array and are asked to indicate when they have visualised the array, their response latencies increase with the number of objects described. Beech found that these latencies were much longer when the subjects read a visually presented description than when they listened to a spoken description, and the rate of increase of the function relating the latencies to the number of objects in the reading condition was ten times that obtained in the listening condition. Thus, both introspective and behavioural investigations seem to agree that reading interferes in a selective manner with the representation of spatial information in the form of mental images.

Earlier in this chapter, it was suggested that mental imagery could operate as a way of maintaining or preserving spatial information in short-term memory. The question arises whether one can find tasks which selectively disrupt the maintenance of mental images. Healy (1975) reported two experiments in which she required the subjects to remember the spatial order in which a sequence of letters was presented, and she manipulated the nature of the irrelevant task interposed between the presentation of the sequence and the signal to recall the sequence. A verbal task, such as naming a sequence of digits, had little effect upon the recall of spatial order, but a spatial task, such as naming the spatial locations of a sequence of digits, severely disrupted the recall of spatial order. Thus, the processing of spatial information seems to interfere in a selective manner with the preservation of mental images. Comparable findings were presented by Den Heyer and Barrett (1971) and by Meudell (1972).

Again, one might ask whether perceptual tasks interfere with the retrieval of information from mental images. One of the experiments reported by Brooks (1967) seemed to indicate this sort of disruption, when it was found that the written recall of a spatial message took much longer than the spoken recall of the same message, but that there was no such difference in the case of non-spatial control messages. Brooks (1968) followed up this idea by requiring his subjects to retain either a visual or a verbal stimulus in memory, and to categorise the elements of the stimulus by either a directional or an oral response. An example of a visual stimulus was an outline diagram of the block letter F, in which case the subject had to identify from memory each vertex of the diagram, either as a corner in the top or bottom of the diagram, or as a corner in between. An example of a verbal stimulus was a sentence, such as *A bird in the hand is not in the bush*, in which case the subject had to identify each word in the sentence either as a noun or as another part of speech. The subjects responded either by saying 'yes' or 'no', or by pointing to a series of symbols 'Y' and 'N' printed on a sheet of paper. The oral response produced faster performance in the case of the visual stimulus, but the pointing response produced faster performance in the case of the verbal stimulus. The subjects themselves reported that it was easier to visualise the outline diagrams while responding orally, and to rehearse the sentences in a verbal manner while pointing.

The most usual interpretation of these results has been elegantly summarised by Bower (1970a):

> If remembering in visual imagery utilizes somewhat the same central mechanisms as are used in visual perception, competition for this limited capacity will result when the person must both visually guide his hand (to indicate answers to various questions about the memorized diagram) and simultaneously remember the spatial diagram in visual imagery. The general idea, therefore, is that two activities in the same modality will compete for a limited analyzer or processing capacity, whereas two activities in different modalities will tend to be less competitive, less disruptive, and less interfering.

Thus, Brooks' (1968) results appear to show that the processing of spatial information interferes in a selective manner with the retrieval of information from mental images (cf. Byrne, 1974).

The control tasks used in these experiments are typically verbal in some sense. Many psychologists would assume that they involve some sort of auditory representation in memory and the same functional systems which might operate in auditory imagery (for example, Bower, 1970a, 1972; Neisser, 1972b). Since these tasks were assumed not to interfere with the use of visual imagery as a representation of spatial information, the results appeared to suggest that the effects of concurrent perceptual tasks upon mental imagery are modality-specific. The basic assumption of this sort of argument is actually incorrect, as will be pointed out in a moment. However, there exists good empirical evidence against the idea of modality-specific interference. Brooks (1968) himself had considered this problem, and demonstrated that a pointing response was equally disruptive of the recall of spatial information whether it was monitored visually or tactually. He concluded that such concurrent activities had their effect by disrupting a general spatial system (see Paivio, 1971c, pp. 147–50, for a discussion of Brooks' argument). A series of unpublished experiments by Baddeley and Lieberman (Baddeley, 1976, pp. 230–1) investigated the problem more systematically. It had previously been demonstrated that performance in Brooks' visual imagery tasks could be disrupted by concurrent pursuit tracking, in which the subject attempts to follow a spot of light moving along a circular path with a stylus (Baddeley, Grant, Wight and Thomson, 1974). Baddeley and Lieberman attempted to separate the visual and the spatial components of this disruption. A visual, non-spatial task was devised in which the subject made successive brightness judgements; similarly, a non-visual, spatial task was devised in which a blindfolded subject followed a pendulum with a flashlight, on the basis of auditory feedback provided through a photocell and tone-generator attached to the pendulum. As Baddeley (1976, p. 231) concluded:

> The results were fortunately very clear. The auditory tracking caused far greater impairment on the Brooks spatial task than on the equivalent verbal task, while for the brightness judgement no such difference occurred. In short, it appears that, for the Brooks tasks at least, disruption is spatial rather than visual.

It is interesting that rather different results are obtained if the situation is reversed, and one considers the extent to which mental imagery may disrupt performance in perceptual tasks (Janssen, 1976, pp. 29–30). This question was extensively investigated in a series of experimental projects by Segal and her collaborators (see Segal, 1971b, for a review), and the major conclusions of this research are quite reliable. First, a subject's sensory sensitivity in a detection experiment is reduced when he is maintaining a mental image (Segal and Fusella, 1969; Segal and Gordon, 1969). Second, the reduction in detection sensitivity is roughly twice as great when the signal and the mental image are in the same sensory modality. Thus, auditory imagery interferes more with the detection of auditory signals, but visual imagery interferes more with the detection of visual signals (Segal and Fusella, 1970, 1971). So, although there is a generalised effect of mental imagery upon perceptual sensitivity, there is also a clear modality-specific effect as well. This latter effect might be taken to support the idea of a functional overlap between mental imagery and perception, but Bower (1972) suggested that it might merely reflect peripheral effects of mental imagery upon modality-specific attentional mechanisms; for example, visual imagery might reduce visual sensitivity by producing pupil dilation and misfocusing.

Unfortunately, recent research by Phillips and Christie (1977*b*) has tended to undermine the conventional interpretation of Brooks' (1967, 1968) original experiments in a radical manner. They observed that Brooks had failed to include adequate control conditions, and so could not legitimately claim to have demonstrated interference specificity. Experiments which incorporated such controls have clearly shown that verbalisation can affect visualisation (Kelly and Martin, 1974; Yuille and Ternes, 1975). They proposed that one should analyse various complex intervening tasks to determine precisely which aspects or components are responsible for the resulting interference.

In previous research, Phillips and Christie (1977*a*) had identified a recency effect in the short-term recognition of novel abstract patterns. This effect was confined to the last item in a sequence and was attributed to a visual short-term memory, which they called visualisation. Accordingly, they carried out a series of experiments to determine which interpolated tasks would remove or interfere with this component. It was found that visualisation was disrupted by mental addition, but not by reading; that the disruption caused by mental addition was independent of the presentation modality of the digits to be added; and that interference from similar stimulus patterns depended upon whether the subjects had to maintain visual representations that outlived iconic storage. Contrary to the usual interpretation of Brooks' findings, that visualisation and perception compete for special purpose visual processing resources, Phillips and Christie took their results to indicate that visualisation requires general purpose resources, and that interference between visualisation and perception might be due to competition for these resources. However, their experiments suggested that visualisation might be disrupted by any concurrent activity which is not pre-programmed and over-learned, but which might compete for the resources of a central executive system or working memory. Previous results may be readily interpreted in these terms. For instance, the experiments by Healy (1975), mentioned earlier, showed that the recall of spatial order would be disrupted by a relatively novel, unpractised task, such as naming the spatial locations of a sequence of digits, but not by a relatively over-learned task, such as naming a sequence of digits. One may conclude, however, that research which attempts to disrupt mental imagery by the specific use of perceptual concurrent tasks is unlikely to be informative concerning the nature and function of mental imagery.

4.5 CONCLUSIONS

This chapter has been concerned with a very limited number of rather specialised areas of experimental research. However, generally speaking, the results of that research indicate that mental imagery may be employed in the representation, preservation and manipulation of spatial and pictorial information. In particular, it may operate as a form of short-term working memory in a variety of experimental tasks to enable the subject to grasp emergent properties of a stimulus array which could not be readily computed or deduced purely on the basis of a propositional description of that array. This use of mental imagery may be disrupted by a concurrent cognitive task involving the processing of spatial information, and possibly by any concurrent task which is not preprogrammed but makes demands upon a central executive system.

5

Pictorial Memory

Having considered the use of mental imagery itself as a form of cognitive representation in immediate memory, I shall now consider the effects of imaging upon the retention of information in long-term memory. Various empirical effects of mental imagery upon memory performance may be demonstrated, but the critical point of the dual coding theory developed by Paivio (1971c, 1975b, 1978b, 1979) is that the use of mental imagery in learning gives rise to a qualitatively different vehicle or 'substrate' of long-term memory. Kosslyn and Pomerantz (1977) have pointed out that this position may be argued from two different points of view. First, it may be proposed that mental imagery produces a form of mnemonic representation which is *structurally* distinct, in the sense that it has different organisational properties (Paivio, 1975c). It is actually very difficult to test hypotheses about mnemonic organisation, since the structure or format employed may be largely independent of what is represented, as Kosslyn and Pomerantz observed. Second, it may be proposed that mental imagery produces a form of mnemonic representation which is *functionally* distinct, in the sense that it is subject to different psychological laws (cf. Anderson, 1978). For example, it might be argued that this representation was less subject to decay (Bower, 1972). However, common coding theorists argue that mental imagery does not give rise to a mnemonic representation which functions differently or which employs a different format, and that all phenomena of human memory can be explained in terms of a single system of underlying propositions.

In the previous chapter, a variety of empirical evidence could be interpreted as indicating an equivalence or isomorphism between mental imagery and perceptual experience (see also Paivio, 1975b). It follows that the use of mental imagery in remembering verbal information might lead to the sort of mnemonic representation which is produced by specific physical objects, events or scenes that are witnessed or experienced. Nevertheless, it is notoriously difficult to control the aspects of such objects, events or scenes to which the observer is attending. One way of introducing such control is to present the subject with a stationary and possibly stylistic representation: in short, a picture. Thus, it might reasonably be assumed that the form of mnemonic representation which is produced by the use of mental imagery is directly aroused by the presentation of pictures (Paivio, 1972). It is therefore important to establish whether pictures are remembered using a distinctive form of mnemonic representation.

5.1 MEMORY FOR PICTURES

It has been well established that the normal adult's ability to recognise pictures is remarkably good. The first systematic investigation of this ability was carried out by Shepard (1967). He compared his subjects' recognition memory for words, sentences and pictures. In each case, the subjects attempted to memorise a series of approximately 600 stimuli, and were then tested on their ability to discriminate these from other, 'new' stimuli using a forced-choice procedure. On immediate testing, the median percentage of correct responses for each of the three kinds of material was 90.0, 88.2 and 98.5. As Shepard concluded:

> Evidently, after 20 or more years of absorbing visual information, *S*s are still able to take in as many as 612 further pictures and, then, discriminate these from pictures not previously seen with (median) accuracy of over 98%.

Comparable performance on pictures with an absolute judgement (yes/no) recognition task was found by Nickerson (1965). Using sequences of 2560 photographs presented over a period of two or four days, Standing, Conezio and Haber (1970) demonstrated performance of approximately 90% correct, even when the presentation interval was only one second per picture. Finally, further evidence for a superiority of pictorial material over verbal material was found by Standing (1973), with a sequence of 10 000 pictures. These and other studies have been discussed by Goldstein and Chance (1974).

These results are consistent with the idea that pictorial presentation gives rise to a distinctive and highly efficient means of storing information. However, it is possible to give an explanation of the superiority of pictures in recognition memory without postulating a separate form of mnemonic representation. It could be argued, for instance, that pictures are usually unique, and are thus less susceptible to forgetting through interference than other sorts of stimuli, such as sentences and words (Ellis, 1975). It is certainly the case that, whatever might be the differences between the mnemonic representations evoked by pictorial and verbal material, there are important similarities between them. For example, it is well known that increased organisation of a list of words will improve their recall (for example, Mandler, 1967), and similar effects may be found with pictorial presentation, so that stimuli presented as interacting pictures are remembered better than stimuli presented as separate pictures (Epstein, Rock and Zuckerman, 1960; Kerst, 1976; Wollen and Lowry, 1974; cf. Webber and Marshall, 1978). The role of such organisational factors in mental imagery will be discussed in the following chapter.

The problem of demonstrating the existence and efficacy of a distinctive pictorial representation in human memory is extremely complicated. Moreover, within the general framework of dual coding theory, it is possible to give two different accounts of the superiority of pictorial material over verbal material (Paivio, 1971c, pp. 207–8). The explanation which is immediately suggested by the early studies on recognition memory is the *image superiority hypothesis*, according to which pictures immediately evoke imaginal representations in memory, and these are inherently more memorable than verbal representations. Although intuitively plausible, this idea has been criticised on conceptual grounds by Reese (1977*a*, 1977*b*). An alternative explanation is the *coding redundancy hypothesis*, which is based upon the idea that memory performance increases directly with the number of alternative memory codes available for an item (Paivio, 1971*c*, p. 181). Specifically, many pictures may be implicitly named or described at the time of presentation, and thus will receive both imaginal and verbal representations in memory. This would enhance the subsequent performance in tests of retention 'because one code could be forgotten during the retention interval without complete loss of the nominal item' (Paivio, 1972; see also Goldstein and Chance, 1971).

The available evidence tends to favour the latter interpretation. First, if pictures and words are presented at a rate which is sufficiently fast to preclude the implicit naming of the pictures, there is no difference in either free recall or recognition memory for the two sorts of stimulus material (Paivio and Csapo, 1969). Presumably the image superiority hypothesis must predict a pictorial superiority even at fast rates of presentation (Paivio, 1972). Second, the pictorial superiority in recognition memory only appears to operate when the pictorial material can be meaningfully interpreted (Bower and Karlin, 1974; Goldstein and Chance, 1971). Indeed, Wiseman and Neisser (described by Anderson and Bower, 1973, p. 454) found that complex visual patterns could be recognised only if they yielded a familiar interpretation at the time of the original presentation, and if they evoked the same interpretation at the time of the recognition test. However, they employed Mooney pictures, which are highly confusable, relatively unstructured arrays derived by deleting the contours of a naturalistic scene, and thus presumably minimised the contribution of pictorial memory to the recognition task. It is known that the organisational effects mentioned above are not merely caused by the use of a more coherent verbal representation: Horowitz, Lampel and Takanishi (1969) found that children would describe both integrated and separated pictorial scenes by giving simple lists of the objects presented, but they showed considerably better performance in recalling the integrated scenes.

One important sort of evidence relevant to this problem is that concerning the effects of instructions to subjects to name the objects depicted. It is well established that such labelling increases the (verbal) recall of pictures (Bahrick and Boucher, 1968; Bower, 1970*a*; Kurtz and Hovland, 1953). Conversely, supplementing verbal material with appropriate pictures leads to improved recall performance (Madigan, McCabe and Itatani, 1972). Although some researchers have suggested that the effects of labelling should be more pronounced in tests of recall (for instance, Sheehan, 1972), it is clear that labelling pictures may also increase subsequent recognition performance (Bacharach, Carr and Mehner, 1976; Calfee, 1970; Davies, 1969; London and

Robinson, 1968; Nelson and Kosslyn, 1976; Reese, 1975; Robinson, 1970; Ward and Legant, 1971). Thus, although it might eventually turn out to be necessary to allow that image superiority contributes to the fact that memory performance is better with pictorial material than with verbal material, it seems essential to incorporate the possibility of redundant and simultaneous codes into an adequate account of the effect, and the coding redundancy hypothesis tends to be accepted by most psychologists who accept the existence of a qualitatively distinct imaginal representation (for example, Bower, 1970a; Paivio, 1971c, 1972). Perhaps more important, it is difficult to see how the evidence on the effects of labelling can be handled by the opposing, common coding theory of imagery and language, which assumes that pictorial and verbal material are encoded into a common mnemonic representation.

In connection with the effects of labelling upon memory performance, it has long been known that, if subjects are asked to recall ambiguous geometrical figures by drawing them, supplying verbal labels may lead to distortion of the figures in the direction of a prototypical instance of the relevant concept (Bruner, Busiek and Mintura, 1952; Carmichael, Hogan and Walter, 1932; Hall, 1936; Herman, Lawless and Marshall, 1957). However, such distortion also occurs if the labels are provided only at the time of recall (Hanawalt and Demarest, 1939), and it does not occur in tests of recognition memory (Prentice, 1954). This suggests that labelling has an effect upon the processes of reconstruction, but not upon the actual storage of the labelled pictures (Reese, 1977b).

Quite a different experiment creates further problems for the common coding hypothesis. Jenkins (described by Bower, 1972) required his subjects to learn paired associates consisting of pictures and words. He found that their learning performance was actually increased if the perspective of the object depicted in the picture was varied from one trial to the next, compared to a control condition in which the same picture was used on each trial. This indicated that the subjects were integrating the successive perspective views into a single three-dimensional representation which was a superior mnemonic cue to the constant two-dimensional representation presumably evoked in the control condition. As Paivio (1975b) remarked, the mnemonic representation produced by mental imagery is a mental construction rather than a product of any specific perceptual experience.

Whether the subject's retention is tested by recall or recognition, it is usually suggested that the contribution of the hypothesised pictorial representation should be more important if a verbal description of what is represented is too complex or is simply not available (Sheehan, 1972). Thus, complex, abstract geometrical patterns for which there exists no obvious label can plausibly only be remembered by means of some pictorial, non-verbal representation (Owens and Richardson, in press). A more interesting class of stimulus is the human face, and a considerable amount of research has been carried out on the specific problem of how one recognises faces.

5.2   FACES: A SPECIAL CASE?

Under normal circumstances, performance in tests of recognition memory with
human faces is very good, and typically better than performance with other
classes of familiar objects (Scapinello and Yarmey, 1970; Yin, 1969). This is not
surprising, since a person's face is the primary source of information for
recognising and thus for re-identifying him as a particular individual. Moreover,
a person's face is also a primary source of information for the purpose of ascribing
feelings, moods and emotional states (Ekman, Friesen and Ellsworth, 1972). On
the other hand, faces are rather difficult to describe, and the connection between
a person's name and his face is invariably quite arbitrary. Indeed, learning
people's names may be difficult task which requires the use of complex strategies
(Morris, Jones and Hampson, 1978). Even when a person's name has been
learned, its role in the total memory system may be mediated almost exclusively
by the pictorial representation of the person's face. In comparing photographs of
the faces of known and unknown people as stimuli in a picture-word learning
task, Bower (1972) found only a slight difference between known faces (which
could all be immediately named) and unknown faces (which presumably could
not be named). These results suggest most strongly that recognising another
person's face is not mediated by verbal descriptions.

Experimental evidence for this suggestion was obtained by Goldstein and
Chance (1971). They found no correlation between the number of verbal
associations given to human faces and the ease with which they could be
recognised. Moreover, they suggested that subjects tend to give similar verbal
descriptions to different faces, so that such descriptions could only be of very
limited assistance in face recognition. A further study by Malpass, Lavigueur
and Weldon (1973) showed that training in visual identification produced a
marked improvement in the recognition of faces, but that training in verbal
description did not. As Ellis (1975) concluded, the evidence indicates that the
recognition of human faces appears to be almost entirely a visual process.

A more specific idea that is sometimes put forward is the hypothesis that the
recognition of human faces is mediated by a specific memory system or by a
specific set of perceptual analysers which are not employed in the recognition of
other classes of visual stimulus. In recent years this hypothesis is associated
especially with the work of Yin (1969, 1970), but it has been suggested by other
researchers and is often implicit in the neurological use of the term *prosopagnosia*
to refer to a relatively specific impairment in the recognition of familiar faces. A
recent critical assessment of the hypothesis of a specific face-recognition system
has been given by Ellis (1975), who considered evidence from the ontogeny of
facial recognition, from experiments involving the recognition of inverted and
upright faces, and from clinical studies of prosopagnosia. In each case, Ellis
concluded that there was no unambiguous evidence that faces are analysed by a
special and specific recognition system. Nevertheless, faces constitute an
especially interesting class of stimulus material for which it is highly plausible on

a priori grounds that the memory system mediating recognition performance employs a pictorial, non-verbal representation.

5.3 PICTURES AND WORDS

One of the critical assumptions of the dual coding hypothesis is that the verbal and non-verbal representations taken to operate in human memory are functionally independent (Paivio, 1975*b*, 1978*b*). To test this assumption, it is necessary to show that the two sorts of mnemonic code have additive effects upon performance in particular experimental situations. Of course, since both codes may in principle be used to remember a given class of stimulus material, the demonstration of additive effects is no easy matter. However, there is some evidence for such effects in the recall of pictures and words.

Paivio and Csapo (1973) reported a series of experiments which used incidental recall and different orienting tasks to induce one code or the other individually, or both simultaneously. They based their research on the fact that repeated presentations of a stimulus in the same modality are typically not additive in their effects upon recall performance. This is consistent with the idea that repeated presentations serve to strengthen a single mnemonic representation, and inconsistent with the idea that each presentation creates a new, separate representation in memory. Conversely, they argued, additive, statistically independent effects of repeated presentations upon memory performance are evidence for separate, functionally independent representations in memory.

Not surprisingly, the experiments demonstrated that repeated presentations of a stimulus produced increased recall performance, and pictorial presentations produced better performance than verbal presentations (that is, names of objects were recalled less well than pictures of the same objects). Picture–picture and word–word repetitions produced poorer performance than would be expected on the basis of stochastically independent effects upon recall performance, but repetitions which pictured previously named objects or which named previously pictured objects were additive in their effects. This supported the hypothesis that pictorial and verbal mnemonic codes are functionally independent.

As Paivio (1975*a*) observed, the empirical observation of stochastic independence cannot be handled by common coding theory without the addition of some purely *post hoc* device. For example, it might be assumed that knowledge of the original presentation modality is preserved by attaching differentiating and independent 'tags' to a 'core' representation in memory. However,

differential tagging could not explain the superior recall for pictures . . . without also assuming that the tags differ in their retrieval effectiveness. Unless they are deducible from other principles within the theories, such additional assumptions would render the common-coding models formally equivalent to dual coding, which simply assumes that the memory representations corresponding to the different events are independent and qualitatively different despite their conceptual relatedness.

A different way of testing the dual coding hypothesis is to compare the presentation modality used at the time of learning and at the time of recall. If pictorial and verbal information is represented in a common memory system, then the method of testing memory performance should be independent of the original presentation modality. This was tested by Weingartner, Walker, Eich and Murphy (1976) using a modified paired-associate procedure in which the stimulus terms were common, concrete nouns, and the response terms were other similar nouns or simple line drawings of objects. The initial learning task required the subjects to select a response term for each stimulus, and the retention test required them to reconstruct these pairings. It was found that a disparity between the learning and recall conditions (presenting a word as a picture, or vice versa) impaired the recall performance, especially for incidentally learned pairs of items. These results support the idea of distinct mnemonic representations in the learning of pictures and words. It should be mentioned, however, that experiments on recognition memory have failed to show any effect of disparity between learning and test modality, either with incidental learning or with intentional learning (Paivio, 1976a; Richardson, 1978c). These results can be handled by dual coding theory on the assumption that subjects can easily translate a test item into either modality, but they no longer serve to discriminate between this theory and the common coding approach.

A few investigations have attempted to compare the recall of pictures and words when the structural complexity of the relevant stimuli is carefully controlled. Wells (1972) compared the retention of visual and verbal stimuli varying in size, colour and form; thus, subjects remembered either a large, red, dotted pattern, or the words 'large red dotted'. In an immediate test of recognition memory, performance was similar under the two conditions, suggesting that the same mnemonic representation was used in both cases. Jones (1978) carried out a similar investigation using stimuli varying in colour, type and physical location in a display; thus, the subjects remembered either a yellow cup in the top left-hand corner of the display or the words 'yellow/cup/top left'. In this case, verbal presentation produced poorer performance, especially in the recall of location information. A similar impairment had been obtained by Pellegrino, Siegel and Dhawan (1975) in studying the short-term retention of drawings and their labels. Jones concluded that pictorial and verbal presentation give rise to functionally separate, though structurally similar mnemonic representations.

Further information on the coding of pictures and words has come from the use of selective interference paradigms. The basic methodology was discussed in chapter 4. Cohen and Granström (1968, 1970) studied short-term memory for irregular geometric figures, and manipulated the type of retention test and the type of material interpolated during a retention interval. They found that a verbal distractor task interfered more with the subsequent recall of the figures than with their subsequent recognition, but that a visual distractor task had the opposite effect. Moreover, the subjects' ability to describe the original stimuli was correlated with their recall performance, but not with their recognition performance. Baddeley (1976, pp. 216–17) summarised the implications of these results as follows:

> It appears then that the *recall* of visual material is relatively poor, shows rapid forgetting . . . , and tends to rely on verbal coding, whereas visual *recognition* shows relatively little forgetting after the first few seconds and is not apparently affected by verbal factors.

However, more recent experiments have produced rather different conclusions. The experiments by Pellegrino *et al.* (1975) interposed either an auditory distractor task (counting backwards aloud) or a visual distractor task (a Hidden Figures Test) between the presentation and recall of picture and word triads. The performance with word triads was affected only by the auditory task, indicating that words were primarily encoded in an acoustic manner in this experiment (see also Wells, 1972). The performance with picture triads was high with either distractor task individually, but was reduced when the two tasks had to be carried out simultaneously. This indicated that pictures were encoded into separate visual and acoustic processing systems, thus supporting the dual coding hypothesis. Warren (1977) investigated the effect of a concurrent pursuit-rotor task upon the recall of pictures and words (cf. Baddeley, 1976, pp. 230–1). In two experiments, he showed that, when subjects attempted to recall and to track concurrently, their recall of pictures was impaired, but their recall of words was not. Thus, however important the verbal component hypothesised by Baddeley might be in the recall of pictures, performance in such a task is nevertheless crucially dependent upon a non-verbal mnemonic code, and the use of this code may be disrupted by a concurrent visuo-spatial task.

5.4 PICTURES AND MENTAL IMAGERY

While there seems to be good evidence that the pictorial presentation of material directly arouses a distinctive, nonverbal representation in human memory, the critical proposition for present purposes is that the same representation is evoked when subjects construct mental images in learning material which is presented in a verbal form. What experimental evidence is there for this idea?

First, if pictorial presentation directly arouses such a mnemonic representation, then presumably the construction of mental images should have little or no effect upon performance. Since the idea of instructing subjects to make up mental images of what is clearly before them is rather bizarre, there is little evidence on this matter. Nevertheless, Robinson (1970) showed that instructions to use mental imagery had little effect upon recognition memory for line drawings, whereas instructions to label the drawings had the usual beneficial effect upon performance. An important exception to the idea that mental imagery should have little effect upon pictorial memory is that it should be helpful if it serves to integrate stimuli which are presented as separate pictures. Kerst (1976) used an incidental paired-associate learning experiment, and found that instructions to generate such interactive images produced a substantial increase in performance, equivalent in magnitude to that produced by actually presenting the pictured objects interacting in some way (see also Wollen and Lowry, 1974). As Paivio (1975*d*) pointed out, the parallel results obtained from the use of interactive pictures and from the use of instructions to make up interactive mental images 'make it reasonable to infer that the instructional sets and the pictures arouse similar representations'. However, the more detailed discussion of the effects in instructions to use mental imagery in learning verbal material contained in chapter 6 will throw considerable doubt upon the idea that such instructions implicate a qualitatively different sort of mnemonic representation.

Second, a verbal stimulus which is reliably associated with some (possibly arbitrary) pictorial stimulus should come to evoke the representation of that stimulus in non-verbal long-term memory. Bower (1972) used this idea to explain why subjects performed better in a paired-associate learning experiment when the stimuli were the names of their personal friends than when they were the names of historical characters whose exact facial appearance was unknown, or when the stimuli were the names of totally unknown people randomly selected from a telephone directory. Indeed, the association with pictorial or actual experience is usually taken to be the basis of the effect of stimulus imageability or concreteness upon memory performance (see chapter 7). But can the operation of such associations be demonstrated more clearly? An experiment by Philipchalk (described by Paivio, 1971*b*; 1971*c*, p. 72) used nonsense syllables as the stimulus terms in a paired-associate learning task, where the response terms were pictures, concrete words or abstract words. In the second phase of the experiment, the same nonsense syllables were paired with randomly chosen, meaningful words. The syllables which had previously been paired with pictures produced better performance than those which had been paired with concrete words, and these in turn produced better performance than those which had been paired with abstract words. However, this variation in performance occurred only when the subjects were instructed to use their previous associations in the subsequent learning task. Philipchalk's results suggested that pictorial associations might subsequently be employed as mental images to mediate new learning, although this mediation might need to be primed or prompted by appropriate instructions. This was confirmed by the use of post-learning questionnaires, in which the subjects reported the greatest use of mental imagery in learning syllables which had previously been paired with pictures, and the least use of mental imagery in learning syllables which had previously been paired with abstract words. However, such images must have been constructed under determinate intentional descriptions, and Philipchalk's results may be taken to show merely that these propositional mediators enhance memory performance.

Finally, can one point to similarities between pictorial presentation and the use of mental imagery in learning in terms of the situations in which they are most effective? The results of Bower (1972) and Kerst (1976) show that both procedures are more effective when they encourage the integration or organisation of the material in a single, interactive representation, than when they promote the use of a separate, unrelated representations. However, in the following chapter, it will be noted that the superiority of *interactive* encoding over *separative* encoding applies equally to verbal representations in memory. Reference has already been made to the work of Jones (1978), who showed that pictorial presentation was especially helpful in retaining location information. Jones demonstrated a similar conclusion in analysing the results of experiments by Anderson and Bower (1973, pp. 305–19), on the effects of instructions to use mental imagery. These studies investigated memory for sentences of the form, 'The *Subject Transitive-Verb*-ed the *Object* who *Intransitive-Verb*-ed in the *Location*' (for example, 'The hippie touched the debutante who sang in the park'). In one experiment the subjects received standard learning instructions, and in the other the subjects received additional instructions 'strongly urging them to form vivid visual images of the sentences to be memorized'. In both cases, the subjects were cued with one, two or three of the five content words and had to produce the entire sentence. Anderson and Bower had concluded that the effect of instructions to use mental imagery upon sentence recall was simply to raise the overall level of performance, but Jones demonstrated that the improvement was relatively specific to the grouping, 'the *Object* who *Intransitive-Verb*-ed in the *Location*' (for example, '. . . the debutante who sang in the park'). As Jones concluded: 'This may be because the coding of information set in a locational context is particularly improved by the imaging operation; this explanation is consistent with the finding reported earlier that recall involving location is particularly improved by pictorial rather than verbal presentation.' Once again, however, since the mental images employed by Anderson and Bower's subjects must have been constructed according to intentional descriptions, the results might be taken to indicate that both pictorial presentation and imagery mnemonic instructions encourage propositional representations which emphasise location information.

5.5 CONCLUSIONS

Although it is extremely difficult to specify experimental situations which would offer a critical decision between dual coding theory and common coding theory, the available evidence on pictorial memory tends to favour the former position, at least with respect to the specific proposals which have been made by the proponents of the respective theories.

The well-established superiority of pictorial presentation in recognition and recall does not discriminate between the alternative positions, but the effects of labelling upon the recall of pictures and the effects of supplementing verbal material with relevant pictures are difficult to handle in terms of a theory based upon a common propositional representation in long-term memory. The same conclusion applies to Paivio and Csapo's (1973) demonstration of the stochastic independence of pictorial and verbal presentations in incidental recall. On *a priori* grounds, moreover, it is difficult not to assume a basically pictorial representation in memory underlying in the retention of complex visual displays which cannot be readily described or labelled, such as abstract geometrical patterns, or the faces of unknown people.

Thus, the empirical evidence favours the theory of dual coding, and within this framework gives specific support to the coding redundancy hypothesis, according to which pictures to be remembered may receive both pictorial and verbal representations in long-term memory. This account is supported further by the effects of selective interference from irrelevant spatial tasks interpolated between presentation and recall. Although, as Anderson (1978) has proved, it is possible in principle to specify versions of common coding theory which are equivalent to dual coding (at least with respect to its predictions for pictorial memory), the various adjustments needed to ensure this equivalence are unlikely to constitute well motivated extensions of the current versions of common coding theory. The dual coding model may therefore be regarded as the most promising and most coherent theoretical approach for investigating pictorial memory.

For the purpose of this book, however, the principal interest in pictorial memory lies in its value as a means of investigating mental imagery. There is nevertheless little direct evidence to permit an identification of the non-verbal representation aroused by the presentation of pictures and the mnemonic code produced by the use of mental imagery. Where experimental investigations have suggested that the two representations have structural or functional properties in common, the question of the intentionality of mental imagery suggests that the relevant information might be adequately represented at a propositional level. Moreover, in subsequent chapters, empirical findings will indicate that any similarities between the two representations are also shared with verbal coding in long-term memory. The crucial assumption of dual coding theory that pictorial presentation gives rise to an imagistic representation in memory may turn out to be empirically testable only by a consideration of the relevant neuropsychological evidence, and this must wait until chapter 9.

6

Imagery Mnemonic Instructions

One of the reasons for the revival of interest in mental imagery was the experimental demonstration of the effectiveness of instructions to subjects to use mental imagery in their learning. The efficacy of such instructions had in fact been known more generally for a very long time. Various techniques prescribed for orators in Greek and Roman times included the use of mental imagery explicitly (see Paivio, 1971c, chap. 6; Yates, 1966), and these techniques survive essentially unchanged in the present day in courses of memory improvement. In this chapter, I shall discuss experimental evidence on the effects of imagery mnemonic instructions and its implications for theories of human memory.

6.1   THE EFFECTS OF IMAGERY INSTRUCTIONS

Experimental research on the value of instructions to subjects to use mental imagery in learning verbal material has generally demonstrated consistent, reliable and substantial improvements in performance. These effects have been demonstrated when comparisons are made between groups of subjects who are given different learning instructions (Bower, 1970b, 1972), when comparisons are made within a single group of subjects before and after they are given instructions to use mental imagery (Richardson, 1976b), and even when comparisons are made between different stimulus items being learned concurrently by the same subject (Schnorr and Atkinson, 1969). The effects have been demonstrated with free recall (Kirkpatrick, 1894; Richardson, 1976b, 1978d), with serial recall (Delin, 1969), with paired-associate learning (Bower, 1970b, 1972; Schnorr and Atkinson, 1969), and with recognition memory using both absolute judgement (yes/no) procedures (Morris and Reid, 1974) and comparative judgement (forced choice) procedures (Bower, 1972).

The elaboration of verbal material by the construction of mental images is known to affect long-term or secondary memory. This has been shown by considering the shape of the serial-position curve in free recall, by quantifying components of the total performance attributable to primary and secondary memory, and by comparing performance on immediate testing and after a delay (Paivio, 1975b; Richardson, 1976b, 1978d; Smith, Barresi and Gross, 1971). Indeed, some results show a somewhat more pronounced effect after a delay

(Bower, 1972; Groninger, 1971; but cf. Hasher, Riebman and Wren, 1976), indicating that mental imagery not only improves memory performance, but also makes the stored material less vulnerable to forgetting. Moreover, Beech (in press) has suggested that the adequate use of mental imagery depends upon an adequate delay between presentation and recall, so that subjects have time to visualise the material to be remembered. It is interesting that he found that immediate recall produced a specific reduction in the accurate recall of location information.

Whether these effects are specifically due to the use of mental imagery and not to other factors must be determined by examination of the experimental evidence. The most plausible alternative explanation is that instructions to use mental imagery simply enhance the subjects' motivation to learn. This was discussed at length by Bower (1972) and by Paivio (1969), and rejected fairly conclusively. The most crucial difficulty for a motivational account is that the effects of imagery instructions are undiminished under incidental as compared to intentional learning conditions (Paivio, 1972). Indeed, incidental and intentional learners operating under imagery instructions may produce comparable levels of performance (Bower, 1972). Further evidence comes from the use of post-learning questionnaires in which the subjects indicate the learning strategies they have employed. These indicate quite clearly that subjects are able to increase their use of mental imagery in response to specific instructions to do so (Paivio and Yuille, 1967, 1969; cf. Bugelski, 1971). However, they also show that subjects frequently use mental imagery spontaneously, especially in learning relatively concrete material, and this tendency increases over trials even when the subjects have been given specific instructions to use alternative mnemonic strategies (see Paivio, 1971c, pp. 361–6, for discussion of this point). The implication is that the substantial observed effects of imagery mnemonic instructions are nevertheless likely to be underestimates of the effectiveness of mental imagery as a mnemonic strategy (Anderson and Kulhavy, 1972; Bower, 1972).

One of the traditional elements of techniques for the improvement of memory is the prescription that the learner should try to produce mental images that are in some way bizarre or peculiar. Instructions to produce bizarre mental images have been found to produce improved recall performance when compared with standard learning instructions (Perensky and Senter, 1970). However, studies which have attempted to separate the effects of bizarreness and of imaging have failed to find any additional effect of constructing bizarre images over and above the benefit of using mental imagery (Hauck, Walsh and Kroll, 1976; Senter and Hoffman, 1976; Wollen, Weber and Lowry, 1972; Wood, 1967). Indeed, bizarre mental images take longer to construct and may result in poorer performance (Nappe and Wollen, 1973); similarly, sentences describing conventional or plausible situations may be more effective mediators in paired-associate learning than sentences describing bizarre or implausible situations (Collyer, Jonides and Bevan, 1972; Kulhavy and Heinen, 1974). Neisser (1976, p. 140) has expressed certain reservations about accepting these negative findings, and there are suggestions that bizarreness may be of benefit after a delay of 24 hours or more (Andreoff and Yarmey, 1976; Delin, 1968; cf. Webber and Marshall, 1978), or if the subjects rate the bizarreness of their mental images at the time of presentation (Merry and Graham, 1978). However, the safest conclusion at present is that bizarreness is not a factor determining the value of mental imagery in improving recall.

The most common explanation of the effectiveness of imagery mnemonic instructions is the *coding redundancy hypothesis* mentioned in the previous chapter, according to which memory performance varies with the number of alternative memory codes available for an item. This is naturally the explanation favoured by adherents of the dual coding theory (for example, Bower, 1970a, 1972; Paivio, 1971c, chap. 11). The specific account runs as follows (Paivio, 1971c, p. 389):

Any superiority observed under imagery mnemonic conditions may result from the addition of imagery to a verbal baseline laid down during the subject's initial representational or associative reactions to the to-be-learned items, i.e., two mediational systems are potentially available rather than one.

However, this account must be evaluated against the findings of an important area of experimental research which has attempted to identify the effective component when subjects are instructed to use mental imagery in their learning.

6.2 INTERACTIVE AND SEPARATIVE IMAGERY

While it has generally been established that instructions to use mental imagery in learning may lead to substantial improvements in recall and recognition performance, there is one important exception to this generalisation which was mentioned briefly in the previous chapter. It is crucial that the mental imagery used by the subjects in such experiments serves to increase the organisation and cohesion of the material to be remembered. Accordingly, instructions to produce separate mental images corresponding to the individual stimulus items may have no effect upon performance at all, and may even lead to a reduction in recall.

This point was first identified by Bower (1972), who compared the incidental learning performance of a group of subjects receiving *interaction* instructions (to construct a mental image depicting two objects interacting in some way) with that of another group of subjects receiving *separation* instructions (to construct a mental image depicting two objects 'separated in their imaginal space, like two pictures on opposite walls of a room'). The first group demonstrated the usual marked superiority in recall when cued with one of the words in each pair, whereas the second group performed at the level expected when subjects were merely instructed to use rote repetition. As Bower concluded: 'Instructions to image the terms per se have relatively little effect on associative learning. The

important component is the interactive relation between the imaged objects.'
Elsewhere, Bower (1970b) replicated this basic effect using intentional learning
conditions and a control group who used overt rote repetition. Bower's
theoretical discussion will be considered in a moment.

Similar findings were obtained by Begg (1973), by Dempster and Rohwer
(1974), and by Rowe and Paivio (Paivio, 1972), although most of this
subsequent research employed slightly different separation instructions, in which
the subjects were merely told to construct a separate mental image for each
individual stimulus item. (The modification does not materially affect the
experimental outcome, and makes the task somewhat more intelligible for the
subjects.) Morris and Stevens (1974) compared the usefulness of interactive and
separative imagery in the free recall of noun triplets, and found that only
interaction instructions facilitated memory performance. This variation in recall
was associated with a concomitant variation in the subjects' mnemonic
organisation of the material, as measured by the extent to which the members of
a triplet tended to be recalled together. Similar results were found by Richardson
(1976b, 1978d), who investigated the free recall of lists of unrelated words, and
measured subjective organisation by the extent to which consecutively presented
pairs of words tended to be recalled together. Whereas interaction instructions
are known to have a selective, beneficial effect upon secondary memory (see
above), Richardson's experiments showed that separation instructions reduced
the contribution of secondary memory but increased that of primary memory; it
was concluded that instructions to make up separate mental images of the items
to be remembered disrupted the subjects' organisation of a list, and required a
greater use of primary memory as a short-term buffer store.

An experiment by Neisser and Kerr (1973) compared the effectiveness of
interactive and separative mental imagery, and also attempted to determine
whether effective mental images have to describe picturable interactive
relationships. They used an incidental learning task in which the subjects were
asked to rate the vividness of the mental imagery evoked by three types of
sentence. Some sentences described a pair of objects in a manner designed to
encourage separative imagery: for example, 'Looking from one window, you see
the Statue of Liberty; from a window in another wall, you see a daffodil.' Some
sentences described a pair of objects in an interacting, picturable relationship:
for example, 'A daffodil is sitting on top of the torch held up by the Statue of
Liberty.' Finally, some sentences described a pair of objects in an interacting
relationship, but not one which could be represented by any ordinary two-
dimensional picture: for example, 'A daffodil is hidden inside the torch held up
by the Statue of Liberty.' The latter, 'concealed' condition produced performance which was superior to the 'separative' condition, and not significantly
different from the 'pictorial' condition. Neisser and Kerr concluded that the
mnemonic efficacy of an image depended only on the spatial relationships which
were represented, and not on the pictorial quality of those relationships. Their

results seem to imply that mental imagery is spatial in nature, and not tied to any specific sensory modality (Baddeley, 1976, p. 231). However, their subjects' reports indicated that they had to make the 'concealed' relationships picturable in order to carry out the task. In the majority of cases, the subjects reported making the concealed object visible directly, imagining being able to 'see through' the concealing surface, or imagining some movement or change of position which brought the object into view (Neisser, 1972*b*). Thus, Neisser and Kerr's experiment cannot be accepted as a valid comparison of 'pictorial' and 'concealed' imagery, although their results supported the general idea of the mnemonic effectiveness of interactive imagery.

Bower (1970*b*) argued that the effects of interactive and separative imagery permitted one to discriminate between two general classes of explanation for the efficacy of mental imagery in human memory: 'One class of explanations supposes that the imagery effect is due to some benefit regarding the differentiation of the individual elements in the pairs; the other class of explanations attributes the effect to the element-to-element association process itself.' He suggested that the poor performance of subjects who used separative imagery showed that the benefit of mental imagery was in the formation of relational associations rather than in the encoding of individual items. Bower also found that interactive imagery instructions enhanced paired-associate learning without increasing the subjects' performance on a test of stimulus recognition, which supported his conclusion. (Of course, other experiments *have* found effects of imagery mnemonic instructions in tests of recognition memory, as was mentioned above. These findings indicate *either* that interactive imagery instructions also affect the encoding of individual stimulus items, *or* that associative retrieval processes operate in tests of recognition memory.)

It is of course well known that subjective organisation is important in verbal learning, and that procedures to increase that organisation which are merely based upon verbal categorisation may also lead to substantial improvements in recall performance (for example, Mandler, 1967). Consequently, Bower's argument tends to undermine the idea, central to dual coding theory, that the use of mental imagery leads to a qualitatively different mnemonic representation. Bower (1970*b*, 1972) continued this line by pointing to parallels between the findings obtained in comparing interactive and separative imagery, and those obtained in the recall of pictures and in the recall of pairs of words. In the previous chapter, I mentioned experiments which demonstrated that two pictured objects are more easily remembered if they are shown in some sort of interaction. It is also known that the recall of noun pairs is facilitated if they are embedded in a meaningful sentence and connected by a verb or preposition; this facilitation does not occur if the sentence is anomalous (in which case performance may actually be reduced) or if the two nouns are merely connected by a conjunction (Bobrow and Bower, 1969; Epstein, Rock and Zuckerman, 1960; Rohwer, 1966). On the basis of the similarity among these experimental results, Bower concluded that 'this recall pattern with pictures, images, and words is probably being produced by the same relational generating system' (see also Anderson and Bower, 1973, p. 457).

More recently, this approach has been developed by Begg (1978), who studied cued recall, free recall and recognition memory for pairs or triads of nouns learned under interaction or separation instructions. Although cued recall performance was substantially better with interactive imagery than with separative imagery, this was not so in the case of recognition memory, and was not so in the case of free recall unless the mnemonic instructions encouraged interunit organisation as well as intraunit organisation. Begg concluded that the results merely reflect general principles of mnemonic organisation, rather than any specific properties of mental imagery. Begg and Young (1977) compared the effects of interactive imagery and type of connective in the retention of pairs of nouns. As mentioned above, verbs enhance organisation and recall more than conjunctions. (Begg and Young demonstrated further that prepositions which imply spatial contiguity, such as *in* or *on*, produce this facilitation, whereas prepositions which merely suggest spatial proximity, such as *near* or *by*, do not.) Interactive imagery instructions were found to remove this *form class effect* by selectively increasing performance on pairs connected by conjunctions; on the other hand, separative imagery instructions were found to remove the effect by selectively reducing performance on pairs connected by verbs. Once again, Begg and Young took the attitude that imagery mnemonic instructions were merely one way of manipulating the likelihood that pairs of items will be jointly encoded in memory.

6.3 IMAGERY AND VERBAL INSTRUCTIONS

The results which have just been described are not formally inconsistent with dual coding theory. As Paivio (1972) pointed out, this position entails that mnemonic instructions may lead to increased performance *either* by providing an alternative memory code (the coding redundancy hypothesis) *or* by increasing the organisation of the material to be remembered within one or both representations. Nevertheless, if the effects of imagery instructions could be explained by a theory which posits only a single form of coding in memory, then on the grounds of parsimony this latter position should be adopted in preference to one which posits two or more representations. Conversely, more evidence on the effects of imagery mnemonic instructions is required if dual coding theory is to be given a sound empirical basis.

One source of evidence involves the comparison of imagery instructions and other mnemonic devices which do not explicitly mention the use of mental imagery. Just as the presentation of a pair of nouns in a meaningful phrase or sentence may lead to improved recall, substantial improvements in performance are also obtained when the subjects themselves are asked to make up a sentence linking two nouns (Bower, 1972). Instructions to generate such verbal mediators may be just as effective in increasing recall as instructions to use interactive mental imagery (Janssen, 1976, p. 42). These findings might be interpreted as further evidence for the idea that constructing mental images and generating sentences are two forms of cognitive processing operating on a common representational system in memory. The stronger idea that this system might be verbal or propositional in nature was considered by Bower (1970a):

> According to this extreme view, therefore, discovering and tagging (or storing) linguistic relationships between items would be assumed to be the basic operational processes in memory, and the 'mental imagery' instructions would act only parasitically, deceptively, indirectly, but nonetheless inevitably through this verbal medium.

However, Bower himself rejected this 'strict verbal hypothesis'. On the one hand, his own experiments had shown that the effects of instructions to use interactive mental imagery are sometimes greater than those of instructions to generate linking sentences; however, he agreed that the differences are typically not very large, and so there may still be considerable overlap between the cognitive processes aroused by the two procedures. On the other hand, it could be argued that the overlap arises not because imagery instructions enhance the organisation of material within a common, propositional representation, but because sentence generation itself depends upon the use of mental imagery (cf. Paivio, 1971b). In support of this idea, Bower (1972) mentioned that his subjects spontaneously reported the experience of imaging the scene described by a generated sentence (but cf. Bugelski, 1971).

Another source of evidence is an extension of the original approach used by Paivio and Csapo (1973) which was mentioned in the previous chapter. It will be recalled that these experimenters attempted to determine whether repeated presentations of pictures and words created new, independent representations in memory, or whether they merely served to strengthen a single, original presentation. Paivio and Csapo carried out further experiments using homogeneous lists of either pictures or words, where the subjects were either to construct a mental image of the object pictured or named, or to pronounce its name to themselves. Particular items could be presented once or twice, and they could be imaged or pronounced at each presentation. An unanticipated recall test produced an analogous pattern of results to that obtained in the original experiment. Not surprisingly, repeated presentations produced an increase in recall performance, and imaging produced better performance than pronouncing. Repeated imaging and repeated pronouncing produced poorer performance than would be expected on the basis of stochastically independent effects, but imaging and pronouncing the same item conformed with the assumption of additive effects. These findings were replicated and extended by Paivio (1975a), and were taken to support the hypothesis of functionally independent imaginal and verbal representations in long-term memory. However, the experiments actually show at most that the phonemic representation produced by pronouncing a word is functionally independent of the semantic representation produced by constructing a mental image of its referent; the results do not determine whether the latter representation is pictorial or propositional in nature, and so they do not distinguish between dual coding theory and common coding theory.

6.4   IMAGERY INSTRUCTIONS AND SELECTIVE INTERFERENCE

In recent years, many psychologists have attempted to establish the form of coding or representation used in memory by investigating which sorts of concurrent task will interfere with recall performance. This idea was discussed in chapters 4 and 5. The analysis rests upon the assumption that a concurrent task will disrupt the ability to remember only if it makes demands on human information processing which are similar to those of the original memory task (Healy, 1975). Paivio (1975*d*) has pointed out that, in a sense, increasing presentation rate may be seen as a way of selectively interfering with cognitive processing. The fact that imagery mnemonic instructions are more effective at slower rates of presentation (Paivio, 1971*c*, pp. 343–4) may therefore be taken as evidence that such instructions give rise to additional forms of representation in memory. However, such findings are clearly only weak evidence for the dual coding position.

The particular problem of interest is the investigation of the effects of concurrent spatial tasks upon the retention of verbal information and the beneficial effect of imagery mnemonic instructions. The first study to investigate this problem was carried out by Atwood (1971), who presented concrete and abstract noun pairs in the context of phrases. Two groups of subjects carried out a concurrent task, in which the digits 1 and 2 were presented during the interstimulus intervals, and where the subjects had to respond orally in each case with the other digit ('1' for 2, '2' for 1); one group responded to visually presented digits, and the other group responded to auditorily presented digits. The paired associates were presented auditorily, and a control group received no signals during the interstimulus intervals. Half of the subjects in each group learned the concrete phrases, and were instructed to visualise the scene described by each. The remaining subjects learned the abstract phrases, and were instructed to 'contemplate the meaning of each phrase as a whole'. The results showed that the auditory task interfered more with the retention of the abstract material, whereas the visual task interfered more with the retention of the concrete material. Atwood concluded that a concurrent visual task interfered selectively with the use of mental imagery.

However, there are several problems with this study (Janssen, 1976, pp. 31–2). First, Atwood completely confounded the effect of varying the mnemonic instructions with the effect of varying the concreteness of the stimulus material.

These are two different ways of investigating mental imagery, and there is no guarantee that they will be affected by a concurrent interfering task in the same manner. Atwood's experiment provides no way of testing the specific hypothesis that a concurrent task will reduce the beneficial effect of imagery mnemonic instructions. (The relationship between such tasks and the effect of stimulus concreteness will be considered in the following chapter.) Second, the experimental material in Atwood's study was somewhat bizarre (for example, 'nudist devouring a bird'). Third, and most crucial, attempts to replicate Atwood's experiment have continually proved unsuccessful (Baddeley, Grant, Wight and Thomson, 1974; Bower, Munoz and Arnold, cited by Anderson and Bower, 1973, p. 459; Brooks, cited by Paivio, 1971c, p. 374; Quinn, cited by Baddeley, 1976, p. 229).

A series of experiments was reported by Janssen (1976) in an attempt to clarify the situation. (In this chapter, only the results bearing upon the effects of imagery mnemonic instructions will be discussed.) The first experiment concerned the intentional learning of paired associates under imagery mediation, verbal mediation and rote rehearsal instructions with Atwood's auditory and visual tasks and a control condition. The second experiment compared the incidental and intentional learning of paired associates under imagery and verbal mediation instructions with the auditory and visual concurrent tasks. The third experiment concerned the free recall of lists of nouns under separative imagery, interactive imagery, separative verbal and standard free-recall instructions with the auditory and verbal tasks and a control condition with no concurrent activity. A further experiment used paired-associate learning under imagery and verbal mediation instructions with Atwood's auditory and visual tasks and a spatial tracking task. In three of these experiments there was a significant main effect of interference type, but in none of the experiments did the interaction between type of instructions and type of concurrent interference even approach statistical significance. Janssen reported one experiment which investigated the effect of a concurrent task upon the *retrieval* of paired associates. This did demonstrate a significant interaction in the expected direction, such that subjects using imaginal mediators were more disrupted by a visual concurrent task, whereas subjects using verbal mediators were more disrupted by an auditory concurrent task. This result is quite different from those of the other experiments, and clearly stands in need of replication. Given the excellent agreement among Janssen's other four studies and previous attempts to replicate Atwood's (1971) findings, the safest conclusion at the present time seems to be that concurrent visual or spatial tasks do not normally have any selective effect upon the use of mental imagery in human learning.

In chapter 4, I mentioned some unpublished experiments by Baddeley and Lieberman on the disruptive effects of concurrent tasks in immediate memory. The same series of experiments included studies of the effects of concurrent pursuit tracking upon performance in long-term memory (Baddeley, 1976, pp. 230–2). In the first experiment, subjects who were instructed to use rote rehearsal were compared with those who were taught the 'one-bun' mnemonic. This technique consists of a nonsense rhyme, 'one is a bun, two is a shoe', and so on, and is used to learn a sequence of items by constructing a compound image relating the first object and a bun, another image relating the second object and a shoe, and so on. Baddeley and Lieberman found that the advantage of using the mnemonic was slightly reduced when the subjects carried out the concurrent pursuit tracking task. However, a further experiment compared subjects using rote rehearsal with those who were taught a location mnemonic. In this technique, the subject learns a sequence of items by constructing an image locating each object at a particular location on a well known route (for example, a walk around the university campus). Baddeley and Lieberman found that the usefulness of this mnemonic was drastically reduced when the subjects carried out the concurrent pursuit tracking task.

On the basis of these results, Baddeley (1976, p. 232) concluded that 'it is possible to interfere with the control process involved in forming, manipulating, and utilizing images'. However, this does not explain why concurrent tracking did not greatly disrupt the use of the 'one-bun' mnemonic, and it ignores Janssen's (1976) continual failure to show any selective interference with the use of mental imagery in learning, either when compared with the use of verbal mediators, or when compared with the use of rote repetition. These latter results indicate that concurrent spatial tasks do not interfere with the primary function of mental imagery which has been identified in this chapter, the elaboration and strengthening of associative connections in long-term memory. On the other hand, it is reasonable to suppose that such concurrent tasks will interfere with other constructive, manipulative or spatial tasks in short-term, non-verbal, working memory. The location mnemonic includes a component which seems to fall within this latter category, namely the manipulation of a pictured geographical representation, and it is therefore not surprising that it is disrupted by concurrent tracking. However, the 'one-bun' system merely involves the use of a well learned set of phonemic associations, and certainly does not place any demands upon the form of working memory defined above. It is thus equally unsurprising that concurrent spatial tasks do not interfere drastically with the use of this mnemonic, nor with the purely associative strategies which were used by Janssen's (1976) subjects. It is of course an implication of this analysis that the constructive and elaborative uses of mental imagery which were described in chapter 4 are functionally independent of one another.

6.5   THE USEFULNESS OF IMAGERY MNEMONICS

It is quite clear that, under the circumstances investigated by cognitive psychologists in their formal laboratory experiments, the elaboration and construction of integrative, interactive, mental images may lead to substantial and reliable improvements in the ability to remember. But what is the value and generality of these techniques, and what is their role in the development of human understanding? Human learning is of course most crucial in schools, yet nothing is really known concerning the potential value in formal education of the technique of using mental imagery. As Hunter (1977) concluded: 'There is, as yet, almost no systematic data on the uses and usages of the technique, nor on whether children can be taught to appreciate its range of utility and to diagnose contexts of appropriate use.'

In order to understand the role of mnemonics in cognitive development, Hunter suggested the concept of 'adaptive cognitive regression': material which cannot be adequately grasped at the intended level of comprehension is provisionally retained at a more primitive cognitive level. Similarly, Bower (1972) made the following suggestion: 'Our prescription to the adult in approaching a new learning task is for him to become as a child again, to tap the wellsprings of his suppressed imaginative talents that have lain buried under years of linguistic development.' Hunter argued that this heuristic approach 'occupies a significant, albeit minor, place in the repertoire of techniques by which people learn and remember information, and a more explicit recognition of that place could be of practical value'. Thus, the formal discussion of the value of a mnemonic in the classroom could help both the teacher and his students to decide whether it should be retained, improved or rejected. A recent example of this is the research by Atkinson (1975; Atkinson and Raugh, 1975) which transformed the informal mnemonic used by individual language learners into a formal, explicit teaching programme for learning the vocabulary of a foreign language (see also Paivio, 1976d).

Nevertheless, most mnemonic techniques are very limited in their range of possible applications. Hunter assessed the location mnemonic in the following manner:

> The Method has such a circumscribed range of utility that it is useless for all practical purposes of learning and remembering. Appropriate task conditions are essential. The presented items must be translatable into imaged objects; the rate of presentation must be slow, not faster than about one item every three seconds; and the Method breaks down if we try to comprehend relationships between items that are not strictly contiguous. These task conditions rarely arise in real life. . . .

Hunter went on to quote with approval Francis Bacon's remark that the mnemonic is 'not dextrous to be applied to the serious use of business and occasions'. Similarly, Morris (1977) suggested that imagery mnemonics are really only of value in learning lists of unrelated, concrete words. Of course, even if mnemonic techniques based upon mental imagery are entirely lacking in general practical utility, this cannot be blamed upon the efforts of psychologists. Such techniques have been devised by ordinary human beings for use in specific mundane activities. Their limitations merely reflect the superficial understanding which ordinary folk have of their own cognitive faculties. Nevertheless, psychologists *can* be blamed for having only recently paid attention to the possible implications of mnemonic techniques for psychological theories of those faculties, and for having so far failed to offer more effective devices for improving memory in real-life situations.

6.6 CONCLUSIONS

While it may be true that mnemonic techniques based upon mental imagery are of only limited value in assisting learning in everyday life, it does not follow that the study of mental imagery will only be of limited value in understanding memory function. This latter point has to be decided by an informed and critical appreciation of the available experimental research.

The evidence which I have reviewed in this chapter indicates that under laboratory conditions instructions to use mental imagery may lead to substantial improvements in memory performance. The comparison of interaction and separation instructions shows that these effects come about by means of increased organisation of the material to be remembered. More generally, the effects of imagery mnemonic instructions are entirely analogous to those of verbal mediation instructions, and the resulting increases in recall performance are typically comparable in the two cases. The study of repetition effects in incidental recall does not permit one to specify the nature of the mnemonic representation produced by mental imagery, and the effects of concurrent spatial tasks upon memory performance are largely independent of the effects of imagery mnemonic instructions, unless the mnemonic technique itself contains a spatial, manipulative component.

The empirical findings on the effects of imagery mnemonic instructions do not permit one to distinguish between dual coding theory and common coding theory. Indeed, both approaches tend to interpret the effects in terms of enhanced relational organisation. However, precisely because both accounts can readily handle the available evidence, considerations of parsimony must favour common coding theory: it is simply unnecessary to postulate an additional, imaginal system of mnemonic representations. A propositional system of representations is necessary to handle the independent corpus of evidence on sentential mediators and the form class effect, and this approach can readily encompass the effects of instructions to use mental imagery without serious modification.

Nevertheless, once again, the property of intentionality compels one to reconsider the implications of the empirical evidence. A subject who constructs a mental image in response to the appropriate mnemonic instructions does so under an intentional description which must be conceived as an abstract propositional representation of the content or object of the image. Such propositions also underlie other mediating devices which might be employed, such as generated sentences. It is therefore totally unsurprising that the propositional structures reported by subjects in using interactive and separative imagery are similar to those produced by subjects who are instructed to generate sentences. Anderson and Bower (1973, p. 457; see also Bower, 1970*b*) describe these in some detail:

> If one examines the verbalizations or descriptions of the images generated by these subjects, the interaction-imagery subjects invariably use verbs or locatives, as in agent–action–object constructions (e.g., 'cow *kicked* lawyer') or agent–preposition–object constructions ('lawyer *on top of* cow'). On the other hand, separation-imagery subjects invariably use simple *conjunctions* to describe the two objects: 'A picture of a *cow* over here and a picture of a *lawyer* over there.' There might be many adjectival embellishments of each object singly, but the primary connective between the two objects was the simple conjunction *and*.

Of course, it is possible that the construction of a mental image according to an intentional description when material is presented for learning gives rise *both* to a propositional representation *and* to a pictorial representation in long-term memory. However, the identity of any mental image generated at the time of the retention test will depend upon the intentional description on the basis of which *it* is constructed, and so whether it is the right image will depend upon whether it is constructed on the basis of the right propositional description (cf. Wittgenstein, 1953, §389, p. 177; 1967, §650). This means that only the propositional description will be functional in remembering, and that any pictorial representation produced by the original imaging experience will be purely epiphenomenal. This conclusion applies whether the subject was deliberately constructing mental images in response to specific mnemonic instructions to do so, or whether he happened to experience mental imagery in carrying out other instructions, such as generating sentences, or in learning without specific mnemonic instructions.

7

Remembering Individual Words

The experimental evidence discussed in the previous chapter showed that subjects can use mental imagery to remember verbal material when specifically instructed to do so. The results indicated that this strategy can produce reliable improvements in recall and recognition performance. However, experiments which have collected 'introspective' reports on the techniques employed in remembering have found that subjects spontaneously use mental imagery in learning verbal material; that is, mental imagery is regularly employed even without specific mnemonic instructions (Paivio, Smythe and Yuille, 1968; Richardson, 1978e). Of course, one would expect that some verbal material would evoke mental imagery more readily than other material. It would not really be surprising that imagery is used to remember material which reliably, immediately and easily evokes such experiences. The principal methodological problem is that of identifying such material, and, more generally, of measuring and quantifying the ease with which words, phrases and sentences evoke mental imagery. In this chapter, I shall consider the idea of mental imagery as a cognitive experience which is differentially evoked by different stimulus materials.

7.1 STIMULUS IMAGEABILITY

An experimenter is at perfect liberty to define the ease with which different words evoke mental imagery on a purely personal, intuitive basis, but if he wishes to ensure that his definition has any generality, and that his intuitions are similar to those of his experimental subjects, he must consult them in order to validate his selection of experimental material. In contemporary research, this is usually carried out with the assistance of questionnaires administered to large groups of subjects, in which evoked mental imagery is scored on a seven-point rating scale. The first large-scale study of this nature was reported by Paivio, Yuille and Madigan (1968), who collected ratings on 925 English nouns. The instructions given to their subjects were as follows:

> Nouns differ in their capacity to arouse mental images of things or events. Some words arouse a sensory experience, such as a mental picture or sound,

very quickly and easily, whereas others may do so only with difficulty (i.e., after a long delay) or not at all. The purpose of this experiment is to rate a list of words as to the ease or difficulty with which they arouse mental images. Any word which, in your estimation, arouses a mental image (i.e., a mental picture, or sound, or other sensory experience) very quickly and easily should be given a *high imagery* rating; any word that arouses a mental image with difficulty or not at all should be given a *low imagery* rating. Think of the words 'apple' or 'fact'. Apple would probably arouse an image relatively easily and would be rated as high imagery; fact would probably do so with difficulty and would be rated as low imagery. Since words tend to make you think of other words as associates, e.g., knife-fork, it is important that you note only the ease of getting a mental image of an object or an event to the word.

A measure of the imagery value or *imageability* of each stimulus item is computed by taking the mean score across the subjects participating in such an experiment.

It is now well established that stimulus imageability is positively correlated with performance in a wide variety of learning tasks (Janssen, 1976, pp. 5–12; Paivio, 1971c, chap. 7). This effect has been demonstrated with free recall (Janssen, 1976, pp. 49–51; Paivio, 1968; Paivio, Yuille and Rogers, 1969; Richardson, 1974a, 1978d), with serial recall (Paivio et al., 1969), with paired-associate learning (Paivio, Smythe and Yuille, 1968; Richardson, 1978e, in press), and with recognition memory (Olver, described by Paivio, 1971c, p. 184). Stimulus imageability has been found to affect both the accuracy with which material is retrieved from memory, and the speed with which it is retrieved (Macht and Scheirer, 1975). It has also been shown to have a selective effect upon long-term or secondary memory, using a variety of procedures for quantifying the relative contributions of primary and secondary memory to total performance (Paivio, 1975b; Richardson, 1974a, 1978d).

It will be noted that the instructions described above tend to emphasise the *ease* with which mental imagery is evoked by a stimulus. However, some researchers have considered that the *vividness* of the evoked imagery is also important. Bower (1972) asked his subjects to rate the vividness of the imagined scenes suggested by pairs of nouns, and found that their ratings predicted their subsequent recall of each pair, even when the recall test was unanticipated. Similarly, Anderson and Hidde (1971) found that ratings of the vividness of the images suggested by individual sentences would predict their subsequent recall. However, in both cases the effect was relatively weak and apparently confounded with that of ease of image arousal. Indeed, Neisser and Kerr (1973) failed to find any difference between recalled and non-recalled items in terms of rated vividness of evoked mental imagery. However, they did find a clear negative correlation between rated vividness and the latency of image arousal, and Paivio (1968) showed that both measures were correlated with the rated ease of image arousal. It is clearly advisable to separate these different attributes if at all possible (Paivio, 1972, 1975d).

One set of evidence on this question comes from the experiment by Neisser and Kerr (1973), which was described in detail in the previous chapter. It will be remembered that this study compared the relative effectiveness of separative imagery, 'pictorial' interactive imagery and 'concealed' interactive imagery (where the relevant interactive relationship could not have been represented in any ordinary two-dimensional picture). The experiment was an incidental learning task in which the orienting task required the subjects to rate the vividness of the mental imagery evoked by each sentence on a seven-point scale. The vividness ratings indicated that the 'pictorial' images were better than the other two types, which were essentially alike. Nevertheless, as was mentioned in chapter 6, the 'concealed' images produced better recall performance than the separative images, and were not significantly different from the 'pictorial' images. Thus, the usefulness of mental imagery appears to be determined by its relational organisation, and not by its vividness.

Further evidence comes from two experiments which Richardson (in press) carried out as extensions of a study mentioned above by Bower (1972). In each case the subjects rated the imageability of the stimulus material in response to instructions similar to those of Paivio, Yuille and Madigan (1968), and then received an unanticipated retention test. When the subjects rated individual nouns, and the test was one of free recall, the average imageability rating given to each item did not show a significant correlation with the number of subjects who recalled that item ($r = +0.28$). However, when the subjects rated pairs of nouns on the ease with which they evoked an interactive mental image, and one member of each pair was given as the cue to the recall of the other member of that pair, there was substantial correlation between the average imageability rating given to each pair and the number of subjects who recalled that pair ($r = +0.67$). These experiments suggest that it is the ease with which a stimulus item evokes an integrative mental image which is the critical property determining how easily it will be remembered.

The question arises as to whether it is really the case that material which is of high imageability is easily remembered *because* it evokes mental imagery when presented for learning. This is by no means a trivial question: the fact that verbal material may display considerable variation both in ratings of evoked mental imagery and in the ease with which it can be recalled in no way guarantees that evoked mental imagery is causally responsible for improved retention. Additional evidence is necessary to substantiate this latter conclusion (cf. Anderson, 1978; Neisser, 1972*b*)

The most important source of evidence is the reports given by the subjects themselves as to the sorts of devices or mediators used in learning experiments. First, the frequency of reported use of mental imagery is substantially greater in the case of material which is of high imageability (Paivio, Smythe and Yuille, 1968; Richardson, 1978*e*; cf. Neisser, 1972*b*). Second, the vividness of reported imagery both at presentation and recall is greater in the case of material of high imageability, and the effect at the time of recall is greater if the retention test is unexpected (Sheehan, 1972). It thus appears that material which is of high imageability is more likely to evoke mental imagery in the context of an experiment on verbal learning, and this produces consequent improvements in memory performance.

Is one to conclude from this that mental imagery is not employed in remembering stimulus material which is rated low in imageability? First, one must recall that the critical dimension measured by this scale appears to be the ease with which a stimulus item evokes an integrative mental image. Moreover, ratings of the *ease* with which a stimulus evokes a mental image are highly correlated with the *speed* with which that stimulus evokes a mental image. It is reasonable to expect, therefore, that items which receive low imageability ratings will evoke mental images eventually if the subjects are allowed an adequate period of time for study. It is interesting in this context to note that there is a curvilinear relationship between rated imageability and the latency of evoked imagery, so that items of moderate rated imageability evoke mental images as quickly as those of high rated imageability (Janssen, 1976, p. 84). Moreover, as one would expect, there is a similar curvilinear relationship between rated imageability and recall performance, so that items of moderate imageability are also recalled as well as those of high imageability (ibid., pp. 50–1). However, the important evidence seems to be that obtained from the use of post-learning questionnaires to identify the relative employment of different sorts of mediator. These show that, under the experimental conditions conventionally employed to investigate human memory, the use of mental imagery with material rated low in stimulus imageability is relatively infrequent (Paivio, Smythe and Yuille, 1968; Richardson, 1978*e*).

Once again, the explanation of the effect of stimulus imageability upon retention which is preferred by dual coding theorists is the coding redundancy hypothesis. Recall increases with stimulus imageability 'because the items are increasingly likely to be stored in *both* the verbal and the nonverbal code . . . . The increased availability of both codes increases the probability of item recall because the response can be retrieved from either code—one code could be forgotten during the retention interval, but verbal recall would still be possible provided that the other is retained' (Paivio, 1971*c*, pp. 207–8; see also Paivio, 1972). Propositional theories of memory are not sufficiently articulated to encompass the findings which I have been discussing, but it would not be unreasonable to suppose that they would attribute the effect of stimulus imageability upon performance, like the effect of imagery mnemonic instructions, to enhanced associative organisation; alternatively, it could be argued that propositions which contain spatial predicates are more likely to be retained.

The use of an additional level of representation has been taken to imply the possibility of decoding errors at the time of recall. Specifically, the use of an additional, pictorial code should increase the likelihood of semantic confusions. This proposal was put forward in the following manner by Paivio (1975*b*; see also 1971*c*, pp. 385–6; 1972):

Since image-mediated verbal recall requires that the image or some component of it be transformed or decoded back into the appropriate verbal response, decoding errors should be a strong possibility. . . . This can be appreciated most readily in the case of paired-associate recall of concrete noun responses that have synonyms which could be mediated by the same response-term image. The image of an adult female, for example, could generate 'lady' or 'woman' as a response. The same process might operate in a more subtle way in other instances.

This idea is not really a new one. As Marks (1972) mentioned, Bartlett (1932) attributed most of the inventions and importations found in repeated reproductions of prose passages to visual imagery. However, it is only recently that there has been any sound evidence for the proposal. Bower (1972) compared subjects using interactive imagery instructions and subjects using rote repetition in learning a paired-associate list containing unique concrete nouns and another paired-associate list containing synonym pairs. The subjects using mental imagery produced poorer performance on the synonym list than on the unique list, but the subjects using rote rehearsal showed no appreciate drop in performance. Moreover, 31% of the errors made by the subjects using mental imagery were synonym intrusions, whereas the corresponding figure for the subjects using rote rehearsal was only 2%.

Similar results have been found in studies of the effects of stimulus imageability. Thus, material of high imageability produces more intrusion errors and fewer omission errors than material of low imageability (Davies and Proctor, 1976; Postman and Burns, 1973). Yuille (1973) showed that the increase in synonym intrusions in recall with material of high imageability or following instructions to use mental imagery was not due to a more rapid degradation of the relevant mediator, and therefore must be attributed to decoding errors (Paivio, 1975*b*). On the other hand, Bower (1970*a*) used a similar basis for arguing that subjects may spontaneously use mental imagery even to remember items of low imageability. His evidence for this was that his subjects sometimes made semantic intrusion errors with such material which took the form of associated concrete words (for example, *church* instead of *religion*). He argued: 'Such errors are entirely understandable in terms of the person's forgetting the linguistic tag on his concrete image, which tag was supposed to remind him to name the abstract concept, not the concrete exemplar.' However, the mere existence of such intrusion errors is at best suggestive of this sort of process. One would prefer to have quantitative data showing that the proportion of concrete intrusion errors given for abstract items was greater than the proportion of abstract intrusion errors given for concrete items. Even this would be far from conclusive, since such results are also consistent with the idea that the use of mental imagery involves a 'deeper' level of coding or processing in long-term memory, and leads to a higher incidence of synonym intrusions merely because it makes more likely the registration of information in a semantic or propositional form. Indeed, the demonstration of an increased number of synonym intrusions shows at most that the subjects are more likely to employ a semantic representation; it does not determine whether this representation is pictorial or propositional in nature, and so it does not distinguish between dual coding theory and common coding theory.

However, Anderson and Bower (1973, pp. 230–2) pointed out that some conceptual relationships may be carried by the propositional description under which an image is constructed, but may not be unambiguously depicted in the image itself. Thus, the pair of sentences 'The lieutenant signed his signature on the cheque' and 'The lieutenant forged a signature on the cheque' are conceptually distinct but would evoke pictorially similar mental images. Another example is the pair of sentences 'George picked up the pen to write on the paper' and 'George picked up the pen to doodle on the paper'. Experiments by Anderson and by Kosslyn showed that such pairs of sentences were confused in tests of recognition memory no more often than pictorially different (though syntactically similar) pairs. Thus, recognition performance is determined by the intentional description under which a sentence might be imaged, and not by pictorial properties of the image. This result is clearly contrary to the expectations of dual coding theory and the interpretation of semantic confusions offered by Paivio (1975*b*).

Other investigations of the effects of stimulus imageability have been concerned with the specific study of paired-associate learning. At a fairly early stage in the development of experimental investigations of mental imagery, it was proposed that the ease with which the stimulus term in a paired associate redintegrates the mediator employed at the time of the original presentation will determine how easily the response term can be retrieved at the time of recall. This was the so-called *conceptual-peg hypothesis* (Paivio, 1963), which at the time constituted a radical departure from conventional theories of associative learning. It led to the specific prediction that the imageability of the stimulus term should be of greater importance than that of the response term in predicting the retention of a paired associate. This was clearly established (Paivio, 1965), and is supported by the fact that the frequency of reported use of mental imagery is also more influenced by the imageability of the stimulus term than by that of the response term (Paivio and Yuille, 1969). Further evidence comes from tests of backward association, where the subjects are unexpectedly cued with the nominal response term, and are required to produce the nominal stimulus term. Under these circumstances, the conceptual-peg hypothesis predicts that the imageability of the response term will be of greater importance in determining the retention of a paired associate, and the results clearly support the hypothesis (Bower, 1972; Lockhart, 1969; Yarmey and O'Neill, 1969).

Whereas the conceptual-peg hypothesis stresses the facilitatory effect of mental imagery upon the retrieval of information from memory, the research of Bower (1970*b*) described in the previous chapter tends to emphasise the role of mental imagery as a relational organiser, and these two approaches are sometimes set up in opposition to one another. However, it should be remembered that both the richness of a subject's mnemonic organisation and his capacity to utilise certain retrieval schemes at the time of recall are determined by the nature of his encoding activities at the time when the material was originally presented for learning. Indeed, the prevailing opinion among proponents of dual coding theory tends towards the compromise view that mental imagery affects both organisation and retrieval (Karchmer, 1974; Macht and Scheirer, 1975; Paivio, 1972).

However, the evidence for the conceptual-peg hypothesis is also entirely consistent with common coding theory, if it is assumed that propositional memory is more effective, in terms of both storage and retrieval, when encoded descriptions incorporate perceptual or spatial predicates. This assumption is entirely plausible, and might be taken to follow from Anderson and Bower's (1970, pp. 154–5, 460) suggestion that 'a propositional system initially evolved to deal effectively with perceptual material, and that language attached itself parasitically onto this propositional base'. Indeed, the conceptual-peg metaphor was originally introduced without reference to mental imagery (Lambert and Paivio, 1956), and other researchers have proposed redintegrative theories of human memory which postulate a single form of representation (e.g. Horowitz and Manelis, 1972; Horowitz and Prytulak, 1969).

7.2   STIMULUS CONCRETENESS

Much of the experimental research on the use of mental imagery in remembering which has concentrated upon the properties of the stimulus material has employed the dimension of imageability. However, many researchers have also investigated the dimension of stimulus concreteness, which they have felt to be closely related to the former attribute. Like imageability, concreteness has been measured by experimental psychologists using questionnaires in which large numbers of subjects rate various stimulus items along seven-point scales in terms of the extent to which they refer to objects which can be experienced by the senses. Although some earlier researchers had attempted to investigate concreteness by these means, notably Spreen and Schulz (1966), the first large-scale study was again that carried out by Paivio, Yuille and Madigan (1968) on 925 English nouns. Their instructions included the following explanation: 'Any word that refers to objects, materials, or persons should receive a *high concreteness* rating; any word that refers to an abstract concept that cannot be experienced by the senses should receive a *high abstractness* rating . . . .'

It is well known (and not at all surprising) that ratings of the imageability of stimulus material are highly correlated with ratings of its concreteness; Paivio, Yuille and Madigan (1968) gave a correlation of +0.83 for their 925 English nouns. Indeed, contemporary research in experimental psychology tends to regard concreteness as merely an alternative index of the image-arousing potential of verbal material. However, this way of conceptualising concreteness is rather different from that which one finds in other disciplines (Richardson, 1978a). For example, in developmental psychology (Brown, 1958), in linguistics (Chomsky, 1965, pp. 230–1; Katz and Fodor, 1963) or in philosophy (Strawson, 1959, chap. 1), the fact that a word or phrase refers to a concrete particular is taken to have implications for its role in a person's conceptual structure. In particular, the dimension of stimulus concreteness is taken as a primary factor determining the structure of semantic memory.

Nevertheless, this sort of account has been overshadowed in recent psychological research by the revival of interest in mental imagery. In particular, Paivio was influential in arguing that imageability and concreteness were alternative measures of the likelihood that verbal material would be processed by the use of mental imagery. Besides pointing to the high correlation between the two variables, he dismissed items which differentiated between the two scales as peculiar (Paivio, 1969; 1971c, p. 79; see also Yuille, 1968). On the other hand, he demonstrated that imageability was better than concreteness in predicting performance in free recall, and concluded that the former scale was the superior index of the image-evoking capacity of verbal material (Paivio, 1968; 1971c p. 201). Thus, the dominant conception of concreteness in contemporary experimental psychology is that of a measure of the image-arousing potential of material, but a measure which is secondary in theoretical importance and in predictive power to imageability.

In a recent series of papers, Richardson (1975a, 1975c, 1976a) criticised the reasoning behind Paivio's position, and attempted to distinguish between the two interpretations of concreteness on an experimental basis. A minimal requirement of the position that imageability and concreteness are not merely alternative measures of image-evoking potential is that stimulus items be found which reliably discriminate between the two scales. One experiment (Richardson, 1976a) required different groups of subjects to rate 244 phrases on their concreteness and imageability, and the analysis of their ratings produced a highly significant interaction between the two scales and the various stimulus items. This implied that imageability and concreteness do deviate from one another, and that it is legitimate to study material which distinguishes between the two scales.

The more specific proposal that concreteness is a feature of semantic organisation would be supported by demonstrating effects of concreteness in experimental tasks which are designed to investigate that organisation. Two further experiments were of this nature (Richardson, 1975a). In the first, the subjects were asked to categorise individual nouns on the basis of their meaning, and a majority sorted the words in a manner related to their concreteness. In the second, the subjects were asked to produce a discrete free associate to each of these words, and the concreteness of a word correlated with the average speed with which the associate was given. In neither experiment was stimulus imageability related to the subjects' performance, which implied that neither task was contaminated by imaginal processing. On the other hand, the significant effects of concreteness in these tasks implied that this variable was not merely an index of the image-arousing potential of verbal material (cf. Postman, 1975).

Nevertheless, the question arises as to the relative importance of imageability and concreteness in verbal learning. The first experiment to manipulate the two scales orthogonally considered the free recall of individual nouns (Richardson, 1975c), and produced an interactive relationship, such that imageability had a positive effect upon the recall of items of low concreteness, but no effect upon the recall of items of high concreteness. This pattern was replicated using noun phrases. A subsequent experiment (Richardson, 1975a) showed that image-ability would affect the recall of items of high concreteness if the subjects were instructed to use mental imagery in learning. Under these circumstances, the memorability of the stimulus items varied with their imageability, but not with their concreteness. These results confirmed, once again, that concreteness should not be regarded as an index of the image-arousing capacity of verbal material, but also that the manipulation of stimulus imageability and the use of imagery mnemonic instructions are alternative ways of affecting the same cognitive processes (see below).

However, an important criticism of these experiments is that they did not employ any material of very high imageability. In order to manipulate concreteness and imageability in an orthogonal fashion, stimulus material was selected from the middle regions of the two scales. It could be argued that mental imagery is a useful mnemonic strategy only if the material readily evokes mental images, and hence that these experiments do not give a valid indication of the circumstances under which mental imagery is employed (Richardson, 1978a). An even more serious problem concerns the replicability of the original findings. Although the same pattern of results was obtained in three different experiments, using both individual nouns and phrases, a recent study by Christian, Bickley, Tarka and Clayton (1978) failed to demonstrate an interaction between concreteness and imageability, even though the stimulus material had been selected according to the criteria used in the original experiments. These researchers found that imageability was correlated with memory performance for words of high frequency, but not for words of low frequency, while concreteness was not correlated with recall.

Richardson (1975a) had concluded that, in the absence of explicit instructions to use mental imagery as a mnemonic aid, subjects would employ imagery to remember only the small number of items which were imageable but of low concreteness. Despite the difficulties which have just been mentioned, this theoretical proposal is open to direct empirical evaluation, insofar as stimulus material which produces high ratings on both scales should show no correlation between imageability and recall performance. On the other hand, the conventional position, that concreteness is merely a secondary index of the image-arousing potential of stimulus material, would predict that imageability would be the effective stimulus attribute even with material of high imageability. An experiment was carried out to test these predictions, using a test of free recall with individual nouns with imageability and concreteness ratings greater than 6.0 (Richardson, 1978a). The partial correlation between imageability and performance (even with this restricted range) was +0.41, but the partial correlation between concreteness and performance was −0.13.

These results clearly demonstrated that the imageability of stimulus material, rather than its concreteness, is the effective attribute determining how easily it can be remembered. They are thus quite consistent with the conventional position on the relationship between concreteness and imageability, but are clearly inconsistent with the proposals of Richardson's (1975a) earlier paper. Accordingly, while it may be of interest to distinguish between concreteness and imageability, both conceptually and theoretically, this recent experiment suggests that conventional accounts, which identify stimulus imageability as the primary determiner of recall performance, are likely to be essentially correct.

7.3 LEXICAL COMPLEXITY

A rather different problem arises over the possibility that certain words have a complex internal structure, and that this dimension of linguistic complexity is correlated and thus confounded with the image-evoking potential of individual words. This problem was first raised by Kintsch (1972a, 1972b), who pointed out that many words commonly referred to as 'abstract' may also be regarded as syntactically complex, whereas 'concrete' items may be regarded as relatively simple. The complexity with which Kintsch was concerned is that which has been ascribed to derived nouns, such as *refusal, destruction* and *eagerness*. At one time, many linguists regarded these nouns as resulting from the application of nominalising transformations to their stems or base forms, *refuse, destroy* and *eager* (Chomsky, 1965, pp. 184–92; Fowler, 1971, pp. 129–31; Katz and Postal, 1964, pp. 123–4; Lees, 1960, pp. 64–9). (More accurately, sentences containing such nouns were considered to result from deep structures containing the corresponding base forms, together with some nominalising morpheme.) The idea that derived nouns are more complex than their stems is intuitively plausible, and suggests that they should be more difficult to deal with in a wide variety of psychological tasks than simple nouns which are not produced in this manner.

Kintsch (1972a) carried out three experiments to examine the relative importance of imageability and lexical complexity in paired-associate learning. The results indicated that the two variables had roughly equal effects, although one experiment produced a complex interaction with word frequency. However, Richardson (1975a, 1975c) suggested that there were various respects in which Kintsch's experiments were unsatisfactory, and he carried out further studies in which the variables of imageability, concreteness and lexical complexity were manipulated in an orthogonal fashion in free recall. These showed that lexical complexity had no effect upon recall performance when the imageability and the concreteness of the stimulus material were both controlled. That is, derived nouns are not more difficult to remember than simple nouns, when one allows for the fact that they may be more abstract and less imageable.

These results are consistent with the more recent linguistic account of lexical derivation, according to which derived nouns and their stems are merely alternative surface forms of the same, neutral lexical entry (Chomsky, 1970); this would not predict that derived nouns were more difficult to remember. However, the results are also consistent with the view that derived nouns and their stems are merely distinct lexical items, and J. T. E. Richardson (1977*b*) has argued for this conclusion on the basis of an extensive series of experimental studies. On this account the intuition of a relationship between a derived noun and its base form should be ascribed to diachronic considerations (pertaining to the historical development of the language), rather than to synchronic considerations (pertaining to a correct account of linguistic competence). Accordingly, the distinction between simple and derived nouns is not relevant to an understanding of the processes operating in learning tasks.

7.4 IMAGEABILITY AND MNEMONIC INSTRUCTIONS

According to the operationist presuppositions of contemporary research on mental imagery, it is important to demonstrate that different experimental procedures are investigating the same set of cognitive processes by showing that the effects of those procedures interact in a meaningful and theoretically significant manner when they are incorporated into the same experimental situation. What might one expect if concrete and abstract items are learned by subjects who are given standard instructions, interactive imagery instructions or verbal mediation instructions? For Paivio (1971*c*, p. 359), the predictions were quite unambiguous:

> In general, the expectations were that imagery instructions would interact with item concreteness in such a manner as to enhance imaginal associations to concrete stimuli more than to abstract, with a consequent facilitating effect on learning when the list items (or at least the stimulus members) are concrete but not when they are abstract. Indeed, an imagery set might be expected to interfere with performance in a learning situation involving abstract items because of the difficulty of discovering images for such pairs. No such interaction would be expected with verbal instructional sets, inasmuch as the availability of verbal mediators is theoretically independent of concreteness.

However, the situation is actually more complex. First, as Janssen (1976, p. 15) noted, Paivio predicted an interactive effect at the level of performance on the basis of an interactive effect at the level of the *availability* of mediators;

however, this required additional assumptions about the relative *effectiveness* of imaginal and verbal mediators. Second, Paivio's argument made certain implicit assumptions about the use of such mediators in the absence of specific mnemonic instructions. As he himself realised in a different though quite analogous context (Paivio, 1971c, p. 502), dual coding theory leads to two alternative predictions concerning the effect of interactive imagery instructions upon the recall of concrete and abstract material. On the one hand, as he suggested in the passage quoted above, the effect might be most pronounced in the case of material which can be readily imaged. On the other hand, such material might be learned through the use of mental imagery even under standard learning conditions; it follows that, if explicit instructions have any effect at all, it should be most pronounced in the case of abstract material. Indeed, subjects' reports indicate that mental imagery is spontaneously used to a considerable extent, especially in the learning of concrete material, and this is actually assumed by the explanation of the effect of stimulus imageability upon recall which is proffered by dual coding theory in the form of the coding redundancy hypothesis. Finally, assumptions about the interaction between the effect of stimulus imageability and that of imagery mnemonic instructions must also specify the role of the presentation rate (cf. Paivio, 1972). Too fast a rate of presentation might inhibit the use of mental imagery even with concrete material (see below). Too slow a rate of presentation might allow adequate time for effective imaginal mediators to be discovered even for abstract material. Thus, the exact manner in which imagery mnemonic instructions affect learning performance is likely to depend not only upon the imageability of the stimulus material, but also upon the efficacy of mental imagery in learning the experimental material, the degree of spontaneous use of mental imagery in the absence of specific mnemonic instructions, and the presentation rate employed.

If one considers published research in which interactive imagery instructions are compared with standard learning or rote repetition instructions, the results are quite clear. Instructions to use mental imagery lead to improved performance in the case of concrete material, but not in the case of abstract material. (Equivalently, such instructions tend to enhance the effect of stimulus imageability upon recall performance.) This has been found in free recall (Gupton and Frincke, 1970), in paired-associate learning (Janssen, 1976, pp. 42–3; Paivio and Yuille, 1967; Yuille and Paivio, 1968), and in recognition memory (Morris and Reid, 1974). This is exactly what one would expect in the light of the comments above: these studies were all conventional experiments of the sort in which mental imagery might be expected to be an effective mnemonic device, where the spontaneous use of mental imagery with concrete material was high but not at a ceiling, and where the presentation rates were such as to inhibit the use of mental imagery with abstract material but not with concrete material. It is interesting to note that the relative effects of intentional and incidental recall are quite different from those of imagery mnemonic instructions: intentional learning instructions lead to improved performance in the case of abstract material, but not in the case of concrete material, and instructions to motivate the subjects to learn accentuate this effect (Sheehan, 1972). The clear discrepancy between these results and the effects of imagery mnemonic instructions constitutes further, excellent evidence that such instructions do not merely affect performance by increasing the subjects' motivation (see chapter 6).

However, if one considers experiments in which interactive imagery instructions are compared with verbal mediation instructions, the findings are rather different. The two types of instructions lead to similar improvements in performance in the case of concrete items, and have no effect upon the recall of abstract items. (Equivalently, the effect of stimulus imageability upon recall performance is roughly the same under both imagery and verbal mediation instructions.) This has been found principally in paired-associate learning (Janssen, 1976, pp. 42–3, 48, 53; Paivio and Yuille, 1967; Wood, 1967; Yuille and Paivio, 1968), but also in free recall (Janssen, 1976, pp. 50–1). However, the different mnemonic instructions seem to be only partially effective in influencing the subjects' learning strategies. Both subjects receiving imagery instructions and those receiving verbal instructions report a greater use of mental imagery with concrete material than with abstract material, and a greater use of mental imagery with repeated presentations of the same paired-associate list (Paivio and Yuille, 1969). These results led Paivio (1971c, p. 362) to conclude 'that associative strategies are only partly controlled by experimental sets and that, over trials, subjects increasingly revert to associative habits aroused by the semantic characteristics of the to-be-learned items'.

In order to resolve these difficulties, Paivio and Foth (1970) compared the effects of imagery and verbal mnemonic instructions with concrete and abstract material when the subjects were forced to specify the mediator employed in learning each paired associate. Different groups of subjects learned concrete or abstract paired associates, but each subject used both types of mediators with different items. Under instructions to use mental imagery, the subjects were required to construct an interactive mental image and to give a sketch drawing of the scene or event depicted. Under instructions to use verbal mediators, they were required to generate a linking phrase or sentence and to write it down. The results showed a significant interaction such that imagery instructions produced better performance than verbal instructions in the case of concrete pairs, but worse performance in the case of abstract pairs. (Equivalently, the effect of stimulus imageability upon recall performance was greater with interactive imagery instructions than with verbal mediation instructions.) These results are of course entirely consistent with dual coding theory, and with the theoretical analysis of the effect of imagery mnemonic instructions which was given by Paivio (1971c) in the passage quoted above. Nevertheless, the procedure used by Paivio and Foth confounded the mnemonic efficacy of constructing an interactive mental image with that of drawing an interactive picture (Janssen, 1976, p. 42); since the subjects instructed to use mental imagery were also required to generate their own pictorial presentation of the material to be remembered, it is not possible to determine which is the effective mnemonic device. Moreover, subsequent research by Janssen (loc. cit.) and by Yuille (1973) has failed to replicate Paivio and Foth's 'elusive interaction'. The safest conclusion in the light of the available results in that it is not merely elusive but actually non-existent.

Finally, these conclusions on the basis of research to date must be carefully considered and possibly qualified in terms of the analysis which was given earlier of the factors likely to influence the interrelationship between the effects of stimulus imageability and those of imagery mnemonic instructions. Although such instructions do not typically lead to improved performance in the learning of abstract material, and although the spontaneous use of mental imagery with such material is relatively infrequent (see above), the possibility remains that subjects instructed to use mental imagery might be able to do so even with abstract material provided that the circumstances of the experiment permit it (cf. Bower, 1970a). Paivio (1971c, p. 365) described a study by MacDonald in which the subjects did sometimes report the use of concrete images as mediators for abstract paired associates (for example, 'boy scout' for the pair *chance-deed*), and in which the recall of the paired associate was shown to be conditional upon the correct recall of the mediating image. There is also evidence that pictorial mediators supplied by the experimenter may increase performance in learning paired associates of low imageability (Paivio, 1971c, pp. 365–6; 1972). These experiments show that improvements in performance will result from the availability of integrative mental imagery; that this may be made avilable either by providing the subject with pictorial mediators or by permitting him an adequate amount of time to discover and generate appropriate mental images; and that, as proposed earlier in this chapter, the critical property underlying the dimension of stimulus imageability is the latency with which integrative mental imagery is aroused.

7.5 IMAGEABILITY AND SELECTIVE INTERFERENCE

Once again, one may examine the forms of coding or representation used in remembering concrete and abstract words by considering which sorts of concurrent tasks will interfere with recall performance. In this case, the particular problem of interest is that of discovering concurrent tasks which interfere in a selective manner with the beneficial effect of stimulus imageability. Such a discovery would count as evidence for the functional independence of the two mnemonic representations postulated by dual coding theory (Paivio, 1975b).

As was mentioned in chapter 6, Paivio (1975d) has pointed out that, in a sense, increasing the presentation rate may be regarded as a way of selectively interfering with cognitive processing. The fact that the effect of stimulus imageability upon performance is greatly attentuated with very fast rates of presentation (Paivio and Csapo, 1969; see also Paivio, 1975*b*) may therefore be taken as evidence that the presentation of concrete material at slower rates of presentation gives rise to additional forms of representation in memory (see Paivio, 1972, for discussion). So, the interaction of the effect of presentation rate and the effect of stimulus imageability upon recall performance provides (very limited) evidence for dual coding theory.

The first empirical study to investigate this problem by requiring the subjects to carry out a clearly defined concurrent task was that of Atwood (1971), which was described in detail in the previous chapter. This study found that a concurrent visual task interfered more with the retention of concrete material under imagery mnemonic instructions than with the retention of abstract material under verbal instructions, but that a concurrent auditory task had the opposite effect. On the other hand, there were various problems with this study, the most important of which was the complete confounding of the manipulation of mnemonic instructions and the manipulation of stimulus imageability (Janssen, 1976, pp. 31–2). Attempts to replicate Atwood's experiment have been unsuccessful (Bower, Munoz and Arnold, cited by Anderson and Bower, 1973, p. 459; Brooks, cited by Paivio, 1971*c*, p. 374; Quinn, cited by Baddeley, 1976, p. 229), and several studies which have looked more carefully at the effect of stimulus imageability have failed to find any interaction with the effect of a spatial concurrent task (Baddeley, Grant, Wight and Thomson, 1974; Byrne, 1974; Elliott, 1973; Warren, 1977). Although Janssen (1976, pp. 41–3, 47, 51–7) did find evidence for the predicted interaction, most authorities consider that concurrent visuo-spatial tasks do not have a selective effect upon the recall of concrete material as opposed to that of abstract material (Anderson and Bower, 1973, p. 459; Baddeley, 1976, pp. 229–32).

This conclusion entails that the cognitive processes which are responsible for the effect of stimulus imageability upon recall performance are functionally independent of those which are disrupted by a concurrent visuo-spatial task. Janssen (1976, pp. 33–4) and Baddeley (1976, pp. 230, 232; Baddeley *et al.*, 1974) have attempted to articulate this point in a more specific manner. Janssen argued that whether two tasks interfere with one another depended upon whether they both employ mental imagery in a spatial or a non-spatial manner. He suggested that the concurrent tasks which are typically employed have a strong spatial component, whereas the use of mental imagery in long-term memory does not. However, the experiment by Neisser and Kerr (1973) shows that effective relational associations in long-term memory may indeed be based upon spatial organisation.

Baddeley's argument was that 'it is possible to interfere with the control process involved in forming, manipulating, and utilizing images, though not with the more basic semantic characteristics which cause subjects to rate a word as being concrete or imageable'. He distinguished between the optional strategy or *control process* of mental imagery, which 'represents an activity of the subject and may thus be disrupted by a concurrent visuo-spatial task', and the concreteness of the stimulus material, which 'depends on the way in which the material has already been registered and thus is not dependent on the current activities of the subject'. Baddeley's discussion implies that these two cognitive modes are functionally independent. However, it does not explain why the effect of a concurrent visuo-spatial task typically does not interact with that of imagery mnemonic instructions (which presumably implicate the 'control process' of mental imagery); nor does it explain why the effect of stimulus imageability typically *does* interact with that of imagery mnemonic instructions.

The interpretation of stimulus imageability which is suggested by the research to date is that of a measure of the ease with which experimental material evokes integrated, relationally organised images. The research on selective interference suggests that concurrent spatial tasks do not interfere with the elaboration and strengthening of such associative connections in long-term memory. The theoretical dichotomy which Janssen and Baddeley were (unsuccessfully) attempting to delimit appears to be that which was defined in chapter 4 between the constructive and elaborative uses of mental imagery. Once again, the implication of the empirical evidence on selective interference and stimulus imageability is that these two sorts of use are functionally independent of one another.

7.6 CONCLUSIONS

The available evidence indicates that stimulus imageability is an excellent predictor of memory performance. The usefulness of the mental imagery evoked by the material to be learned seems to depend upon its relational organisation, rather than upon its subjective vividness. In learning tasks, imageability is the effective attribute of the experimental material, rather than its concreteness or its lexical complexity. The effects of concurrent visuo-spatial tasks upon memory performance are largely independent of the effects of stimulus imageability.

These results are entirely analogous to those obtained in the study of imagery mnemonic instructions. Both areas of research emphasise the role of organisational factors in determining memory performance. The two 'operational procedures' interact in the anticipated manner, so that the beneficial effect of imagery mnemonic instructions is largely on material of high imageability, and the effect of stimulus imageability is increased with imagery mnemonic instructions. Imagery and verbal mediation instructions yield similar improvements in performance.

However, the empirical findings on the effects of stimulus imageability do not permit one to distinguish between dual coding theory and common coding theory, and considerations of parsimony must once again favour the latter approach. As was pointed out in the previous chapter, the property of intentionality implies that the propositional description under which a mental image is constructed will be the functional representation determining memory performance. This idea was supported empirically by the experiments of Anderson and Kosslyn (Anderson and Bower, 1973, pp. 230–2), who showed that synonym confusions in recognition memory were determined by conceptual similarities, rather than pictorial similarities, among the recognition test items.

8

Remembering Connected Narrative

The research which I described in the previous chapter indicated that stimulus imageability was an important factor determining a person's ability to remember individual, unrelated words. However, it is important to remember that human beings rarely encounter lists of unrelated words outside the confines of the psychological laboratory. If this research is to have any relevance to remembering in everyday life, similar findings must be demonstrated in more realistic situations. More generally, the role of mental imagery in retaining connected material must be carefully determined. Although this is the most important task in any area of experimental research, the specific question of the relevance of mental imagery to everyday remembering has really received no clearly articulated answer. Nevertheless, in this chapter, I shall try at least to sketch out an answer by considering evidence on the function of mental imagery in the retention of narrative. To do this, I shall consider findings obtained with simple noun phrases, with individual sentences, and finally with connected discourse.

8.1 MEMORY FOR PHRASES

One of the simplest ways of constructing linguistically structured phrases is by adding relevant modifying adjectives to individual nouns. Of course, once again it is true that isolated noun phrases are rarely experienced in everyday life. However, it is interesting to consider experiments using such material, since their results were directly responsible for much of the research on mental imagery. The original finding was obtained by Lambert and Paivio (1956), and concerned the sequential learning of groups of words, each consisting of a noun and three modifying adjectives. Performance was found to be better when each noun was presented before the relevant adjectives than when it was presented afterwards. This result was explained in terms of a *conceptual-peg hypothesis*, according to which nouns were superior to adjectives in redintegrating a whole phrase. The basic pattern of results has also been obtained with adjective–noun paired associates (Paivio, 1963), and has been obtained both with English subjects and material (for which the superior mode of presentation violates the conventional order) and with French subjects and material (for which the superior mode of presentation follows the conventional order) (Yuille, Paivio and Lambert, 1969). However, these results are not found with the free recall of adjective–noun phrases, where the performance is determined by the gram-matical order of the component words (Richardson, 1978*f*).

Paivio (1963) proposed that the conceptual-peg hypothesis should be reinterpreted specifically in terms of the use of mental imagery as a mnemonic representation. As was mentioned in the previous chapter, this suggestion has received confirmation from experiments using unrelated words. Research using adjective–noun phrases has similarly shown that concrete phrases are better remembered than abstract phrases, regardless of presentation order (Kusyszyn and Paivio, 1966; Paivio, 1963), and that the stimulus imageability of the cue is more important than that of the item cued in determining recall performance (Yuille *et al.*, 1969). Paivio (1963) also suggested that the effects of presentation order could be attributed to the fact that nouns are typically more concrete or imageable than adjectives. Consistent with this idea, Horowitz and Prytulak (1969) found that the recall of nouns was better than the recall of adjectives in the free recall of adjective–noun phrases; and Lockhart (1969) found that nouns were more effective cues than adjectives in prompting the recall of complete phrases, independent of the order of presentation. Moreover, Yuille *et al.* (1969) showed that the adjective–noun presentation order would promote better performance in paired-associate learning if the noun were of low imageability but if the adjective were of high imageability.

Evidence on the role of mental imagery in redintegrative memory was obtained by Begg (1972), who compared performance in the free recall and cued recall of concrete and abstract adjective–noun phrases. First, Begg found that both the recall of adjectives and of nouns and the efficacy of adjectives and nouns as cues were comparable when they were matched in terms of their imageability (see also Peterson, 1971). This confirmed a suggestion made by Paivio (1971*c*, p. 276) that recall performance is largely dependent upon stimulus imageability, and not upon grammatical category. Second, Begg's subjects could recall the same proportion of words from a list of adjective–noun phrases as from a list of unrelated words when the material was of high imageability, but only half as many words when the material was of low inageability. This suggested that concrete phrases were stored as functional units in memory, whereas abstract phrases were stored as separate words. Finally, Begg found that providing one word in a phrase as a cue to the recall of the other word increased performance relative to free recall, but only for material of high imageability. This confirmed that redintegration was only possible in the case of concrete phrases. However, in chapter 6, it was mentioned that Begg's position is that such findings 'reflect general organization rather than some peculiarity of imagery' (Begg, 1978).

A more complex way of constructing a noun phrase is by combining a parti-ciple of a verb and a relevant noun. Such expressions are usually referred to as *nominalisations*, and two main classes of these are of particular interest. *Subject* nominalisations (for example, *growling lions*) are nominal expressions which are intuitively related to complete sentences in which the relevant noun is the grammatical subject of the verb (*lions growl*). *Object* nominalisations, on the other hand (for example, *digging holes*), are nominal expressions which are intuitively related to complete sentences in which the relevant noun is the grammatical object of the verb, and in which the grammatical subject is indefinite (*someone digs holes*). Linguists are generally agreed that these intuitive relationships reflect a process of derivation by means of grammatical transformation (Chomsky, 1970; J. T. E. Richardson, 1977*b*). (More accurately, sentences containing nominalisations result from deep structures in which nominal expressions are replaced by embedded clauses which are the deep structures underlying the associated complete sentences.) Rohrman (1968) found that subject nominalisations were easier to remember than object nominalisations; since the deep structures underlying the former class contain only two elements, whereas those underlying the latter class contain three elements (*lions + growl* vs. *someone + digs + holes*), he concluded that such phrases were stored in terms of their deep-structure representations.

However, Paivio (1971*a*) showed that the subject nominalisations used by Rohrman were also more imageable on average than his object nominalisations. He carried out a series of experiments in which stimulus imageability and nominalisations type were varied independently; in each case, there was a clear effect of imageability, but no difference between subject and object nominalisations in terms of recall performance. More recently, Richardson (1975*b*) pointed out certain faults in Paivio's study, and carried out further experiments along those lines. The results were even more unambiguous, with no sign of any effect of nominalisation type upon recall performance. The effect of stimulus imageability was present in tests of free recall, but was much more pronounced when the subjects were cued with either the participle or the noun and had to produce the entire phrase. As in the experiment by Begg (1972) mentioned above, the two elements in each phrase were equally effective as cues to the recall of the whole phrase; and cued recall was substantially better than free recall, but only in the case of material of high imageability.

In short, research on connected phrases is quite consistent with the theory of dual coding in memory. However, the evidence is also entirely consistent with common coding theory, if it is assumed that propositional memory is more effective when encoded descriptions incorporate perceptual or spatial predicates. The experimental findings support the notion of redintegration in human memory, without determining whether or not a single form of representation is employed.

8.2 MEMORY FOR SENTENCES

In recent years there has been a considerable amount of research on how people remember individual sentences, and the results can be summarised fairly easily (see, for example, Johnson-Laird, 1970, 1974). First, under most circumstances, subjects demonstrate a retention of the precise wording of a passage only for the last sentence presented, and possibly only for the last clause presented (Jarvella, 1970; Jarvella and Herman, 1972; Sachs, 1967; but cf. Kintsch and Bates, 1977). Even this ability may be limited in tests of incidental learning (Johnson-Laird and Stevenson, 1970). Second, subjects' retention of the meaning of a passage is typically good, and may be maintained despite considerable interpolated information (Begg, 1971; Sachs, 1967). A corollary of this is that the incidence of semantic confusions is relatively high in both recognition and recall (Bransford, Barclay and Franks, 1972; Fillenbaum, 1973; Johnson-Laird and Stevenson, 1970; Sachs, 1967). These findings imply that the verbatim expression of a sentence is lost once a semantic interpretation has been achieved, and must be reconstructed on the basis of that interpretation at the time of recall (Bregman and Strasberg, 1968; Sachs, 1967).

The most important immediate question is whether mental imagery is involved in the storage and retrieval of such semantic interpretations. One sort of evidence comes from studies of cued recall analogous to those mentioned in the previous section. Several studies have found that the efficacy of a word in a sentence as a prompt for the recall of the entire sentence appears to depend upon the syntactic function of the word within that sentence. For example, the final noun in a passive sentence was found to be a more effective cue when it functioned as the logical subject of the sentence (as in *Gloves were made by tailors*), than when it was merely contained in an adverbial phrase (as in *Gloves were made by hand*) (Blumenthal, 1967); an adjective which modified a whole sentence or proposition embedded within the sentence to be remembered (as in *John is easy to please*) was found to be a more effective cue than an adjective which merely modified a noun within that sentence (as in *John is eager to please*) (Blumental and Boakes, 1967); and a noun which functioned as the grammatical subject of a sentence was found to be a more effective cue than a noun which functioned as the grammatical object of the sentence (Horowitz and Prytulak, 1969). However, it now appears likely that these effects were produced by a confounding of stimulus imageability: as in the case of connected phrases, when the imageability of a word in a sentence is controlled, its grammatical status seems to be unimportant in determining performance (James, 1972).

The critical predictions to be made on the basis of dual coding theory depend upon the mnemonic representations which are assumed to be available for encoding concrete and abstract sentences. Paivio (1971b; see also 1971c, pp. 450–1) stated his position in the following way:

> Extended to connected discourse, the dual process model implies that concrete phrases or sentences, like concrete words, can be coded and stored in memory, not only verbally, but also in the form of nonverbal imagery . . . . Although high imagery words or paired associates are generally easier to learn and remember than low imagery ones, the model does not imply that high imagery

sentences will necessarily be remembered better than low imagery sentences. If concrete material indeed tends to be coded in a nonverbal form, then it must be decoded back in order to generate the correct verbal output. Decoding errors are therefore possible, especially in regard to such features of language as its grammatical form and precise wording.

Paivio's position thus attempted to ascribe the general phenomenon of semantic confusions in the long-term retention of sentences to the particular problem of retrieving a verbal expression on the basis of a non-verbal memory code. The crucial assumption in his analysis was that abstract sentences cannot be encoded in the form of mental images, and are thus more likely to be remembered in terms of their specific verbal expression. This assumption is actually highly questionable, as will be argued in the following section, but it appeared to lead to a quite clear-cut prediction. Just as subjects are more sensitive to changes in the meaning of concrete sentences than to changes in their wording (Sachs, 1967), they should be more sensitive to changes in the wording of abstract sentences than to changes in their meaning. This was confirmed by Begg and Paivio (1969), who employed a recognition test in which the subjects had to detect changes in sentences that had previously been presented in the context of passages of connected discourse. The results showed exactly the predicted interaction between the imageability of the stimulus material and the nature of the change to be detected.

The validity of this conclusion clearly depends upon the two sets of stimulus material being comparable in respects other than their image-evoking potential (most especially, in their intelligibility), and also upon the changes introduced in the sentences presented being roughly equivalent. Subsequent research has tended to focus upon these issues. Paivio and Begg (1971) showed that the two sets of sentences employed in their earlier study were approximately equal in terms of the times taken by subjects before they indicated that they had understood each sentence. However, Johnson, Bransford, Nyberg and Cleary (1972) found that subjects tended to rate Begg and Paivio's abstract sentences as more difficult to comprehend than their concrete sentences. Their subjects also tended to consider equivalent changes in the meaning of sentences to be more significant in the case of the concrete sentences. Thus, it could be concluded that the original study had not effectively controlled either the comprehensibility of the material presented for learning, or the amount of change in meaning employed in the recognition test. As Johnson-Laird (1974) suggested, 'the most that can be safely concluded from the original experiment is that individuals retain the sense of sentences, as opposed to verbiage, in proportion to their grasp of it.'

Klee and Eysenck (1973) used a more sensitive latency measure, by timing how quickly subjects could say whether a sentence made sense. They found that concrete sentences produced shorter latencies than abstract sentences, and agreed with Johnson *et al.* that Begg and Paivio had probably confounded comprehensibility with imageability (see also Holmes and Langford, 1976). They argued that concrete sentences were more likely to have a single dominant meaning which could be readily grasped, whereas abstract sentences tended to have several potential interpretations. This explains why the presentation of a relevant context for a sentence brings about a selective improvement in detecting changes in meaning with abstract material (Pezdek and Royer, 1974).

Moeser (1974) carried out a systematic series of experiments in which the material had previously been matched in terms of rated comprehensibility. In three experiments, the subjects were faster and more accurate in detecting both meaning and wording changes in concrete sentences than in abstract sentences. (See also Anderson and Bower, 1973, pp. 232–3; Sacks and Eysenck, 1977.) An interaction of the sort found by Begg and Paivio was only obtained under certain critical circumstances in a fourth experiment, and was attributed to the operation of response biases towards the detection of changes in wording in the case of abstract sentences. The subjects took longer to encode and decode the abstract sentences, even though they were no more difficult to comprehend. From these results, Moeser arrived at three conclusions. First, she pointed out that the imageability of a sentence had a pronounced effect upon how easily her subjects could store and retrieve that sentence. This applied whether the subjects were instructed to encode the meaning of a sentence or its wording, and it applied whether they were tested on changes in meaning or changes in wording. She argued that these facts could best be handled by a single semantic system. Second, she suggested that the interaction between sentence concreteness and the type of change to be detected which was reported by Begg and Paivio was due not to any confounding of concreteness and comprehensibility, but rather to the specific experimental design which they had used (see also Anderson and Bower, 1973, p. 233). Their results could be better explained in terms of subjects' response biases than in terms of their memory coding processes. Her own findings did not support the dual coding model, at least as interpreted by Paivio (1971b, 1971c; Begg and Piavio, 1969). Third, Moeser argued that the specific propositional models that had been put forward up to that point could not explain differences in the storage and retrieval of sentences which differed only in terms of their imageability:

A better explanation, I believe, can be offered by an analog semantic coding model which proposes that memory representation is organized in terms of iconic groupings, functionally unitary, integrated memory structures. They are described as iconic in the sense that they utilize principles similar to, although not necessarily analogous with, the imaginal representation of the sentence; it is assumed that sentences that are easier to represent in imagery are also easier to translate into this memory code.

The first two points made by Moeser seem to be largely correct, and constitute a firm rebuttal of Begg and Paivio's position. Nevertheless, her third suggestion is not sound. Her 'analog semantic coding model' is sketched out only in a very vague manner, and it is not possible to see clearly how it differs from standard propositional models. Moreover, even when her paper was written, some propositional theorists had already incorporated into their models the explicit assumption of a more favourable mnemonic representation for imageable material (Anderson and Bower, 1973, p. 452). This idea is typically handled either by assuming that concrete sentences lead to more distinctive representations or that they are encoded in more closely interconnected sets of propositions. Thus, it must be concluded that Moeser's results are entirely consistent even with the specific proposals which had been made by propositional theorists. Conversely, however, her results provide no clear support for the dual coding position, and are actually inconsistent with the interpretation of that position offered by Begg and Paivio.

Further evidence on the memory representations available for concrete and abstract sentences comes from the use of interference tasks designed to interfere with a particular form of coding in a relatively specific manner. In previous chapters, it has been observed that Atwood's (1971) original findings obtained with concrete and abstract phrases have not proved to be replicable, and that visuo-spatial tasks usually have equal effects upon the recall of both sorts of material. A series of experiments carried out by Sasson (1971; Sasson and Fraisse, 1972) investigated the effect of interpolated learning upon the recall of concrete and abstract sentences. The first two experiments required subjects to recall concrete sentences under conditions of negative transfer or retroactive interference (from the learning of unrelated pictures or concrete sentences interpolated between the presentation and recall of the critical material) and under conditions of positive transfer (from the learning of interpolated pictures and sentences which respectively depicted and were identical to the critical material). Interpolated pictures and concrete sentences were found to produce similar amounts of positive and negative transfer, and Sasson concluded that sentences were stored and retrieved primarily in the form of visual images. In a third experiment, the subjects were required to recall abstract sentences under conditions of retroactive interference from unrelated pictures, unrelated concrete sentences or unrelated abstract sentences. The interpolated abstract sentences produced substantial negative transfer, but the interpolated pictures and concrete sentences did not. Sasson and Fraisse concluded that abstract sentences were stored and retrieved primarily in a verbal form.

However, there are two major difficulties which prevent one from accepting Sasson's conclusions. First, all of the pictures employed in his experiments depicted events or scenes which could be readily described even under the rapid presentation conditions used. In fact, the pictures were outline drawings produced 'such that each drawing would exactly depict the event described' by one of the concrete sentences. That is, each picture was a symbolic representation constructed by an artist under an intentional description which was exactly contained within one of the simple affirmative concrete sentences. The finding that pictures and concrete sentences have equal effects upon the recall of concrete and abstract sentences shows at most that pictures and concrete sentences have similar mnemonic representations; it does not specify whether those representations are pictorial or propositional in nature, and so does not distinguish between dual coding theory and common coding theory.

The second problem is that the abstract sentences employed in the third experiment were rather obscure or bizarre, and had to be interpreted metaphorically (for example, 'Religion teaches charity'). Under the presentation conditions which Sasson and Fraisse employed, it is possible that most of the time subjects simply did not grasp the meanings of the sentences to be learned. The finding that interpolated abstract sentences impair the recall of the original abstract sentences, whereas interpolated pictures or concrete sentences do not, shows at most that pictures and concrete sentences have a different mnemonic representation from abstract sentences; it does not specify whether those representations are pictorial and propositional, pictorial and verbatim, or propositional and verbatim. Two features of their results give strong support to the idea tha the abstract sentences were only remembered in terms of their verbatim expression. On the one hand, interpolated concrete sentences had no effect upon the recall of abstract sentences, and yet they had presumably been encoded in terms of meanings, and this should have interfered with any retention of the semantic content of the abstract sentences. On the other hand, the retention of the abstract sentences was essentially non-existent after a delay of two days. (The performance in delayed recall was less than 5% even in a control condition with no interpolated learning.)

Further experiments on selective interference were reported by Davies and Proctor (1976), who used a distractor task which involved verbal coding (counting backwards) and one which involved perceptual coding (visual tracking). The recall of abstract sentences was more impaired by the verbal task, whereas the recall of concrete sentences was more impaired by the perpetual task. Errors with the abstract sentences tended to be omissions, whereas errors with the concrete sentences tended to be intrusions. Moreover, a greater proportion of the intrusion errors obtained with concrete sentences involved a change of meaning from the original following the perceptual task. These results indicated that qualitatively different encoding processes operate in the retention of concrete and abstract sentences. However, the fact that a visual tracking task was found to have a selective effect upon the recall of concrete material is inconsistent with most of the other research which has been carried out on selective interference effects using phrases and unrelated words (chapter 7). Inspection of their abstract material suggests that these sentences were rather obscure or opaque, and so a failure to control the intelligibility of the stimulus material might have been a factor influencing the results.

8.3 IMAGERY, MEANING AND UNDERSTANDING

One of the problems in interpreting the results obtained in the experiment by Begg and Paivio (1969) mentioned above was that material which they had selected in order to manipulate stimulus imageability might not have been comparable in terms of its intelligibility. The usual reaction to this suggestion is to regard the experiment as inconclusive on the ground that two possible determiners of memory performance were confounded. This is entirely reasonable, and gave rise to a series of interesting papers by Johnson *et al.* (1972), Moeser (1974) and others. However, there is a different sort of reaction which might be considered. As a radical alternative, it could be argued that stimulus imageability is a factor determining both how easily a sentence may be remembered, and how easily it may be understood. The idea that the comprehension of sentences might be mediated by mental imagery was considered briefly by Paivio (1971*b*), but it is important because it is related to the conception of meaning which is to be found throughout his writings.

Within traditional behaviourist associationism, the concept of meaning is extremely problematic. There have been many different approaches (see Paivio, 1971*c*, pp. 40–50), but none of them is at all satisfactory. One major source of difficulty is that behaviourist psychology tends to regard speech as a complex system of conditioned responses, and the meaning of a linguistic utterance as the fractional anticipatory goal response which mediates the actual production of the utterances. This sort of account typically postulates a representation of verbal information in terms of its acoustic or articulatory properties, and thus has great difficulty in giving any elucidation of what one might ordinarily mean by the 'meaning' of an utterance. Nevertheless, this model of symbolic representation is incorporated within Paivio's version of dual coding theory with very little modification: the presentation of words, phrases or sentences is assumed to produce a direct activation of 'implicit auditory-motor representations' within the subject (Paivio, 1971*b*; 1971*c*, p. 53).

As it stands, this account of linguistic meaning seems to be clearly naive and oversimplistic. The addition of mental imagery as a second major cognitive representation within Paivio's model serves to relieve this impression and to make the total system both more flexible and more plausible. It immediately makes possible the specification of the three levels of meaning or levels of processing which were discussed in chapter 2, and gives rise to many testable predictions which have continued to motivate the work of Paivio and his colleagues. On the other hand, one might suggest, somewhat cynically, that mental imagery was postulated to fill some of the more glaring holes in the standard associationist account of language. Nevertheless, it must be admitted that Paivio regards the concept as being of the utmost importance in understanding the nature of language, and seriously postulates mental imagery as a substrate for both semantics and syntax (Paivio, 1971*b*).

But is this account of sentential meaning really adequate? First, one must surely agree that many abstract sentences can be understood and remembered without recourse to mental imagery (Johnson-Laird, 1974), and yet one would be extremely unhappy about describing that understanding merely as the arousal of an 'implicit auditory-motor representation' of such a sentence. Davies and Proctor (1976) suggested that even concrete sentences may not arouse mental imagery if they are tautologies or merely make a statement about the general nature of the world (for instance, *The shoes are a product of the skin of the cow*). Although subjects do report using mental imagery when carrying out sentence comprehension tasks, Garrod and Trabasso (1973) found that this was considerably attenuated when the sentences were presented visually, presumably a selective interference effect of the sort discussed in chapter 4 (see also Klee and Eysenck, 1973). Moreover, Holmes and Langford (1976) argued that response latencies in such tasks are too short to permit mental imagery to have any effective role. Bugelski (1977) has claimed that 'to argue that all of meaning cannot be accounted for by imagery is to attack a straw man', since no one has ever denied this. But the point is that no dual coding theorist has ever given a clear account of the meaning of abstract sentences which is at all plausible to someone who does not subscribe to a rigorous form of behaviourism. My personal inclination is to regard the account given by propositional theorists as essentially correct as a solution to this latter problem, without prejudice to the question of the status or the functional utility of mental imagery. But, even in their most recent publications, dual coding theorists continue to regard propositional theory as inherently contradictory to their own position, and not as a possible extension of that position (Bugelski, 1977; Paivio, 1978*b*).

Nevertheless, if one wishes to relate these positions to the nature of sentential meaning, one must ask: What is it to understand a sentence? There are several different answers which have been given to this question, and they are associated with different methods for measuring whether the process of understanding a sentence is affected by its imageability (cf. Moeser, 1974). These were mentioned in discussing the experiment by Begg and Paivio (1969) earlier in this chapter, but it will be useful to consider them once more.

1. One might say that a person had understood a sentence when he had imposed some interpretation on it. This is the sort of idea which seems to have been behind Paivio and Begg's (1971) use of a simple latency measure to investigate comprehensibility. It will be recalled that they found no difference between concrete and abstract sentences (cf. Ernest and Paivio, 1971*b*; Yuille and Paivio, 1967), though Holmes and Langford (1976) criticised their measure as crude and insensitive, and their conclusion as erroneous.

2. One might say that a person had understood a sentence when he had made the absolute judgement that it was meaningful, and had discriminated it from other sentences in terms of their meaningfulness. This seems to have been involved in the study by Johnson *et al.* (1972), in which the subjects rated the sentences on a comprehension scale; and also in the experiments by Klee and Eysenck (1973) and by Holmes and Langford (1976), which measured the

reaction times to classify sentences as meaningful or as anomalous. In both cases, concrete sentences were found to be more comprehensible than abstract sentences.

3. One might say that a person had understood a sentence when it had been fully encoded into long-term memory and integrated with all relevant previous knowledge. This is the notion which was adopted by Moeser (1974). She demonstrated significant differences between concrete and abstract sentences in terms of encoding latencies and in terms of retention even when they were matched in terms of rated comprehensibility (see also Holmes and Langford, 1976).

Moeser suggested that, in research on human memory, it would be most helpful to employ this last criterion of understanding. That is, comprehension should be defined as the integration of the ideas contained within a sentence into a holistic semantic representation in long-term memory. She argued that concrete sentences were more likely to be encoded in an integrated form, whereas abstract sentences 'were more likely to be represented in a partial form because their complete representation involved more complex integrative operations'. To examine whether this explanation holds good as a general account of the comprehension and retention of connected discourse, one must now consider the abstraction and integration of information across sentences.

8.4   SCHEMATA AND THEMATIC STRUCTURE

The most common situation in which a person attempts to retain and to integrate the information contained in a series of sentences is where he tries to learn a story. The first systematic investigation of story recall was carried out in the 1920s by Bartlett (1932). He was concerned with understanding the extent to which the interpretation placed upon a story reflected the reader's social and cultural background. His best known study employed a North American folk-tale called *The War of the Ghosts*. Bartlett expected that the unusual social conventions embodied in the story and the apparently disconnected narrative would create considerable difficulties for his British subjects; their attempts at recalling the story would therefore shed light upon the processes of interpretation which had been used. Each subject was asked to recall the story as accurately as possible on several occasions over many months. The version recalled by any given subject showed considerable omissions and distortions, but it remained relatively fixed from one test to the next. It remained a single passage, and was more coherent than the original in terms of the subject's own culturally induced expectations. Bartlett suggested the term, *schema*, to refer to the abstract mnemonic representation of a narrative, distorted so as to be consistent with already existing schemata, acquired on the basis of past cultural experience.

Although Bartlett's ideas are generally recognised as being very important, his empirical investigations were not followed up for a considerable time. In the

1960s, some psychologists turned their attention to the role of thematic structure in remembering narrative. One of the original findings in this area was that both the total verbal recall and the incidence of semantic confusions in the retention of connected discourse are greater when its thematic structure is obvious than when it is obscure (Pompi and Lachman, 1967). This suggested that such material is encoded in the form of *surrogate processes*, general ideas or themes from which the narrative itself is reconstructed at the time of recall. It was subsequently shown that the comprehension and recall of an obscure or vague passage would be increased by supplying an appropriate and relevant picture or title (Bransford and Johnson, 1972; Dooling and Lachman, 1971). Yuille and Paivio (1969) showed that thematic organisation had a greater effect upon the recall of concrete passages than upon the recall of abstract passages. On the other hand, Pezdek and Royer (1974) showed that the provision of relevant context paragraphs enhanced the ability to detect changes of meaning in abstract sentences more than in concrete sentences. These two results are entirely consistent with one another, if one assumes (1) that the thematic structure of concrete material is typically obvious, promotes semantic encoding, and does not stand in need of support from the context; but (2) that the thematic structure of abstract material is typically obscure, promotes literal encoding, and benefits from the provision of a context. These results might be taken to be consistent with the idea that thematic structure in the case of concrete passages permits the construction of interactive, integrative mental imagery, from which the verbal content may be reconstructed or redintegrated at the time of recall (Paivio, 1971*b*). However, they are in no way inconsistent with the view that concrete and abstract passages receive exactly the same sort of semantic representation. Indeed, these findings are entirely analogous to those obtained with individual sentences, which were described earlier in this chapter.

These experiments had the disadvantage that the notion of thematic structure was poorly defined, and there was little experimental control over how it was introduced. This problem was handled by Bransford and Franks (1971), who introduced a novel experimental technique to demonstrate the operation of Bartlett's schemata. The subjects were asked to listen to component sentences which together defined a complex idea. For example, the sentences, *The ants were in the kitchen*, *The jelly was on the table*, *The jelly was sweet* and *The ants ate the jelly*, each connote a single proposition, and jointly define the complex idea, *The ants in the kitchen ate the sweet jelly which was on the table*. The acquisition sentences in the original experiment contained one, two or three of the components in a given idea. The subjects then received a recognition test with sentences containing one, two, three or four components. The subjects' confidence that a particular sentence had been presented for learning varied directly with the number of components which it contained; in particular, the sentences containing four components were judged as 'old' with the highest confidence, even though they had never been presented. A subsequent experiment showed that the subjects' confidence ratings in such a test were predicted by the number of components which a sentence contained, but not at all by whether the sentence had actually been presented. Bransford and Franks concluded that their subjects had integrated the information communicated by sets of individual sentences to construct *holistic semantic ideas*. These ideas 'need not be communicated by single sentences. They may result from the integration of information expressed by many different sentences experienced successively and often nonconsecutively in time.' Bransford and Franks explicitly related their ideas to the research carried out by Bartlett, and suggested that their methodology might lend some precision to the concept of a schema as what is learned when subjects are exposed to connected discourse.

These original findings were replicated both by Bransford and Franks (1972) and by other researchers (Cofer, 1973; Singer, 1973). Bransford, Barclay and Franks (1972) demonstrated similar integrative processes operating among the clauses within a single sentence, and Bransford and Franks (1972) produced similar findings on the integration of information expressed by sentences within connected paragraphs. It has been shown that the basic pattern of results may break down under certain circumstances (Flagg, 1976; Pezdek, 1978), and they may also be open to alternative interpretations, at least when material other than sentences is used (Reitman and Bower, 1973). Nevertheless, it is obvious that the experimental tasks employed by Bartlett and by Bransford and Franks are considerably more typical of remembering in everyday life than experiments on the learning of individual sentences, phrases or words; and some process of abstraction and integration such as is postulated by these writers must be assumed to operate in the comprehension and retention of connected narrative.

The material which was employed in the original experiments was typically concrete and easily evoked mental imagery (Franks and Bransford, 1972). Indeed, the experimental subjects spontaneously commented that they had constructed mental images of the situations described by the sentences to be remembered (Bransford *et al.*, 1972; cf. Anderson and Bower, 1973, p. 314). It is therefore interesting to consider whether a holistic semantic idea might consist, in whole or in part, in a composite, interactive mental image (Neisser, 1972b). Bartlett (1932, pp. 64–5, 220–4, 303–4) himself considered and rejected the suggestion that mental imagery might be of importance in the retention of narrative. Similarly, Bransford *et al.*, (1972) commented that their 'constructive' approach to sentence memory was based upon the construction of semantic descriptions, and not upon the concretisation of information in the form of mental images.

However, Franks and Bransford (1972) noted a clear implication of the research of Begg and Paivio (1969) on the retention of individual sentences. If concrete sentences are stored as mental images, while abstract sentences are stored in a superficial verbal form, the integration of information in the form of holistic semantic ideas should be much more difficult in the case of abstract sentences, and so the subjects should be better able to remember the particular sentences which were presented for learning. Franks and Bransford repeated their earlier experiments using abstract ideas, and obtained essentially the same results. The confidence ratings given to a sentence in a test of recognition memory were directly related to the number of components which it contained, and not at all to whether it had actually been presented. This indicated that, for both concrete and abstract ideas, the subjects were integrating the information contained in the individual sentences presented for learning, and storing holistic representations of the complete ideas in memory. Franks and Bransford did not consider that their results constituted a strict refutation of Begg and Paivio's position, but they did demonstrate an important functional similarity between the mnemonic representations of concrete and abstract ideas.

The studies of Bransford and Franks demonstrated virtually complete integration of both concrete and abstract material. They could therefore be regarded as suffering from a ceiling effect if one wished to consider the specific hypothesis that concrete material is more easily integrated than abstract material. Unpublished experiments carried out at Brunel University have tried to remedy this by severely attenuating the acquisition conditions so that only partial integration was achieved. That is, when the number of acquisition sentences was reduced to a minimum, the subjects were able to discriminate between these sentences and 'new' sentences which related to the same complex ideas. The recognition test also included sentences relating to entirely different ideas, so that the subjects were actually being tested both on their ability to remember the particular sentences used in the acquisition phase, and on their ability to remember the general ideas described by those sentences. Not surprisingly, concrete *ideas* were remembered better than abstract ideas. However, the results also showed quite clearly that the subjects could discriminate between 'old' and 'new' sentences relating to concrete ideas just as well as they could discriminate between 'old' and 'new' sentences relating to abstract ideas; that is, concrete material showed no more integration than abstract material. Another way of describing these results is to say that the subjects were more accurate in detecting changes in meaning but no less accurate in detecting changed in wording in concrete sentences than in abstract sentences. It will be recalled that similar findings were obtained by Moeser (1974) in studying the retention of individual, unrelated sentences.

This research also included conditions where the subjects were instructed to use mental imagery to help them to remember the sentences. These instructions did not affect the subjects' ability to remember the general ideas, nor did they affect their discrimination of 'old' and 'new' sentences in the case of concrete ideas. However, they produced poorer discrimination of 'old' and 'new' sentences in the case of abstract ideas. This suggests that the use of mental imagery may produce better integration of the material to be remembered, at least in the case of abstract material, provided that the subjects receive explicit instructions to this effect. However, when the subjects do receive such instructions, their discrimination of 'old' and 'new' sentences relating to concrete ideas is actually better than of those relating to abstract ideas; that is, they showed less integration and a superior ability to detect changes in wording in the case of concrete material than in the case of abstract material. This seems quite inconsistent with the proposals of Begg and Paivio. Moreover, since in the absence of imagery mnemonic instructions concrete material produced no more integration than abstract material, it is unlikely that mental imagery normally plays any important role in the construction of holistic semantic ideas.

It would be of considerable interest to know whether this system of mnemonic representations were distinct from whatever form of storage is employed in remembering pictures, or totally encompassed that form of storage. An important study along these lines was carried out by Baggett (1975), who presented simple stories consisting of four pictures, and tested her subjects either immediately or after a delay. In her first experiment, the subjects were presented with individual pictures and had to indicate whether each was consistent with the original story. On immediate testing, the responses to 'old' pictures were faster than those to 'new' pictures which were consistent with the story; this suggested that the responses were made partly on the basis of an immediate memory for the specific pictures presented. After a delay of 72 hours, 'old' pictures no longer showed this superiority, indicating that the responses were made on the basis of a conceptual representation of the story which was neutral with respect to the original pictures presented. In the second experiment, the subjects had to indicate whether each specific picture had been one of those originally presented. They were able to reject 'new' pictures with perfect accuracy, even when they were consistent with the original story, and even when the test followed a delay of 72 hours. This implied that a mnemonic representation of the original pictures was available even after 72 hours, and could be accessed by the subjects if the task demanded it (but cf. Pezdek, 1978). Finally, the third experiment required the subjects to respond to written yes/no questions on the basis of whether they were consistent with the original story. The response latencies were independent of whether the answer had to be inferred from the events actually depicted in the original pictures. This suggested, once again, that the responses were made on the basis of a conceptual representation of the story.

Thus, Baggett's results appear to support the idea of a long-term memory for specific pictorial presentations, and a separate conceptual, propositional, nonpictorial representation. She concluded her paper in the following manner:

> Our study has focused on the memory representations arising when a viewer bridges the gaps in the continuity of action in a picture story in order to integrate the surface structure into a meaningful succession of incidents related over time. We believe that the viewer, at least with our simple stories, makes inferences at the time of viewing to aid his comprehension; that these inferences, when stored in memory, are essentially nonpictorial in nature; and that 3 days later the subject can still separate the inferences from the pictures he saw, if the task requires it.

These conclusions have two important corollaries. First, any theory of human memory which attempts to model all cognitive processes in terms of a single system of propositional representations, and which includes no provision for a specific pictorial memory (for example, Anderson and Bower, 1973; Pylyshyn, 1973) is inherently inadequate. Although the propositional system may be able to represent most of the important knowledge which is employed in cognitive tasks, it cannot handle the excellent retention of pictures demonstrated in Baggett's study (cf. the discussion in chapter 5). Second, the comprehension and retention of picture stories does not give rise to any additional pictorial representations in the form of mental imagery. Otherwise, the subjects would be unable to distinguish efficiently between the original pictures and 'new' but appropriate pictures which happened to have been imaged. This in turn suggests one of two possibilities. Either mental imagery does not give rise to a pictorial representation in memory; or mental imagery does give rise to such a representation, but is not employed in the retention of picture stories.

8.5 CONCLUSIONS

Research with phrases, sentences and connected narrative has consistently demonstrated that concrete material is remembered better than abstract material. To this extent, investigations of memory for connected linguistic material are consistent with studies of the retention of individual words. However, any further evidence that has been obtained in the case of memory for phrases may be readily interpreted in accordance with standard redintegrative accounts of human memory, and does not imply any new principles of mnemonic organisation or function as a result of the use of mental imagery in remembering. In the case of memory for individual sentences, the general methodological problem has been that of measuring and controlling the intelligibility of the material to be remembered. When careful procedures are employed to match the comprehensibility of concrete and abstract sentences, subjects are faster and more accurate in detecting both changes in meaning and changes in wording in concrete sentences than in abstract sentences. This is inconsistent with the specific interpretation of dual coding theory given by Paivio (1971b; Begg and Paivio, 1969), but is entirely consistent with standard propositional accounts of the representation of sentences in human memory. In the case of connected discourse and in the case of picture stories, there is good evidence that the information expressed by various sentences or pictures is integrated in memory into holistic semantic ideas; however, there is no evidence at all that mental imagery is involved in this process.

9

Individual Differences

We come now to one of the most complex and least conclusive of the areas of experimental investigation concerning mental imagery: the study of differences between individual subjects in their ability to use mental imagery and in their preference for using mental imagery in various cognitive tasks. Of course, the study of how individuals differ in their cognitive strategies and abilities has always formed a significant part of psychological research. It is therefore not surprising that the investigation of individual differences is one of the oldest approaches to the understanding of mental imagery.

In chapter 3 it was argued that mental imagery was a typical example of the class of ordinary-language concepts relating to psychological states and processes, in that 'having a mental image' exhibits an asymmetry between its first-person present-tense use and its third-person present-tense use. The exact nature of the asymmetry is a matter of some philosophical controversy, but one can certainly agree that each person has a peculiar authority for asserting that he himself has a mental image, an authority which others lack. Whether he is having a mental image is not something about which he can be mistaken. It would therefore be reasonable to start an investigation of individual differences in the use of mental imagery by comparing people on the basis of what they are inclined to say about their own images. (In contemporary psychology, this is seen as a 'subjective' approach to the study of individual differences; however, for reasons explained previously, I regard this as a misnomer.)

Accordingly, this chapter will consider first the comparison of individual subjects in terms of their reports concerning the vividness or manipulability of their experienced mental imagery. This is the oldest method used by psychologists for studying individual differences in mental imagery, but it will be argued on both conceptual and empirical grounds that it does not constitute a useful approach for psychological research. Nevertheless, certain recent experiments have been concerned with subjects' reports on the strategies or mediators used in verbal learning tasks. This approach has produced quite clear and reliable findings, and it seems to constitute a potentially important way of studying individual differences in the use of mental imagery.

Many psychologists have been dissatisfied with these 'introspective' techniques for comparing individual subjects, and have sought instead for objective measures of performance which can be taken as indices of the ability to employ mental imagery in cognitive tasks. Some researchers have interpreted tests of spatial thinking (similar to certain of the procedures discussed in chapter 4) in this manner, and they have tried to use such tests as predictors of the ability to retain information in long-term memory. Unfortunately, the available evidence will indicate that this approach does not help an understanding of the contribution of mental imagery to long-term retention. However, there is some evidence that one can derive an objective measure of the preferred form of coding in long-term memory.

An important respect in which individuals may vary in their cognitive capacities and strategies is as the result of neurological disorders. Various well-replicated findings show that neurological damage at different locations within the brain affects imagery and language skills in different ways. Neuropsychological research of this nature also suggests that mental imagery consists of several components, each of which again may be differentially affected by neurological damage at different cerebral locations. Finally, I shall examine the suggestion that an analysis of learning tasks as involving the use of mental imagery can provide a better understanding of the impaired mnemonic performance which arises in various sorts of neurological conditions.

9.1   INTROSPECTIVE QUESTIONNAIRES

If a person's account of his own mental imagery enjoys the sort of epistemological priority which was discussed in chapter 3, then it seems that he should be in the best position to specify not only *when* he is experiencing mental imagery, and *what* is depicted in his mental imagery, but also how vivid, distinct and efficacious are his mental images. Psychologists usually interpret these judgements as introspective evaluations of the subject's ability to produce concrete mental images (for instance, Marks, 1972), and formal questionnaires on the vividness of experienced mental imagery have elsewhere been referred to as 'tests of subjective imagery ability' (Richardson, 1978c). The use of such questionnaires has a long history in psychology, going back to the work of Galton (1883). Recent reviews of this research have been given by A. Richardson (1977) and by White, Sheehan and Ashton (1977). Research using these questionnaires has typically demonstrated a considerable variation among individual subjects in terms of reports concerning the vividness of their experienced imagery. Since other experimental approaches have indicated that the use of mental imagery is a highly effective strategy for acquiring new information (chapters 6 and 7), it would be reasonable to expect that the vividness of a person's mental imagery should predict how easily such information can be retained.

The most detailed technique for evaluating the subjective vividness of a person's experienced mental imagery is possibly the Questionnaire upon Mental Imagery (QMI), which was developed by Betts (1909) from Galton's original procedure. This included 150 items, and studied seven major modalities: visual, auditory, cutaneous, kinesthetic, gustatory, olfactory and organic. For example, subjects were asked to think of the sun sinking below the horizon, the mewing of a cat, the prick of a pin, running upstairs, the taste of salt, the smell of fresh paint and the sensation of fatigue. They judged the vividness of the evoked images on a seven-point scale, from 'Perfectly clear and vivid as the actual experience' to 'No image present at all, you only *knowing* that you are thinking of the object'. Sheehan (1967a) developed a shortened form of Betts' original QMI, containing five questions from each of the seven modalities, and it is this version which has been used in recent research. Sheehan's test is reprinted in full in Appendix A of Richardson (1969).

As in the case of any technique for evaluating individual differences, it is important to determine the reliability and validity of the QMI. Measures of the internal consistency of the scale are very good (Juhasz, 1972), while the test-retest reliability varies from moderate to high, depending upon the test-retest interval (Evans and Kamemoto, 1973; Sheehan, 1967b; White, Ashton and Brown, 1977). The question of the test's validity is more difficult to answer. On conceptual grounds, it is difficult to know what other sort of evidence could have the epistemological status of introspective reports; as was mentioned in chapter 3, there appear to be no non-verbal criteria for mental imagery. As Durndell and Wetherick (1975) put this point: 'It is difficult to obtain an external criterion for this subjective phenomenon.' In general, most discussions of the validity of the QMI have fallen back on the use of factor analysis, in order to demonstrate that it has a coherent internal structure, or to show that it correlates with other, similar tests (White, Sheehan and Ashton, 1977). Normative data have been presented by White, Ashton and Brown (1977).

The predictive validity of introspective questionnaires has been investigated in a wide variety of cognitive tasks. However, this chapter will only be concerned with the available evidence concerning human learning and memory; in any case, a useful review of the remaining literature is available elsewhere (Ernest, 1977). In his initial investigations of the predictive capacity of the shortened form of the QMI, Sheehan (1966b, 1967c) had some success in relating the reported vividness of experienced mental imagery to the accuracy of visual memory. However, these results failed to stand up in a more careful replication (Neisser, 1972b; Sheehan and Neisser, 1969). Since then, investigations of the usefulness of introspective judgements in predicting performance in learning and memory tasks have consistently produced negative findings (Calvano, 1974; Danaher and Thoresen, 1972; Janssen, 1976, pp. 44, 51; Morelli and Lang, 1971; Neisser and Kerr, 1973; Rehm, 1973; Richardson, 1978c). Moreover, the rated vividness of experienced imagery does not affect the benefit gained from imagery mnemonic instructions (Baddeley, 1976, p. 222; Danaher and Thoresen, 1972; Janssen 1976, pp. 44, 48, 51), the benefit gained from the concurrent presentation of relevant pictures (Morelli and Lang, 1971), nor the effect of stimulus imageability upon recall (Janssen, 1976, pp. 44, 48, 51; cf. Sheehan, 1972). Sheehan and Neisser (1969) did find that scores on the QMI were related to the incidental recall of block designs, such that vivid imagers were superior to non-vivid imagers. This was not replicated in a further study using concrete and abstract nouns as stimulus material (Sheehan, 1972), but a similar relationship between reported vividness and incidental recall has been found in at least two other investigations (Janssen, 1976, p. 48; Morris and Gale, 1974). Nevertheless, the most appropriate conclusion at present seems to be that the QMI has little predictive validity in the study of human memory.

The negative findings obtained by Sheehan and Neisser (1969) led Neisser (1970) to conclude that the vividness of experienced mental imagery was quite unrelated to its usefulness or accuracy as a memory code. However, this conclusion was challenged by Marks (1972, 1973), who ascribed the negative results to two basic shortcomings of Sheehan's research. First, he suggested that it would not be helpful to evaluate the vividness of each subject's evoked mental imagery by averaging across all seven sensory modalities (see also Durndell and Wetherick, 1976*b*). Rather, 'it would seem more appropriate to select subjects according to their scores in the imagery modality most likely to function in the experimental task to be performed.' In experiments on the recognition and reconstruction of visual patterns and designs, the relevant modality would be vision; indeed, whatever the material, it could be argued that visual imagery is the most easily aroused and of most importance in determining memory performance (Putnoky, 1975; White, Ashton and Brown, 1977). Therefore, Marks devised a Vividness of Visual Imagery Questionnaire (VVIQ), containing sixteen items to be rated in terms of evoked visual imagery along five-point rating scales. The internal consistency of this test is good, the test-retest reliability is high, and factor analysis yields a single underlying dimension (Dowling, described by White, Sheehan and Ashton, 1977; Marks, 1972, 1973; McKelvie and Gingras, 1974).

Marks' second objection was that Sheehan's experiments had employed abstract geometrical patterns of little inherent interest or meaning of the subjects. He suggested that 'it is not unreasonable to assume that vividness will be related to the interest, affect, meaning, and overall level of arousal evoked by a stimulus.' Accordingly, he carried out three experiments in which the stimuli were coloured photographs of objects or scenes, and in which a forced-choice recognition test subsequently required the subjects to recall details of the pictures presented. In each case, the 'good visualisers' produced better performance than the 'poor visualisers'. Subsequent applications of the VVIQ have, however, produced less convincing results. Marks (1977) found a weak positive correlation with recognition memory for pictures, but a weak negative correlation with recognition memory for words (though presumably vivid visual imagery should be useful in both cases). McKellar, Marks and Barron (reported by Marks, 1972) found no relationship between VVIQ scores and performance in the serial learning of lists of words, nor between VVIQ scores and the benefit gained from the location mnemonic (see chapter 6). Nevertheless, some interesting findings were obtained in an experiment by Gur and Hilgard (1975) in which the subjects had to detect differences between pairs of pictures. The subjects were classified as 'good' or 'poor' imagers according to their scores on the VVIQ, and the two stimuli in each pair were presented either simultaneously or separated by an interval of 20 seconds. The response latencies showed a highly significant interaction, such that the poor imagers were worse with successive presentation, but the good imagers were not. Conversely, the good imagers responded faster than the poor imagers, but only under conditions of successive presentation. This is of course exactly the pattern to be expected on the assumption that introspective judgements of the vividness of evoked visual imagery are a measure of the efficiency of pictorial memory.

However, there is a serious problem to be faced by any method for investigating mental imagery which is based upon introspective reports, and this is the extent to which the results might be influenced by the subjects' expectations. The idea that subjects might vary their responses according to their task expectations was first suggested by Angell (1910). More recently, Holt (1964) pointed out that the experimental results in any experiment on mental imagery will be influenced by expectations set up in the subjects 'by the specific experimental conditions, by their general reading, rumor, and other sources of notions about what to anticipate, and by the attitude towards imagery that prevails in their particular subculture'. The first experimental investigation of this problem was carried out by Di Vesta, Ingersoll and Sunshine (1971), who found a significant positive correlation between scores on the QMI and scores on the Marlowe-Crowne Social Desirability Scale (Crowne and Marlowe, 1964), measuring the extent to which an individual is dependent upon the recognition and approval of others (see Durndell and Wetherick, 1975). Di Vesta *et al.* carried out factor analyses on performance in a large number of tests of individual ability, and found that introspective questionnaires on mental imagery contributed only to a factor defined by the Social Desirability Scale. This correlation between reported vividness of experienced imagery and social desirability has not always been replicated (Durndell and Wetherick, 1975; White, Sheehan and Ashton, 1977); for example, A. Richardson (1977) found a clear relationship in the case of male subjects, but not in the case of female subjects. Nevertheless, it remains possible that under certain circumstances introspective reports may be contaminated by a disposition to respond in a socially desirable manner. For instance, this might explain the finding of a study by Huckabee (1974) that introverts produce higher ratings of evoked mental imagery than extraverts.

These sorts of expectations are probably not fixed, but may well be influenced by the subjects' perceptions of the psychology experiment as a social situation. For example, as Bower (1970a) suggested: 'The normal person's introspections are frequently neither very discriminating nor particularly valid, and they are easily influenced by loaded or leading questions.' More generally, one may consider whether introspective reports might be influenced by the manner in which the experimental instructions are presented. Durndell and Wetherick

(1975) administered 'positive' instructions (emphasising the role of mental imagery in creative thought) or 'negative' instructions (characterising mental imagery as a primitive, childish mode of thought). They also compared a 'high-status' experimenter (a senior lecturer soberly dressed in suit and tie) with a 'low-status' experimenter (a postgraduate student dressed in old jeans and a creased, open-necked shirt). Neither manipulation affected reported mental imagery. However, Ashton and White (1975) compared neutral instructions, 'low motivating' instructions (associating vivid mental imagery with 'dull, uncreative people'), and 'high motivating' instructions (associating vivid mental imagery with 'intelligent, creative people'), and found significant differences in scores on the QMI. High motivating instructions had no effect, but low motivating instructions produced scores indicating less vivid imagery in all seven sensory modalities. Similar results were found in a replication by Ashton, White and Brown (mentioned by White, Sheehan and Ashton, 1977).

If the performance of experimental subjects may be manipulated by changes in the manner in which the experiment is presented, then it follows that the results of such an experiment may be contaminated by cues from the experimenter concerning the desired outcome. Several researchers have suggested that experiments using introspective questionnaires involve rather ambiguous, ill-defined tasks, in which the subjects are likely to respond in such a manner as to produce the results which they believe the experimenter to want (Berger and Gaunitz, 1977; Marks, 1972; Neisser, 1972b; 1976, p. 104; Pinker and Kosslyn, 1978); in short, these are situations in which demand characteristics (Orne, 1962) and experimenter effects (Rosenthal, 1966) might well operate. This contamination is especially likely when the investigator identifies his experimental groups before administering the criterion task; unfortunately, this procedure has been followed in almost all of the research on individual differences in mental imagery (see, for example, Ernest and Paivio, 1971a, 1971b; Marks, 1972; Sheehan, 1966a, 1977b, 1967c, 1972). The possibility of such effects can of course be minimised either by using a 'double-blind' procedure in which different experimenters are responsible for identifying the experimental groups and for administering the criterion task; or by identifying the experimental groups *after* the criterion task has been administered. Sheehan and Neisser (1969) employed a double-blind procedure in relating scores on the QMI to the recall of geometric patterns; they found no correlation between the two variables, but a clear difference between the two experimenters in terms of the imagery ratings produced, and an increase in the rated vividness of experienced mental imagery after an initial introspective inquiry. Neisser (1972b) concluded:

These findings confirm in a modern context what was perhaps already obvious: that introspective reports of imagery can be affected by experimenter effects and perceived demand characteristics. This is not because such biasing factors are all-powerful (they had no effect on *accuracy* of reconstruction in our experiment) but because introspection is particularly vulnerable to them.

Berger and Gaunitz (1977) repeated Gur and Hilgard's (1975) investigation of the relationship between scores on the VVIQ and visual memory, but they identified their experimental groups after the memory task had been carried out. They found no sign of any difference in performance between 'good' imagers and 'poor' imagers. Similarly, Richardson (1978c) found no correlation between scores on the QMI and performance in the free recall of lists of common nouns when the experimental groups were identified after the criterion task.

Because of the abundance of negative findings on the relationship between rated vividness of experienced mental imagery and memory performance, and because of the serious possibility of contamination by experimenter effects, some psychologists have questioned whether introspective reports are a valid measure of individual differences in cognitive ability at all. For example, in the light of their finding that introspective reports (as measured by several tests, including the QMI) loaded only on a factor of social desirability, Di Vesta *et al.* (1971) concluded that such reports did not possess construct validity as measures of the use of mental imagery. However, there are good reasons for not accepting this sort of conclusion. The first is the conceptual point made earlier in discussing the problem of validation. Statements about a person's mental imagery are ultimately to be justified and verified on the basis of his verbal utterances. Introspective questionnaires such as the QMI consist of central examples of such utterances, albeit distorted slightly so as to produce a numerical measure of the vividness of experienced imagery. Any alternative notion of mental imagery, any alternative measure that might be proposed, would only be contingently related to what is indicated by the ordinary-language concept. It would therefore have to be validated (in the sense used by Di Vesta *et al.*) by demonstrating that it was empirically correlated with the subjects' introspective reports.

A second reason for rejecting the idea that introspective reports do not possess construct validity is that relatively similar reports have proved very successful in predicting performance in a wide variety of learning tasks when interpreted as measures of the imageability of the stimulus material. In particular, the procedure of Paivio, Yuille and Madigan (1968) computes the average rating of evoked mental imagery across groups of subjects, and the resulting measure shows a high correlation with memory performance on individual items or samples of items in a wide variety of tasks (chapter 7). However, if introspective reports are to be rejected for the purpose of comparing individual *subjects* because they lack construct validity as measures of the vividness of experienced imagery, then to be consistent they should also be rejected for the purpose of comparing individual stimulus items. This would clearly remove an important source of experimental evidence. Conversely, if introspective reports are methodologically acceptable for studying differences among stimulus items in the vividness of evoked mental imagery, then additional justification must be given for refusing to accept them for the purpose of studying individual differences among the experimental subjects.

Nevertheless, the problem remains: even if introspective ratings are methodologically sound, why do they lack predictive power as measures of the vividness of experienced imagery when averaged across stimulus items, but not when averaged across experimental subjects? One possible explanation is that the apparent similarity between the two sorts of task hides crucial procedural differences which prevent variation among subjects from having predictive capacity in investigations of human memory. This can be easily tested by obtaining measures of stimulus imageability and subjects' introspective reports within the same experimental situation. Investigations which have used this approach have consistently demonstrated that introspective reports predict memory performance within subjects and between stimulus items, but not between subjects and within stimulus items (Marks, 1972; Richardson, in press; Sheehan, 1966a, 1966b; Sheehan and Neisser, 1969).

The solution seems to lie in the nature of the judgements which are required in the two sorts of task. In research on the effect of stimulus imageability, the instructions attached to the rating scales determine the possible range of judgements by fixing the end-points of the scale in terms of the individual subject's own vividness of experienced imagery. His subsequent responses are comparative judgements made in the context of this scale. At no point is the subject required to determine in absolute terms how vivid is his mental imagery. Moreover, this sort of experimental research usually compares different samples of stimulus items which have been rated by the same group or groups of subjects. Thus, the absolute rating assigned to a given item by a particular subject is largely immaterial.

However, in research on individual differences in the use of mental imagery, each subject is required to make an absolute judgement of the vividness of his experienced imagery, and the absolute rating which he assigns to himself is critical. However, since each person can only experience his own mental images (see chapter 3), and since mental imagery is qualitatively different from any other sort of experience, the subject has no absolute or intersubjective criteria for evaluating the vividness of his experienced imagery. As Marks (1972) commented: 'The validity of verbal reports concerning image vividness constitutes a difficult problem since no individual can directly compare his imagery with that of another.' Richardson (in press) has explained the implications of this point in the following manner:

In particular, it is likely that subjects lack a definite origin and a definite unit of measurement for making these subjective judgements, and that in consequence their appreciation of the vividness of mental imagery can be taken to define at best an ordinal scale. It is probable that such judgements are adequate to ensure that relatively gross comparisons among different stimulus items predict variations in the memorability of those items. Nevertheless, since there is no unique mapping of this ordinal subjective scale of vividness onto the seven-point rating scale (which may be variously interpreted as representing either an interval scale or a ratio scale), the absolute value assigned by a subject to a given stimulus will have no meaning, and comparisons among different subjects in terms of their average ratings will not predict variations in memory performance.

An analogy from the area of perception may help to clarify this point. Under normal conditions, when an observer views a distant object, he can easily give an accurate estimate of the object's size. However, one may eliminate any information about the distance of the object in the following manner. The object is rendered luminous and is presented in a totally dark room. The observer views the object with one eye through a pinhole in a screen, with his head held stationary. Under these conditions, the only information available to the subject is the visual angle which the object subtends, and he is unable to ascribe a unique objective size to the object. However, if the observer then looks through another pinhole at a different object, he is able to judge, quite accurately, which looks larger, that is, which object subtends the larger visual angle (Epstein and Landauer, 1969; Hastorff and Way, 1952; Rock, 1975, p. 37; Rock and McDermott, 1964).

The subject who is presented with a questionnaire on the vividness of his experienced mental imagery seems to be in an analogous situation. He can judge whether he has a mental image or not, just as the observer in the above experiment can report the presence or absence of a perceptual object. He can judge whether one item evokes a more vivid mental image than another, just as the observer is able to say whether one perceptual object looks larger than another. However, he is unable to make an absolute judgement of the vividness of a single image, just as the perceiver is unable to say in absolute terms how large an object looks. If the argument given above is sound, it follows that comparisons among experimental subjects in terms of their ratings of evoked mental imagery are neither valid nor meaningful, and it is quite unsurprising that they should fail to predict performance in learning tasks.

(An interesting question is whether a subject can make comparative judgements across modalities, for example, comparing the vividness of a visual image with that of an auditory image. It could be argued that mental imagery in one modality is qualitatively different from that in another. So, just as it makes no sense for a subject to ascribe a unique vividness rating to a mental image, neither does it make any sense for him to judge whether a given visual image is more or less vivid than a given auditory image. On this view, the high correlations which have been found among introspective ratings in different modalities of mental imagery do not reflect a genuine, general imagery trait, but are to be ascribed to general suggestibility or to social desirability; cf. Richardson, 1969, p. 46; Sheehan, 1967a; Wagman and Stewart, 1974; White, Ashton and Law, 1974; White, Sheehan and Ashton, 1977.)

9.2　IMAGERY CONTROL

Given this conclusion, it might be reasonable to devote more attention to alternative ways of eliciting introspective reports on mental imagery. An idea which was discussed long ago by such psychologists as Fechner (1860) and Galton (1889) is that mental imagery will be helpful in carrying out cognitive tasks to the extent that it can be controlled and manipulated by the individual. The first formal test of imagery control was devised by Gordon (1949). This contained eleven questions to be answered in a yes/no manner, although Richardson (1972) recommended that it should be supplemented by a formal interview. Richardson (1969) revised the scale by adding a twelfth item, by including an 'unsure' response category, and by suggesting a standardised set of printed instructions. The twelve questions are as follows:

1. Can you see a car standing in the road in front of a house?
2. Can you see it in colour?
3. Can you now see it in a different colour?
4. Can you now see the same car lying upside down?
5. Can you now see the same car back on its four wheels again?
6. Can you see the car running along the road?
7. Can you see it climb a very steep hill?
8. Can you see it climb over the top?
9. Can you see it get out of control and crash through a house?
10. Can you now see the same car running along the road with a handsome couple inside?
11. Can you see the car cross a bridge and fall over the side into the stream below?
12. Can you see the car all old and dismantled in a car-cemetery?

The internal consistency of this test is good, and the test-retest reliability is adequate (Juhasz, 1972; McKelvie and Gingras, 1974; White, Sheehan and Ashton, 1977). However, given that the questions are limited to the visual modality, it is perhaps surprising that the test appears to have a complex internal structure. Factor analyses by Ashton and White (1974) and by White and Ashton (1977) identified four separate factors, which they called 'movement' (Questions 6, 7 and 8), 'misfortune' (Questions 4, 9, 11 and 12), 'colour' (Questions 2, 3 and 10), and 'stationary' (Questions 1, 5 and possibly 4). However, it should be mentioned that unpublished studies at Brunel University have failed to replicate this factorial solution.

Gordon's test of visual imagery control has shown a significant correlation with the QMI in some studies, but not in others (Ernest, 1977; Morelli and Lang, 1971; Morris and Gale, 1974; A. Richardson, 1977; Spanos, Valois, Ham and Ham, 1973; Starker, 1974; White, Sheehan and Ashton, 1977). However, they are loaded on the same factor in factor analytic studies (Di Vesta *et al.*, 1971;

Forisha, 1975; A. Richardson, 1977). A strong positive correlation has also been reported between Gordon's test and Marks' VVIQ (McKelvie and Gingras, 1974). Nevertheless, each of these is a pencil and paper test of mental imagery, and so it is entirely possible that an instrument factor might have been operating (White and Ashton, 1977; White, Sheehan and Ashton, 1977). Finally, the available research on effects of social desirability suggests that Gordon's test is rather less vulnerable to variations in demand characteristics than the QMI (Di Vesta *et al.*, 1971; Durndell and Wetherick, 1975; A. Richardson, 1977; White, Sheehan and Ashton, 1977).

Once again, the predictive validity of Gordon's test has been investigated in a variety of cognitive tasks (Ernest, 1977; Richardson, 1972), but only the very few studies of memory performance need to be mentioned here. Morelli and Lang (1971) compared scores in Gordon's test with paired-associate learning, and found a significant correlation only when the stimulus pairs were supplemented by relevant pictures; they concluded that the ability to control one's mental imagery was only employed in learning when imagery was directly aroused by pictorial presentation. Morris and Gale (1974) reported a positive correlation between imagery control and the incidental recall of individual words. However, experiments at Brunel University have failed to find any sign of a relationship either between imagery control and the recall of paired associates, or between imagery control and the effect of stimulus imageability. Even when the total scores in Gordon's test were broken down into the four factors suggested by White and Ashton (1977), the only correlation to reach statistical significance was that between the 'movement' score and the recall of concrete pairs. It is really too soon to decide whether Gordon's test will prove useful in predicting memory performance. Nevertheless, it should be explored, since the questions contained in the test do not seem to be subject to the conceptual and methodological criticisms which may be directed at the QMI.

9.3   REPORTED MEDIATORS

There are certain other procedures which have been suggested for eliciting introspective reports on the use of mental imagery, such as the Imaginal Processes Inventory (Singer and Antrobus, 1972), for the analysis of daydreaming, the Imagery Survey Schedule (Tondo and Cautela, 1974), for use in behaviour therapy, and the Individual Differences Questionnaire, which was devised by Paivio (1971c, p. 495) to investigate cognitive style. However, these techniques have not been adequately tested in the context of experiments on human learning and memory. There is nevertheless one further method which has been found to have excellent predictive capacity, and which is totally consistent with the methodological attitudes of this book.

In chapters 6 and 7, experiments were described in which the subjects received post-learning questionnaires which asked them to describe the sorts of strategies which they had used to remember different stimulus items. These reports were analysed in terms of the different sorts of item used and in terms of the subjects' performance. The main findings were as follows. First, the number of subjects who report the use of images as mediators is greater with concrete, imageable material. Second, the number of subjects who report the use of imagery for a given item correlates with the memory performance on that item. Third, items for which subjects report images as mediators are recalled better than items for which subjects report verbal mediators. Finally, subjects will tend to report the use of images as mediators in the case of concrete, imageable items, even when instructed to use other learning strategies.

These empirical results seem to have an immediate corollary, that the number of items for which a *subject* reports the use of images as mediators should correlate with that *subject's* memory performance. Although open to immediate empirical verification and although clearly relevant to the study of individual differences in the use of mental imagery, this idea has hardly ever been seriously considered, let alone experimentally tested. One reason for this, of course, has been the idea that such reports are subjective, mentalistic and invalid as a source of scientific data. Another reason, and one that is rather better founded, is the feeling that the causal determiners of psychological performance may not be open to conscious inspection (cf. Pylyshyn, 1973). Nevertheless, while other areas of psychological research have systematised the collection of introspective reports in the method of protocol analysis (Newell and Simon, 1972), such reports have not been collected in research on human memory.

One of the first psychologists to relate memory performance to the subjects' learning strategies was Bartlett (1932, pp. 59–61, 109–12). He found that his subjects could be classified roughly as either visualizers, who claimed to rely mainly upon visual imagery in remembering, or vocalisers, who claimed to rely mainly upon words rather than mental images. Although the vocalisers tended to be less confident in their recall, the two groups produced comparable recall performance. However, Bartlett's experimental procedure was rather peculiar, involving the learning of arbitrary associations between words and simple figures, and rather different results might be obtained with more conventional learning tasks.

One experiment in recent years which compared subjects in terms of the sorts of mediators which they employed was carried out by Hulicka and Grossman (1967). They compared a group of old subjects (whose median age was 74.1 years) with a group of young subjects (whose median age was 16.1 years) in a paired-associate learning task with pairs of common nouns. In a post-learning questionnaire, it was found that the older group reported more verbal mediators and fewer imaginal mediators than the younger group. However, it is obvious that the difference in age between the two groups was entirely adequate to explain any difference in memory performance, without any appeal to differences in preferred encoding strategy.

Another experiment which briefly considered the subjects' reported use of mental imagery was carried out by Wells (1972). She showed that the recall of verbal stimuli was more disrupted by an interpolated backwards-counting task than the recall of pictorial stimuli, and suggested that this was because the pictorial stimuli had been retained as mental images. However, she mentioned that many subjects also seemed to retain the verbal stimuli in the form of images, and found that the greater their reported use of mental imagery, the better their recall (but cf. Hasher, Riebman and Wren, 1976).

Marks (1972) pointed out a possible problem with the use of post-experimental reports, which is that a subject's responses may be influenced by whether his recall was actually successful. Demand characteristics might operate either if the subject cannot remember the mediators he employed, or if he fails to understand the experimenter's instructions. In either event, 'his perception of the purpose of the experiment would presumably be based on the naive (although probably correct) assumption that vivid imagery is expected to accompany high accuracy', and any correlation between recall performance and the use of mental imagery would be artefactual. To illustrate this, Marks repeated the experiment of Sheehan and Neisser (1969), and found that, within subjects, variations in the reported vividness of mental imagery only correlated with variations in recall when reports were obtained after the recall test. Nevertheless, in the same paper, Marks reported an experiment by McKellar, Marks and Barron which showed that the improvement in recall resulting from the use of the location mnemonic was not related to the subjects' scores on the VVIQ, but that it was highly correlated ($r = +0.67$) with the number of reported visual images. In this instance, Marks accepted the evidential value of post-learning reports, and concluded: 'This result strongly supports the notion that visual imagery is the effective mediator of the improved recall.'

Richardson (1978e) carried out an experiment to test the hypothesis mentioned above in a direct fashion. The subjects learned a list of paired associates, attempted to recall the response terms when cued with the stimulus terms, and then completed a post-learning questionnaire of the sort devised by Paivio, Smythe and Yuille (1968). Various measures of the use of mental imagery were considered, but the best predictor of a subject's recall performance ($r = +0.80$) was the absolute number of pairs for which he reported the use of imaginal mediators. A subsequent experiment showed that this correlation applied in the case of concrete material, but not in the case of abstract material. This goes some way to rebutting an objection of the sort made by Marks (1972), that the mediator reports might have been based upon the accuracy of recall; on this interpretation, it is difficult to see why the frequency of reported imaginal mediators did not correlate with the recall of abstract material, or why the frequency of verbal mediators did not show a similar relationship with recall when the subjects had as much opportunity to report such mediators as they did the use of mental imagery (Paivio, 1971c, p. 359; personal communication). In general, as Paivio (1972) has pointed out, the usefulness of mental imagery as a mnemonic device will be demonstrated by interactive relationships between mediator reports, mediation instructions, stimulus imageability and recall performance. The use of subjects' protocols has been neglected in the past, but it may well turn out to be the most effective way of investigating individual differences in the use of mental imagery, and of integrating research on individual differences with investigations based upon the other sorts of experimental procedures.

9.4 SPATIAL ABILITY

One way of trying to study mental imagery in a more 'objective' manner would be to investigate how subjects carry out tasks which plausibly can only be carried out by manipulating some pictorial representation (that is, tasks for which more abstract verbal encoding would be relatively unhelpful). This sort of task was discussed at length in chapter 4. Although the processes operating can only be inferred from the subjects' behaviour, success in these tasks can be defined according to an absolute, public criterion, namely the correctness of the subjects' responses. Moreover, one can also measure the latency of these responses, and thus evaluate the speed with which the tasks are carried out. It is therefore not surprising that psychologists have used such measures as indices of imagery ability. (In contradistinction to introspective methods, these sorts of task have elsewhere been referred to as 'tests of objective imagery ability': Richardson, 1978c.)

In his analysis of factors underlying human intelligence, Thurstone (1938) defined the space factor as the ease with which a subject employs spatial and visual imagery. This factor is measured by tests of *spatial thinking*, an example of which is the Flags test (Thurstone and Jeffrey, 1956). This contains 21 questions, each of which comprises one test figure and six examples, where each figure is the schematic representation of a flag (perhaps a rectangle with a symbol in one corner). The subject has to say whether each example depicts the same side of the flag as the test stimulus (usually rotated) or the opposite side (the mirror-image of the test stimulus, again usually rotated). The subject's performance is derived from the number of correct responses given during a five-minute period. This test is obviously quite similar to the mental rotation task devised by Shepard and Metzler (1971). Other tests that have been employed in experimental research to define imagery ability include the Minnesota Paper Form Board (Likert and Quasha, 1941) and the Space Relations test (Bennett, Seashore and Wesman, 1947). Such tests correlate moderately well with one another (Durndell and Wetherick, 1976a; Ernest, 1977), they load on the same factor or factors in investigations which have employed factor analysis (Di Vesta *et al.*, 1971; Forisha, 1975; Paivio, 1971c, p. 496), and scores are often combined from two or more of a battery of tests. On the other hand, tests of spatial thinking have failed to show any consistent relationship with ratings produced in introspective questionnaires on mental imagery (Danaher and Thoresen, 1972; Durndell and

Wetherick, 1976a; Ernest, 1977; Rehm, 1973; Richardson, 1978c; Starker, 1974), and the two sorts of test typically load on different factors in the solutions obtained by factor analysis (Di Vesta *et al.*, 1971; Forisha, 1975; A. Richardson, 1972, 1977; cf. Paivio, 1971c, p. 496).

In the 1960s, two studies appeared which suggested that tests of spatial thinking might offer a way of investigating the role of mental imagery in long-term memory. A doctoral dissertation by Kuhlman (1960; subsequently published in part as Hollenberg, 1970) compared the spatial ability of children with their performance on a (relatively concrete) memory test using geometric shapes and on a (relatively abstract) conception-formation task. The children were divided into groups of high and low imagery ability by their combined performance on four tests of spatial thinking, including Flags. It was found that the children of high spatial ability were more accurate in recalling geometric shapes, but that the children of low spatial ability were superior in concept formation.

Kuhlman considered that the effect of spatial ability would become less important with age, as adult linguistic categories acquired more importance in thinking and remembering. However, another doctoral dissertation by Stewart (1965) argued that imagery ability would continue to be influential in adults, especially in handling concrete material, and reported three experiments to examine this idea. In the first study, female university students learned paired associates in which the stimulus terms were pictures or words and the responses were digits. The subjects were judged as high or low imagers according to their combined scores on two tests of spatial thinking. The high imagers produced better performance than the low imagers when the stimulus terms were pictures, but the reverse was true when the stimulus terms were words. Stewart replicated this interaction between imagery ability and task concreteness in a second experiment which examined recognition memory for pictures and words. This study provided interesting additional information concerning the sort of coding used by high and low imagers, which will be discussed presently. In a third experiment, Stewart compared high and low imagers in their free recall of word lists which varied in imageability. However, this failed to show a significant interaction between spatial ability and stimulus imageability, so her general theoretical approach was not supported.

Unfortunately, despite the promise of these initial investigations, more recent research has failed to show any consistent relationship between spatial ability and memory performance. Although one or two studies have found a positive correlation between the two measures (for instance, Christiansen and Stone, 1968), most investigations have not (Calvano, 1974; Ernest and Paivio, 1969, 1971a; Paivio, Rogers and Smythe, 1968; Richardson, 1976b, 1978c). Similarly, the relationship between spatial ability and stimulus imageability is quite unclear. Whereas Stewart (1965) found no interaction between these variables in the free recall of unrelated words, Richardson (1976b) found a small but statistically significant correlation between the effect of stimulus imageability and the spatial ability of the subjects (and cf. Christiansen and Stone, 1968). However, in the paired-associate learning of noun-adjective pairs, Di Vesta and Ross (1971) found a clear *negative* correlation, such that subjects of high spatial ability were superior to subjects of low spatial ability only in learning pairs of low rated imageability. Again, Stewart's original study had compared the recall and recognition of pictures and words; Paivio, Rogers and Smythe (1968) found no effect of spatial ability upon the free recall of either sort of material, and Richardson (1978*c*) found no effects in a test of recognition memory. One interesting, though as yet unreplicated result was obtained by Di Vesta and Sunshine (1974), who investigated serial learning assisted by mnemonic devices of the 'one-bun' variety (see chapter 6), and who defined imagery ability according to three spatial tests. This study found that subjects of high imagery ability produced better performance than subjects of low imagery ability when operating under imagery mnemonic instructions, but not when operating under instructions to use verbal mediators. Imagery instructions produced poorer performance than verbal instructions in the case of subjects of low imagery ability, but not in the case of subjects of high imagery ability.

This last result is consistent with the idea that tests of spatial thinking predict the extent to which the subject is able to employ mental imagery as an effective elaborative code in long-term memory. Nevertheless, it clearly stands in need of further investigation, and contrasts markedly with the negative findings obtained by other researchers on the value of spatial tests in memory research. It should also be pointed out that research on the effects of spatial ability may be just as vulnerable to experimenter effects as the investigations reviewed earlier on introspective reports. Unfortunately, as Ernest (1977) has pointed out, there is simply no experimental evidence on this point. In the circumstances, one must remain sceptical of the vast majority of the experiments on the effects of spatial ability on the grounds that the experimental groups were identified before the administration of the criterion task. When the experimental groups are identified after they have completed the recall task, variations in spatial ability seem to have no effect upon performance in long-term memory (Richardson, 1978*c*).

This conclusion is entirely consistent with the general theoretical suggestions made in chapters 6 and 7, that the constructive and elaborative uses of mental imagery are functionally independent of one another. On this analysis, one would expect a person's performance in long-term memory to vary with his use of mental imagery as a form of elaborative encoding, and this receives excellent confirmation from the use of post-learning questionnaires (see above). Nevertheless, it is by no means clear how the *ability* to employ mental imagery as a form of elaborative encoding might be measured objectively, except (trivially) by performance in another long-term memory task. The next section describes an alternative approach.

9.5   CODING PREFERENCE

In discussing the negative findings of research on introspective reports and spatial ability, Richardson (1978c) made the following suggestions:

> A possible conclusion is that neither subjective nor objective tests of imagery ability are appropriate measures of the critical dimensions on which subjects vary in their use of different modes of symbolic representation. In studying individual differences in memory coding, I would suggest that the crucial question is not how well a subject employs a given mode of symbolic representation, but which is his preferred mode of representation. We should therefore not be interested in the ability to construct and manipulate mental iamges, but in the preference for mental imagery as a mnemonic code.

If one distinguishes between these two concepts of *coding ability* and *coding preference*, it is clear that almost all of the research on individual differences in the use of mental imagery has been concerned with the former. It has been assumed that the preference for using mental imagery is correlated with the ability to use mental imagery (Ernest and Paivio, 1971b), but there has been little serious attempt to measure imagery coding preference directly.

An exception is the second experiment reported by Stewart (1965), which investigated recognition memory for pictures and words. The test required her subjects to judge not only whether an item had been presented for learning, but also whether it had been originally presented as a picture or as a word. If subjects vary in their preference for mental imagery as a way of encoding information, this should affect the extent to which they can make the latter sort of judgement with accuracy. Specifically, the judgement which a subject makes should reflect the sort of coding employed. The results indicated that the subjects of high spatial ability were more likely to encode a word as a pictorial image than were those of low spatial ability, whereas subjects of low spatial ability were more likely to encode a picture verbally than were those of high spatial ability.

However, Di Vesta *et al.* (1971) mentioned that they had been 'only partially successful' in replicating Stewart's findings. Richardson (1978c) also asked his subjects to identify whether an item had originally been presented as a picture or as a word. Although the judged presentation modality accurately reflected the original presentation modality, the degree of accuracy was not influenced in any way either by introspective reports (as measured by the QMI) or by spatial ability (as measured by the Flags test). Richardson concluded that coding ability and coding preference are relatively independent dimensions along which individuals may vary, at least with regard to the use of mental imagery. If coding *preference* is the crucial determiner of performance in memory tasks, than this would explain why research employing measures of imagery *ability* has produced confusing, contradictory and unreplicable findings.

Richardson went on to argue that, in order to understand how a subject carried out a verbal-learning task, one must measure the extent to which he tends to encode word stimuli as mental images. Stewart's recognition task enables one to derive just such a measure of coding preference. To be more specific, a subject's preference for imaginal encoding can be estimated from his accuracy in judging the original presentation modality of verbally presented items. To the extent to which he tends to encode such items as pictorial images, his capacity for making such judgements will be reduced. Richardson measured his subjects' preference for imaginal coding in just this fashion, and found that subjects who preferred to encode verbally produced better recall performance than subjects who preferred to encode pictorially. He suggested that the latter subjects were employing mental imagery in a separative manner, and, to support this conclusion, he pointed out certain fine-grain similarities between the results of his experiment and the effects of separative imagery instructions. It was concluded that coding preference is an important determiner of performance in memory tasks, but that a preference for imaginal encoding, as measured according to the above procedure, leads to discrete representations in human memory, which actually impairs the subject's ability subsequently to recall the information thus encoded.

Although this approach appears to be promising, three points should be made concerning Richardson's procedure. First, it is basically a measure of response bias, and there is no guarantee that such bias reflects only variations in mnemonic coding. Second, the superiority of pictorial material (see chapter 5) in both the retention test and the test of presentation modality meant that performance was at a ceiling for all subjects. Only the items presented verbally provided a basis for discriminating among the subjects on the basis of their coding preference. Third, the subjects were therefore discriminated on the basis of whether they could remember that particular items had been presented verbally. However, the fact that a subject could not remember that an item had been presented verbally does not entail that it was remembered in a pictorial form, as a mental image, nor in any other specific representation. The results thus show at most that subjects who could not remember the modality in which an item was presented in one test remember fewer items in another test; they do not show that these subjects employ mental imagery, and they certainly do not show that mental imagery employs a quasi-pictorial representation in human memory.

9.6 NEUROPSYCHOLOGICAL EVIDENCE

An important respect in which individuals can vary in their capacities for different modes of thinking and remembering is when these capacities are affected by damage to the physiological mechanisms of the brain. Neuropsychological evidence of this sort has been considered important in research on mental imagery because it has been taken to support the dual coding theory of functionally separate verbal and imaginal cognitive systems. However, accounts of mental imagery which appeal to such evidence usually fail to assess it in a critical manner or to relate it explicitly to the theoretical positions under discussion. If one wishes to identify mental imagery as an important form of coding in memory tasks, one must go beyond a mere functional dissociation of verbal and non-verbal cognitive systems, to show how the two sorts of system might contribute jointly to performance.

As a very gross approximation, one can say that, on the available evidence, the vehicles of linguistic faculties seem to be localised within the left cerebral hemisphere in most subjects. Damage to the right cerebral hemisphere may lead to an impairment of non-verbal functioning, but typically leaves speech unimpaired. Independent of this distinction between verbal and non-verbal function, one may identify a different sort of organisation within each of the cerebral hemispheres. Again as a rough approximation, one can say that the posterior regions of the hemispheres are responsible for the reception, elaboration and storage of received information; whereas the anterior regions of the hemispheres are responsible for programming, regulating and controlling human actions (see Luria, 1974, chap. 2; Milner, 1971; Walsh, 1978, chap. 8). (It should be obvious that this account ignores individual differences in the cerebral representation of psychological function.) Within this very approximate and imprecise framework, one may attempt to determine the cerebral structures whose integrity is of most importance in the three sorts of mnemonic faculty which have been discussed in the earlier chapters of this book: immediate memory (chapter 4); pictorial memory (chapter 5); and verbal memory (chapters 6–8).

The experimental research reviewed in chapter 4 suggested that mental imagery might operate as a short-term working memory in the representation, preservation and manipulation of spatial and pictorial information. Damage to the posterior regions of the brain, and expecially to the *parietal* lobes of the cerebral cortex, tends to produce impaired performance in these tasks (Miller, 1972, chap. 4; Teuber, 1963). Although deficits in spatial thinking may result from damage to either side of the brain, they are more likely following damage to the right cerebral hemisphere (Arrigoni and De Renzi, 1964; Piercy, Hécaen and Ajuriaguerra, 1960; Piercy and Smyth, 1962). However, the relative frequency of deficit in patients with damage to the right hemisphere varies from task to task (Benton, 1969). Thus, physiological mechanisms in both hemispheres may contribute to the use of mental imagery as a short-term, non-verbal, working memory, but different tasks may make different requirements of the components in the two parietal lobes.

The role of the right cerebral hemisphere is more obvious in considering pictorial memory. The need to postulate a non-verbal representation in long-term memory is perhaps most readily accepted in the case of the retention of complex visual displays which cannot be readily described or labelled. While damage to the left cerebral hemisphere typically leaves performance on such tasks unimpaired, the retention of non-verbal patterned stimuli is especially affected by damage to the right *temporal* lobe. While it is true that a person's ability to recognise such material may be affected in more generalised right posterior lesions, the study of patients who have undergone unilateral temporal lobectomy has clearly implicated the structures of the right temporal lobe in non-verbal long-term memory, and specifically the hippocampus (Milner, 1965, 1966, 1971).

Thus, the available evidence suggests that the parietal lobes constitute the neuroanatomical basis of non-verbal short-term memory, whereas the right temporal lobe contains the neuroanatomical basis of non-verbal long-term memory. This is an interesting conclusion, since an analogous distinction for *verbal* memory has been made with respect to the left parietal and left temporal lobes (Shallice and Warrington, 1970). Since there exists a 'double dissociation' (Teuber, 1955) between the effects of damage to the parietal lobes and the effects of damage to the right temporal lobe (that is, the two components of non-verbal memory appear to be vulnerable to lesions at distinct and non-overlapping anatomical sites), it may be concluded that the short-term and long-term non-verbal stores are functionally independent.

These ideas are confirmed by results obtained with a task devised by Corsi as a non-verbal analogue of the conventional test of digit span (Milner, 1971). In this task, which was mentioned in chapter 4, the subject is presented with nine blocks in an irregular array. The experimenter taps some of the blocks in a particular sequence, and the subject is required to tap out exactly the same pattern immediately afterwards. The maximum number of blocks which he is able to tap in the correct order is his spatial span. In its basic form, this is clearly a test of immediate, non-verbal memory. De Renzi and Nichelli (1975) found that a subject's spatial span might be reduced by posterior lesions in either hemisphere, but Corsi found no impairment following either right or left temporal lobectomy (Milner, 1971). This supports the hypothesis of a parietal basis for non-verbal short-term memory. However, Corsi also employed this task according to the supraspan method devised by Hebb (1961). Each subject was tested on sequences of the same length, one block longer than his spatial span. Unknown to the subject, every third sequence was exactly the same, but other sequences occurred only once. With normal subjects, recall of the recurring sequence increased with repeated presentation, but the non-recurring sequences remained at the same initial level. The improvement on the recurring sequence thus reflects the contribution of non-verbal long-term memory, cumulating with repeated presentation (cf. Baddeley and Warrington, 1970). However, this improvement was reduced following right temporal lobectomy; indeed, if there was radical damage to the hippocampus, the patients showed no benefit from repeated presentation (Milner, 1971). These results support the hypothesis that the vehicle of non-verbal long-term memory is localised within the right temporal lobe.

The distinct neuroanatomical correlates of short-term and long-term non-verbal memory are also illustrated by findings obtained with two maze tasks (cf. Ratcliff and Newcombe, 1973). In a locomotor maze, the subject walks among points arrayed on the ground along a specific path shown on a map. The map is held in a constant orientation relative to the subject, but its orientation relative to the ground changes as he walks. The subject does not have to 'learn' the maze in any sense, but he has to carry out mental rotations in immediate memory in order to relate his perception of the map with his perception of the maze. Performance on this task is affected by parietal lesions of either hemisphere, but not by temporal lesions (Semmes, Weinstein, Ghent and Teuber, 1955, 1963; Teuber, 1963). On the other hand, in a visually-guided stylus maze, the subject has to learn a specific path among a set of points in a rectangular array, tracing a path with a stylus over a series of trials. This requires the subject to encode a complex visual pattern in long-term memory, but he does not have to transform the visual array in any way. Patients with lesions of the right temporal lobe are impaired in this task, but those with lesions confined to the parietal lobes or to the left temporal lobe obtain normal scores (Milner, 1965).

As was mentioned earlier, the neuroanatomical basis of linguistic functioning tends to be localised within the left cerebral hemisphere in most subjects. It is certainly true that verbal learning and memory tend to be disrupted by damage to the left hemisphere (Newcombe, 1969, chap. 6); and, as in the case of non-verbal retention, the structures of the temporal lobe appear to be of particular importance (Miller, 1972, pp. 56–9; Milner, 1971). As Milner (1966) commented: 'It is now well established that a left temporal lobe lesion in the dominant hemisphere for speech impairs the learning and retention of verbal material, whether aurally or visually presented, and regardless of whether retention is measured by recognition, free recall, or rate of associative learning.'

This functional dissociation of the two cerebral hemispheres with respect to the processing of verbal and non-verbal information has been taken to support the dual coding theory of symbolic functioning in a fairly direct manner (Paivio, 1971*c*, pp. 522–3; 1978*b*; Sheikh, 1977). However, the assumption of independence–interconnectedness of the two systems does not appear to be strictly in accord with the neuropsychological evidence. Specifically, the notion of interconnectedness, as encapsulated in the coding redundancy hypothesis, implies that there should *not* be a radical hemispheric dissociation. This argument may be spelled out in the form of two premises, each of which is a central plank of dual coding theory (though neither of which is clearly supported by empirical findings), together with a conclusion which is completely contradicted by the available evidence.

1. Dual coding theory interprets many findings in verbal learning and memory as showing that mental imagery is involved in such tasks. This is a consequence of the coding redundancy hypothesis, which states that both imaginal and verbal processing are involved in verbal remembering. Although many of the findings discussed in chapters 6–8 are consistent with this

framework, very little of the evidence serves to distinguish dual coding theory from common coding theory.

2. Dual coding theory also assumes that mental imagery is the form of mnemonic representation which is involved in pictorial memory. Although it might be parsimonious to explain the effects attributable to the operation of mental imagery in terms of the mnemonic coding aroused by pictorial presentation, the research discussed in chapter 5 failed to provide any convincing evidence for this. Insofar as pictorial memory in particular, and non-verbal cognitive processing in general are vulnerable to lesions of the right cerebral hemisphere, it would be reasonable to conclude that the neuroanatomical vehicle of mental imagery is contained in that hemisphere. The only evidence for this is an experiment on short-term recognition memory reported by Seamon and Gazzaniga (1973). They required their subjects to use either interactive imagery or subvocal rehearsal, and presented recognition probes to either the left or the right cerebral hemispheres by means of a tachistoscope. The subjects produced faster responses for probes to the left hemisphere when they were using subvocal rehearsal, but they produced faster responses for probes to the right hemisphere when they were using interactive imagery. This is the only clear evidence directly associating mental imagery with the functions of the right cerebral hemisphere, but it is actually contradicted by evidence from studies of temporal lobectomy which will be discussed presently.

3. Nevertheless, the two premises which have just been outlined imply that verbal learning and memory should be affected not only by damage to the left cerebral hemisphere (because of the obvious verbal component), but also by damage to the right cerebral hemisphere (because of the involvement of mental imagery). However, the neuropsychological evidence on this matter is quite unequivocal: damage to the right or non-dominant hemisphere virtually never gives rise to an impairment in verbal learning tasks (Miller, 1972, p. 57; Milner, 1966; Newcombe, 1969, chap. 6; Walsh, 1978, p. 174). Thus, the two hemispheres do not seem to contribute jointly to verbal learning and memory. Conversely, their complete functional dissociation seems to be quite inconsistent with usual accounts of dual coding theory.

The two cerebral hemispheres *do* seem to contribute jointly to the recognition of nameable pictures. Milner (1966) devised a test in which the subjects were asked to name the objects depicted in each of four pictures, and subsequently (after an interval occupied by a digit repetition task) to select the original four pictures from a series of nine pictures. The task was administered to 123 patients who were undergoing carotid amytal tests prior to neurosurgery. (In this procedure, the functioning of one of the cerebral hemispheres is selectively interrupted by the injection of a solution of sodium amytal into the common carotid artery.) Failures of recognition tended to occur only when the patient had a pre-existing unilateral temporal lesion, and when the injections were made into the contralateral hemisphere. This suggests that the relevant information is normally stored in both cerebral hemispheres and can be utilised provided at least one of the temporal lobes is functioning. Thus, there is some neuropsychological evidence for a coding redundancy account of the retention of nameable pictures.

Unfortunately, it is unlikely that such evidence can be more than suggestive by itself. As Anderson (1978) has pointed out, the demonstration of a functional dissociation of the two cerebral hemispheres is entirely consistent with the idea that all information has a propositional form, but that propositions encoding visual information are stored in the right hemisphere and propositions encoding verbal information are stored in the left hemisphere; or with the idea that all information is stored in a propositional form in both hemispheres, but that procedures for performing verbal tasks are located in the left hemisphere and procedures for performing spatial tasks are located in the right hemisphere. Either version of common coding theory would be consistent with the available evidence. Unless one is to accept Anderson's conclusion that it is in principle impossible to decide between the two frameworks, future research must devise more intricate experimental techniques for investigating the neuroanatomical basis of psychological function.

Although research on the role of mental imagery in *verbal* memory has received little support from clinical studies of memory impairment, several recent studies have approached the problem by applying experimental procedures to specific clinical populations. Four of these investigations will be briefly summarised.

1. Baddeley and Warrington (1970, 1973) studied patients with a severe global deficit in learning tasks, the amnesic syndrome (Warrington, 1971). Their first series of experiments used tests of verbal learning, and identified this condition as a selective impairment of long-term memory. The second series demonstrated that amnesic patients were able to improve their recall performance when the material was organised on either a phonemic or a semantic basis; however, they did not benefit at all when unrelated words were linked by sentences which they were instructed to visualise. This suggested that amnesic patients were specifically impaired in the use of mental imagery as a form of coding in long-term memory.

2. Jones (1974) examined the usefulness of an imagery mnemonic in patients following unilateral and bilateral temporal lobectomy, who were required to learn heterogeneous lists of concrete and abstract paired associates. As one would have expected, the patients with bilateral lesions showed no retention throughout the experiment. The patients with lesions of the left temporal lobe showed a significant impairment, but were able to improve their performance when instructed to use mental imagery. Indeed, they showed a normal superiority on concrete material, and a normal benefit from imagery mnemonic instructions. This implies that their deficit cannot be attributed to a failure to use mental imagery, and, conversely, that the neuroanatomical basis of mental imagery is not contained within the structures of the left temporal lobe. The patients with lesions of the right temporal lobe showed no impairment, a normal superiority on

concrete material, and a normal benefit from imagery mnemonic instructions. This confirms the point made above, that damage to the right cerebral hemisphere does not give rise to an impairment in verbal learning and memory, and implies that the neuroanatomical basis of mental imagery is not contained within the structures of the right temporal lobe. Further, since damage to the right temporal lobe typically leads to an impairment in learning pictorial material, Jones' results suggest that the effects of stimulus imageability and of imagery mnemonic instructions do not reflect the use of a pictorial representation in long-term memory.

3. Richardson (1978*b*) investigated verbal learning and intelligence in two cases of spontaneously arrested congenital hydrocephalus. They were found to be impaired in free recall when compared with control subjects matched for age and educational attainment. They were also selectively impaired on the performance subtests of an intelligence scale. Richardson concluded that their memory impairment resulted from a reduced ability to use mental imagery as an elaborative code. However, the discussion earlier in this chapter shows that there is no independent support for the idea that performance tests of spatial ability measure the ability to use mental imagery as an elaborative code in long-term memory. Indeed, Richardson's subjects were equally impaired on concrete and abstract material. This suggests that the memory impairment and the deficit in performance IQ were unrelated aspects of a more general reduction in intellectual ability. In fact, congenital hydrocephalus is a disorder which is likely to produce damage in a wide variety of cerebral regions.

4. Richardson (1979) examined 40 adult male patients admitted to hospital following head injuries, and compared them with a control group of orthopaedic patients. The patients with head injuries were impaired in the recall of concrete material, but not in the recall of abstract material. While the control subjects showed the normal pattern of superior recall of concrete material, the patients with head injuries showed no significant difference between the recall of concrete and abstract material. Richardson concluded that head injury leads to an impairment of imaginal encoding, but does not affect verbal encoding. However, in personal discussion, Alan Baddeley has suggested that the performance of the head-injured patients might merely reflect a floor effect in the contribution of secondary memory to the total recall performance. That is, a normal primary-memory component was manifested by both groups of subjects on both sorts of stimulus material, but the secondary-memory component was attenuated *either* with abstract material *or* following closed head injury. On this account, the idea of an impairment in secondary memory would be adequate to explain the results without appeal to mental imagery.

Clearly this is an inadequate amount of empirical evidence on which to establish a neuropsychological theory concerning the role of mental imagery in memory tasks. However, future research might seriously consider the suggestion that an analysis of such tasks as involving the use of mental imagery will be of help in understanding the impaired memory performance which results from neurological damage. On the other hand, the work of Jones (1974) and the more general background of neuropsychological literature seem to have important consequences for the status of current theories of imagery and memory.

9.7 CONCLUSIONS

Contemporary research on individual differences in mental imagery employs two approaches. The 'subjective' approach relies on the subjects' introspective reports concerning their mental images and the use which they make of them. Introspective questionnaires on the vividness of experienced imagery have been frequently used, but they have produced no reliable conclusions. On the other hand, the types of mediator reported in post-learning questionnaires do seem to be important in understanding the role of mental imagery in learning tasks. The 'objective' approach relies on measures of the subjects' performance in tasks requiring the use of mental imagery. Tests of spatial thinking have failed to produce replicable correlations between imagery ability and memory performance.

The reported vividness of experienced mental imagery is independent both of the subject's ability to use mental imagery as a non-verbal working memory, and of his ability to use mental imagery as an elaborative code in long-term memory. There are serious conceptual reasons for questioning whether such reports constitute legitimate or meaningful judgements. The subject's ability to use mental imagery as a non-verbal working memory appears to be dependent upon the operation of physiological mechanisms within the parietal lobes. It is independent of the subject's ability to use mental imagery as an elaborative code in long-term memory. Long-term memory of a nonverbal, pictorial nature appears to be dependent upon the operation of physiological mechanisms within the right temporal lobe; whereas long-term memory of a verbal nature seems to be dependent upon the integrity of the left temporal lobe. The use of mental imagery as an elaborative code in long-term verbal memory does not seem to be dependent upon the mechanisms of either temporal lobe, and should not be considered to give rise to pictorial representations in long-term memory.

Finally, I should mention three further areas in which individual differences in mental imagery have been considered. The first is the study of individuals who experience particularly vivid, detailed and persistent visual imagery. This is often referred to as *eidetic* imagery, and has received some attention from cognitive psychologists in recent years (for example, Gray and Gummerman, 1975; Haber, 1969; Stromeyer and Psotka, 1970). However, Haber (1969) argued that eidetic imagery was quite different from the type of imagery normally employed in memory tasks, and Baddeley (1976, p. 222) has recently concluded that the study of eidetic imagery 'seems to represent an intriguing but relatively unimportant byway on the road to understanding normal human memory'. The second approach is the study of individuals who might be expected to be lacking in certain sorts of mental imagery. Some evidence has been obtained in the case of blind subjects, who are presumably lacking in visual imagery (Paivio and Okovita, 1971), and in the case of deaf subjects, who are presumably lacking in auditory imagery (Conlin and Paivio, 1975). However, these are really only preliminary investigations which have yet to make a positive contribution to the understanding of the role of mental imagery in remembering Finally, one may investigate the performance of individuals who appear to have radically superior mnemonic abilities. Baddeley (1976, pp. 357–68) has given an interesting summary of several such cases, and the role of mental imagery is frequently implicated. Nevertheless, it is also obvious that there are many differences among the mnemonists who have been studied in detail, and it is difficult to come to any general conclusions concerning the origins of super-normal memory.

10

Conclusions

The preceding chapters have attempted to summarise a great deal of experimental research. Indeed, a substantial amount of research resources has been devoted to the investigation of mental imagery during the last twenty years. This book has been concerned only with that portion of this research which bears upon the nature and function of human memory; this has certainly been a major focus of experimentation and theorising, but other important areas have had to be excluded. It is clear that research on mental imagery has given rise to a great many facts and ideas which have proved most interesting and useful to cognitive psychologists, and the heuristic value of investigating mental imagery and its role in human memory cannot be seriously questioned. However, what assessment can one now make of the theoretical proposals which have been made during the course of that research?

Throughout this book, I have tried to emphasise the intentional property of mental imagery, according to which the identity and the functional origin of mental images lie in the abstract propositional descriptions under which they are constructed. The notion of intentionality is a difficult philosophical concept, and a great deal of further analysis needs to be carried out to understand this property and its implications for the epistemological status of mental imagery. Nevertheless, it is also clear that mental images are representations which possess emergent properties (that is, properties which could not be readily computed or deduced on the basis of the relevant propositional descriptions), and these emergent properties can be utilised in many cognitive tasks. Chapter 4 characterised this constructive use of mental imagery as a form of non-verbal, short-term, working memory, which may be widely employed in the representation, preservation and manipulation of spatial and pictorial information. This function of mental imagery may be disrupted by a concurrent cognitive task which involves the processing of spatial or pictorial information, and possibly by any concurrent task which is not pre-programmed but which makes demands upon a central executive system. The operation of this form of working memory appears to be dependent upon the physiological integrity of the parietal lobes of the cerebral cortex.

Much of the research on the function of mental imagery in long-term memory has been concerned with the retention of visual displays such as pictures and faces. On *a priori* grounds, it seems to be necessary to postulate a form of non-verbal storage to explain the capacity for recognising pictorial stimuli which cannot be readily described, named or labelled. Excellent evidence for such a representation comes from the investigation of face recognition, which seems to be almost entirely a visual process. On the other hand, there is fairly good experimental evidence for a coding redundancy hypothesis, according to which nameable pictures and picture stories receive both non-verbal, pictorial representations and verbal, conceptual representations in long-term memory. This idea of functionally independent mnemonic representations is supported by neuropsychological evidence of a 'double dissociation' between pictorial long-term memory, whose neuroanatomical basis appears to lie in the right temporal lobe, and verbal long-term memory, whose neuroanatomical basis appears to lie in the left temporal lobe. However, there is little direct experimental evidence to suggest that this pictorial representation is the form of mnemonic coding aroused by the use of mental imagery, and there is neuropsychological evidence which strongly implies that this identification should not be made. Although it is possible in principle to specify a version of propositional or common coding theory which could handle the experimental and neuropsychological findings on pictorial memory, the various adjustments needed to ensure this consistency with the empirical data are unlikely to constitute well motivated revisions of current examples of common coding theory. A dual coding model may therefore be regarded as the most appropriate theoretical approach for the future investigation of pictorial memory.

In the area of verbal learning, three sorts of experimental procedure have been employed for investigating the role of mental imagery: the administration of instructions to the experimental subjects to use mental imagery in their learning; the comparison of samples of stimulus material in terms of their concreteness or imageability; and the comparison of individual subjects in terms of their ability or preference to use mental imagery in learning. Under the appropriate circumstances, each of these experimental procedures has been found to produce substantial and reliable effects upon memory performance; moreover, they also have been found to yield meaningful interactions in terms of their effects upon recall. Nevertheless, several important considerations need to be appreciated in evaluating this research. First, the relational organisation of mental imagery appears to be important in determining its mnemonic efficacy, rather than its subjective vividness. Second, the empirical evidence does not necessitate any additional principles of learning which are specific to the use of mental imagery as a mnemonic strategy. Rather, all of the findings may be discussed in terms of such general notions as organisation, integration and semantic representation. Third, this elaborative use of mental imagery appears to be functionally distinct (on both experimental and neuropsychological evidence) from the constructive use of mental imagery in immediate memory, and from the representation of pictorial information in long-term memory. Indeed, a clear neuropsychological basis for this function of mental imagery has yet to be identified. Since both common coding and dual coding positions appear to be consistent with the available evidence under this heading, considerations of parsimony seem to require that common coding theory be recommended as the appropriate theoretical framework for the future investigation of verbal learning and memory.

This conclusion is exactly that which was suggested initially on the basis of a discussion of the implications of intentionality for the epistemological status of mental imagery. On these purely conceptual grounds, it was suggested that the functional origin of mental imagery lies in a system of knowledge which is 'essentially *conceptual* and *propositional*, rather than sensory or pictorial, in nature' (Pylyshyn, 1973). Nevertheless, there are a few items of evidence which actually speak in favour of an adoption of common coding theory. These include: the finding that verbal mediation instructions and imagery mnemonic instructions produce comparable effects upon performance; the finding that semantic confusions in recognition memory for sentences are determined by conceptual relationships expressed in the sentence itself, rather than by any pictorial properties of an evoked mental image; and the functional independence of mental imagery as an elaborative code and the retention of pictorial information. Certainly, there exists experimental evidence on the retention of sentences and connected discourse, as well as neuropsychological evidence, which creates fundamental problems for the interpretation of dual coding theory which was offered by Paivio (1971c). Within common coding theory, the empirical effects attributed to the use of mental imagery can be explained by assuming the greater efficacy of propositional structures which incorporate perceptual or spatial predicates. This assumption has always been incorporated into propositional theories of human memory, and can be supported by conceptual arguments similar to those given by Strawson (1959, chap. 1). If such structures are better remembered, whatever the absolute level of recall performance, then this would go some way to explaining why lesions of the left temporal lobe lead to an impairment of memory without reducing either the effect of stimulus imageability or the benefit of imagery mnemonic instructions.

Finally, some remarks are in order concerning the methodology of research on mental imagery. This book has attempted to argue for the evidential priority of the reports given by experimental subjects concerning both the strategies which they employ in carrying out cognitive tasks, and the psychological states which they experience in doing so. However, it is also clear from the discussion of the previous chapter that not all questions which are superficially meaningful to the subject or of interest to the experimenter are legitimate ones to ask. The psychologist who wishes to carry out a serious investigation of personal experience must devote time and effort to ensure that the tasks with which he confronts his subjects are conceptually and methodologically sound.

A second problem concerns the reliability and replicability of the experimental findings. In some cases the empirical effects of interest are substantial and appear regularly in different experiments. However, in other cases, the conclusions of one experiment simply fail to appear in another, quite similar study. Of course, in any experiment there are uncontrolled sources of variation, and these may lead to inconsistencies between different studies. However, an important, and potentially controllable source of variation in virtually all of the experiments reviewed in this book is the idiosyncratic properties of the experimental material employed. Inconsistencies between different papers may often be attributed to the experimenters' failure to take this source of variation into account in analysing their results. Of course, statistical methods have been available for some time for incorporating an estimate of the variation among the experimental stimuli into an analysis of quantitative data (Clark, 1973; Richardson, 1975*d*). However, such methods are unfortunately not widely used. In this book, therefore, it will have been noted that the replicability of experimental findings between different investigations has been regarded as an important criterion determining whether such findings should be used to evaluate the principal theoretical positions being discussed.

A third problem concerns the possibility of experimenter effects in research on mental imagery. This was discussed in some detail in the previous chapter, but is mentioned again here to excuse the omission of an otherwise interesting topic in the study of individual differences in cognitive abilities. This is the study of sex differences, which are implicated because of a well established tendency of female subjects to report more vivid imagery than male subjects (White, Sheehan and Ashton, 1977), and because of speculations in recent years concerning sex differences in hemispheric specialisation. There are also suggestions in the literature that effects of imagery ability are more pronounced in female subjects than in males. However, on inspection, it appears that these suggestions tend to be propagated by female experimenters (for instance, Ernest, 1977; Stewart, 1965; Wells, 1972). This is not an idle observation, since Gralton, Hayes and Richardson (in press) have found that the pattern of results obtained in an experiment may depend upon both the sex of the subject and the sex of the experimenter; they suggested specifically that being tested by an experimenter of the opposite sex may inhibit the use of mnemonic strategies which might otherwise enhance recall performance. Given the likelihood of experimenter effects in such experiments, one may echo their conclusion that 'no comparison of male and female subjects should be accepted until it has been replicated with both male and female experimenters'.

Despite these methodological problems, I must repeat the point that research on mental imagery has given rise to a vast body of empirical findings, and these observations are among the most interesting facts about human memory and human cognitive functioning in general that are available. A considerable amount of the credit for this must go to the work of Paivio and his collaborators, and to the theory of dual coding which he proposed as the first major theoretical interpretation of the growing body of empirical evidence. This evidence must be encompassed by any satisfactory theory of mental imagery and human memory. Nevertheless, after considering the evidence, I must conclude that there is inadequate empirical support for dual coding theory, and that there are certain findings which present grave difficulties for that position. Propositional theories appear to be a more promising means of developing future investigations of the faculty of memory.

References

Anderson, J. R. (1978). Arguments concerning representations for mental imagery. *Psychological Review*, **85,** 249–77.

Anderson, J. R. and Bower, G. H. (1973). *Human Associative Memory.* Washington, D.C.: Hemisphere Press.

Anderson, R. C. and Hidde, J. L. (1971). Imagery and sentence learning. *Journal of Educational Psychology*, **62,** 526–30.

Anderson, R. C. and Kulhavy, R. W. (1972). Imagery and prose learning. *Journal of Educational Psychology*, **63,** 242–3.

Anderson, R. E. (1976). Short-term retention of the where and when of pictures and words. *Journal of Experimental Psychology: General*, **2,** 378–402.

Andreoff, G. R. and Yarmey, A. D. (1976). Bizarre imagery and associative learning: A confirmation. *Perceptual and Motor Skills*, **43,** 143–8.

Angell, J. R. (1910). Methods for the determination of mental imagery. *Psychological Monographs*, **13,** 61–107.

Armstrong, D. M. (1968). *A Materialist Theory of the Mind.* London: Routledge and Kegan Paul.

Arrigoni, G. and De Renzi, E. (1964). Constructional apraxia and hemispheric locus of lesion. *Cortex*, **1,** 170–97.

Ashton, R. and White, K. (1974). Factor analysis of the Gordon Test of visual imagery control. *Perceptual and Motor Skills*, **38,** 945–6.

Ashton, R. and White, K. (1975). The effects of instructions on subjects' imagery questionnaire scores. *Social Behavior and Personality*, **3,** 41–3.

X Atkinson, R. C. (1975). Mnemotechnics in second-language learning. *American Psychologist*, **30,** 821–38.

X Atkinson, R. C. and Raugh, M. R. (1975). An application of the mnemonic keyword method to the acquisition of a Russian vocabulary. *Journal of Experimental Psychology: Human Learning and Memory*, **1,** 126–33.

Atwood, G. (1971). An experimental study of visual imagination and memory. *Cognitive Psychology*, **2,** 239–89.

Bacharach, V. R., Carr, T. H. and Mehner, D. S. (1976). Interactive and independent contributions of verbal descriptions to children's picture memory. *Journal of Experimental Child Psychology*, **22,** 492–8.

Baddeley, A. D. (1976). *The Psychology of Memory.* New York: Basic Books.

Baddeley, A. D., Grant, S., Wight, E. and Thomson, N. (1974). Imagery and visual working memory. *In* Rabbitt, P. M. A. and Dornic, S. (eds) *Attention and Performance V*. London: Academic Press.

Baddeley, A. D. and Warrington, E. K. (1970). Amnesia and the distinction between long- and short-term memory. *Journal of Verbal Learning and Verbal Behavior*, **9,** 176–89.

Baddeley, A. D. and Warrington, E. K. (1973). Memory coding and amnesia. *Neuropsychologia*, **11,** 159–65.

Baggett, P. (1975). Memory for explicit and implicit information in picture stories. *Journal of Verbal Learning and Verbal Behavior*, **14,** 538–48.

Bahrick, H. P. and Boucher, B. (1968). Retention of visual and verbal codes of the same stimuli. *Journal of Experimental Psychology*, **78,** 417–22.

Baker, G. P. (1974). Criteria: A new foundation for semantics. *Ratio*, **16,** 156–89.

Banks, W. P. (1977). Encoding and processing of symbolic information in comparative judgments. *In* Bower, G. H. (ed.) *The Psychology of Learning and Motivation: Advances in Research and Theory*, Vol. 11. New York: Academic Press.

Banks, W. P. and Flora, J. (1977). Semantic and perceptual processes in symbolic comparisons. *Journal of Experimental Psychology: Human Perception and Performance*, **3,** 278–90.

Bartlett, F. C. (1932). *Remembering: A Study in Experimental and Social Psychology*. London: Cambridge University Press.

Beech, J. R. (1977). Effect of selective visual interference on visualization. *Perceptual and Motor Skills*, **45,** 951–4.

Beech, J. R. (in press). Image latency and recall as functions of array size. *American Journal of Psychology*.

Beech, J. R. and Allport, D. A. (1978). Visualization of compound scenes. *Perception*, **7,** 129–38.

Begg, I. (1971). Recognition memory for sentence meaning and wording. *Journal of Verbal Learning and Verbal Behavior*, **10,** 176–81.

Begg, I. (1972). Recall of meaningful phrases. *Jounal of Verbal Learning and Verbal Behavior*, **11,** 431–9.

Begg, I. (1973). Imagery and integration in the recall of words. *Canadian Journal of Psychology*, **27,** 159–67.

Begg, I. (1978). Imagery and organization in memory: Instructional effects. *Memory and Cognition*, **6,** 174–83.

Begg, I. and Paivio, A. (1969). Concreteness and imagery in sentence learning. *Journal of Verbal Learning and Verbal Behavior*, **8,** 821–7.

Begg, I. and Young, B. J. (1977). An organizational analysis of the form class effect. *Journal of Experimental Child Psychology*, **23,** 503–19.

Bennett, G. K., Seashore, M. G. and Wesman, A. G. (1947). *Differential Aptitude Tests*. New York: Psychological Corporation.

Benton, A. L. (1969). Constructional apraxia: Some unanswered questions. *In* Benton, A. L. (ed.) *Contributions to Clinical Neuropsychology*. Chicago: Aldine Publishing Co.

Berger, G. H. and Gaunitz, S. C. B. (1977). Self-rated imagery and vividness of task pictures in relation to visual memory. *British Journal of Psychology*, **68**, 283–8.

Berlyne, D. E. (1965). *Structure and Direction in Thinking*. New York: Wiley.

Betts, G. H. (1909). *The Distribution and Functions of Mental Imagery*. New York: Teachers College.

Blumenthal, A. (1967). Prompted recall of sentences. *Journal of Verbal Learning and Verbal Behavior*, **6**, 203–6.

Blumenthal, A. and Boakes, R. A. (1967). Prompted recall of sentences. *Journal of Verbal Learning and Verbal Behavior*, **6**, 674–6.

Bobrow, S. A. and Bower, G. H. (1969). Comprehension and recall of sentences. *Journal of Experimental Psychology*, **80**, 455–61.

Bousfield, W. A. and Sedgewick, C. H. (1944). An analysis of sequences of restricted associative responses. *Journal of General Psychology*, **30**, 149–65.

Bower, G. H. (1970a). Analysis of a mnemonic device. *American Scientist*, **58**, 496–510.

Bower, G. H. (1970b). Imagery as a relational organizer in associative learning. *Journal of Verbal Learning and Verbal Behavior*, **9**, 529–33.

Bower, G. H. (1972). Mental imagery and associative learning. *In* Gregg, L. W. (ed.) *Cognition in Learning and Memory*. New York: Wiley.

Bower, G. H. and Karlin, M. B. (1974). Depth of processing pictures of faces and recognition memory. *Journal of Experimental Psychology*, **103**, 751–7.

Bransford, J. D., Barclay, J. R. and Franks, J. J. (1972). Sentence memory: A constructive versus interpretive approach. *Cognitive Psychology*, **3**, 193–209.

Bransford, J. D. and Franks, J. J. (1971). The abstraction of linguistic ideas. *Cognitive Psychology*, **2**, 331–50.

Bransford, J. D. and Franks, J. J. (1972). The abstraction of linguistic ideas: A review. *Cognition*, **1**, 211–49.

Bransford, J. D. and Johnson, M. K. (1972). Contextual prerequisites for understanding: Some investigations of comprehension and recall. *Journal of Verbal Learning and Verbal Behavior*, **11**, 717–26.

Bregman, A. S. and Strasberg, R. (1968). Memory for the syntactic form of sentences. *Journal of Verbal Learning and Verbal Behavior*, **7**, 396–403.

Brooks, L. R. (1967). The suppression of visualization by reading. *Quarterly Journal of Experimental Psychology*, **19**, 289–99.

Brooks, L. R. (1968). Spatial and verbal components in the act of recall. *Canadian Journal of Psychology*, **22**, 349–68.

Brown, R. (1958). How shall a thing be called? *Psychological Review*, **65**, 14–21.

Bruner, J. S., Busiek, R. D. and Minturn, A. L. (1952). Assimilation in the immediate reproduction of visually perceived figures. *Journal of Experimental Psychology*, **44**, 151–5.

Buckley, P. B. and Gillman, C. B. (1974). Comparisons of digits and dot patterns. *Journal of Experimental Psychology*, **103**, 1131–6.

Bugelski, B. R. (1971). The definition of the image. *In* Segal, S. J. (ed.) *Imagery: Current Cognitive Approaches*. New York: Academic Press.

Bugelski, B. R. (1977). Imagery and verbal behavior. *Journal of Mental Imagery*, **1**, 39–52.

Byrne, B. (1974). Item concreteness vs. spatial organization as predictors of visual imagery. *Memory and Cognition*, **2**, 53–9.

Calfee, R. C. (1970). Short-term recognition memory in children. *Child Development*, **41**, 145–61.

Calvano, M. A. (1974). Predicting the use of imagery as a mediation strategy. *AV Communication Review*, **22**, 269–77.

Carmichael, L., Hogan, H. P. and Walter, A. A. (1932). An experimental study of the effect of language on the reproduction of visually perceived form. *Journal of Experimental Psychology*, **15**, 73–86.

Chomsky, N. (1964). *Current Issues in Linguistic Theory*. The Hague: Mouton.

Chomsky, N. (1965). *Aspects of the Theory of Syntax*. Cambridge, Mass.: MIT Press.

Chomsky, N. (1970). Remarks on nominalization. *In* Jacobs, R. A. and Rosenbaum, P. S. (eds) *Readings in English Transformational Grammar*. Waltham, Mass.: Ginn.

Christian, J., Bickley, W., Tarka, M. and Clayton, K. (1978). Measures of free recall of 900 English nouns: Correlations with imagery, concreteness, meaningfulness, and frequency. *Memory and Cognition*, **6**, 379–90.

Christiansen, T. and Stone, D. R. (1968). Visual imagery and level of mediator abstractness in induced mediation paradigms. *Perceptual and Motor Skills*, **26**, 775–9.

Clark, H. H. (1973). The language-as-fixed-effect fallacy: A critique of language statistics in psychological research. *Journal of Verbal Learning and Verbal Behavior*, **12**, 335–59.

Clark, H. H. and Chase, W. G. (1972). On the process of comparing sentences against pictures. *Cognitive Psychology*, **3**, 472–517.

Cofer, C. N. (1973). Constructive processes in memory. *American Scientist*, **61**, 537–43.

Cohen, R. L. and Granström, K. (1968). Interpolated task and mode of recall as variables in STM for visual figures. *Journal of Verbal Learning and Verbal Behavior*, **7**, 653–8.

Cohen, R. L. and Granström, K. (1970). Reproduction and recognition in short-term visual memory. *Quarterly Journal of Experimental Psychology*, **22**, 450–7.

Collyer, S. C., Jonides, J. and Bevan, W. (1972). Images as memory aids: Is bizarreness helpful? *American Journal of Psychology*, **85**, 31–8.

Conlin, D. and Paivio, A. (1975). The associative learning of the deaf: The effects of word imagery and signability. *Memory and Cognition*, **3**, 335–40.

Cooper, L. A. (1975). Mental rotation of random two-dimensional shapes. *Cognitive Psychology*, **7**, 20–43.

Cooper, L. A. and Shepard, R. N. (1973). Chronometric studies of the rotation of mental images. *In* Chase, W. G. (ed.) *Visual Information Processing*. New York: Academic Press.

Cooper, L. A. and Shepard, R. N. (1979). Transformations on representations of objects in space. *In* Carterette, E. C. and Friedman, M. (eds) *Handbook of Perception. Vol. VIII: Space and Object Perception.* New York: Academic Press.

Craik, F. I. M. and Watkins, M. J. (1973). The role of rehearsal in short-term memory. *Journal of Verbal Learning and Verbal Behavior*, **12**, 599–607.

Crowne, D. P. and Marlowe, D. (1964). *The Approval Motive.* New York: Wiley.

Curtis, D. W., Paulos, M. A. and Rule, S. J. (1973). Relation between disjunctive reaction time and stimulus differences. *Journal of Experimental Psychology*, **99**, 167–73.

Danaher, B. G. and Thoresen, C. E. (1972). Imagery assessment by self-report and behavioral measures. *Behavior Research and Therapy*, **10**, 131–8.

Davies, G. and Proctor, J. (1976). The recall of concrete and abstract sentences as a function of interpolated task. *British Journal of Psychology*, **67**, 63–72.

Davies, G. M. (1969). Recognition memory for pictured and names objects. *Journal of Experimental Child Psychology*, **7**, 448–58.

Delin, P. S. (1968). Success in recall as a function of success in implementation of mnemonic instructions. *Psychonomic Science*, **12**, 153–4.

Delin, P. S. (1969). The learning to criterion of a serial list with and without mnemonic instructions. *Psychonomic Science*, **16**, 169–70.

Dempster, R. N. and Rohwer, W. D. (1974). Component analysis of the elaborative encoding effect in children's learning. *Journal of Experimental Psychology*, **103**, 400–8.

Den Heyer, K. and Barrett, B. (1971). Selective loss of visual and verbal information in STM by means of visual and verbal interpolated tasks. *Psychonomic Science*, **25**, 100–2.

De Renzi, E. and Nichelli, P. (1975). Verbal and non-verbal short-term memory impairment following hemispheric damage. *Cortex*, **11**, 341–54.

Di Vesta, F. J., Ingersoll, G. and Sunshine, P. (1971). A factor analysis of imagery tests. *Journal of Verbal Learning and Verbal Behavior*, **10**, 471–9.

Di Vesta, F. J. and Ross, S. M. (1971). Imagery ability, abstractness, and word order as variables in recall of adjectives and nouns. *Journal of Verbal Learning and Verbal Behavior*, **10**, 686–93.

Di Vesta, F. J. and Sunshine, P. M. (1974). The retrieval of abstract and concrete materials as functions of imagery, mediation, and mnemonic aids. *Memory and Cognition*, **2**, 340–4.

Doob, L. W. (1972). The ubiquitous appearance of images. *In* Sheehan, P. W. (ed.) *The Function and Nature of Imagery.* New York: Academic Press.

Dooling, D. J. and Lachman, R. (1971). Effect of comprehension on retention of prose. *Journal of Experimental Psychology*, **88**, 216–22.

Durndell, A. J. and Wetherick, N. E. (1975). Reported imagery and social desirability. *Perceptual and Motor Skills*, **41**, 987–92.

Durndell, A. J. and Wetherick, N. E. (1976a). Reported imagery and two spatial tests. *Perceptual and Motor Skills*, **43**, 1050.

Durndell, A. J. and Wetherick, N. E. (1976b). The relation of reported imagery to cognitive performance. *British Journal of Psychology*, **67,** 501–6.

Ekman, P., Friesen, W. V. and Ellsworth, P. (1972). *Emotion in the Human Face*. Oxford: Pergamon Press.

Elliott, L. (1973). Imagery versus repetition encoding in short- and long-term memory. *Journal of Experimental Psychology*, **100,** 270–6.

Ellis, H. D. (1975). Recognizing faces. *British Journal of Psychology*, **66,** 409–26.

Epstein, W. and Landauer, A. (1969). Size and distance judgments under reduced conditions of viewing. *Perception and Psychophysics*, **6,** 269–72.

Epstein, W., Rock, I. and Zuckerman, C. B. (1960). Meaning and familiarity in associative learning. *Psychological Monographs*, **74** (4, whole No. 491).

Ernest, C. H. (1977). Imagery ability and cognition: A critical review. *Journal of Mental Imagery*, **2,** 181–216.

Ernest, C. H. and Paivio, A. (1969). Imagery ability in paired-associative and incidental learning. *Psychonomic Science*, **15,** 181–2.

Ernest, C. H. and Paivio, A. (1971a). Imagery and sex differences in incidental recall. *British Journal of Psychology*, **62,** 67–72.

Ernest, C. H. and Paivio, A. (1971b). Imagery and verbal associative latencies as a function of imagery ability. *Canadian Journal of Psychology*, **25,** 83–90.

Evans, I. M. and Kamemoto, W. S. (1973). Reliability of the short form of Betts' Questionnaire Upon Mental Imagery: Replication. *Psychological Reports*, **33,** 281–2.

Fechner, G. T. (1860). *Elemente der Psychophysik*. Leipzig: Breitkopf und Härtel.

Fillenbaum, S. (1973). *Syntactic Factors in Memory*. The Hague: Mouton.

Fillenbaum, S. and Rapoport, A. (1971). *Structures in the Subjective Lexicon*. New York: Academic Press.

Flagg, P. W. (1976). Semantic integration in sentence memory? *Journal of Verbal Learning and Verbal Behavior*, **15,** 491–504.

Fodor, J. A. (1975). *The Language of Thought*. New York: Thomas Y. Crowell.

Fodor, J. A., Bever, T. G. and Garrett, M. F. (1974). *The Psychology of Language*. New York: McGraw-Hill.

Forisha, B. D. (1975). Mental imagery and verbal processes: A developmental study. *Developmental Psychology*, **11,** 259–67.

Fowler, R. (1971). *An Introduction to Transformational Syntax*. London: Routledge and Kegan Paul.

Franks, J. J. and Bransford, J. D. (1972). The acquisition of abstract ideas. *Journal of Verbal Learning and Verbal Behavior*, **11,** 311–15.

Friedman, A. (1978). Memorial comparisons without the 'mind's eye'. *Journal of Verbal Learning and Verbal Behavior*, **17,** 427–44.

Galton, F. (1883). *Inquiries into Human Faculty and Its Development*. London: Macmillan.

Garner, W. R., Hake, H. W. and Eriksen, C. W. (1956). Operationism and the concept of perception. *Psychological Review*, **63,** 149–59.

Garrod, S. and Trabasso, T. (1973). A dual-memory information processing interpretation of sentence comprehension. *Journal of Verbal Learning and Verbal Behavior*, **12,** 155–67.

Goldstein, A. G. and Chance, J. (1971). Visual recognition memory for complex configurations. *Perception and Psychophysics*, **9,** 237–41.

Goldstein, A. G. and Chance, J. (1974). Some factors in picture recognition memory. *Journal of General Psychology*, **90,** 69 85.

Gordon, R. (1949). An investigation into some of the factors that favour the formation of stereotyped images. *British Journal of Psychology*, **40,** 156–67.

Gralton, M. A., Hayes, Y. A. and Richardson, J. T. E. (in press). Introversion extraversion and mental imagery. *Journal of Mental Imagery*.

Gray, D. R. and Gummerman, K. (1975). The enigmatic eidetic image: A critical examination of methods, data, and theories. *Psychological Bulletin*, **82,** 383–407.

Groninger, L. D. (1971). Mnemonic imagery and forgetting. *Psychonomic Science*, **23,** 161–3.

Gupton, T. and Frincke, G. (1970). Imagery, mediational instructions, and noun position in free recall of noun–verb pairs. *Journal of Experimental Psychology*, **86,** 461–2.

Gur, R. C. and Hilgard, E. R. (1975). Visual imagery and the discrimination of differences between altered pictures simultaneously and successively presented. *British Journal of Psychology*, **66,** 341–5.

Haber, R. N. (1969). Eidetic images. *Scientific American*, **220,** 36–44.

Hacker, P. M. S. (1972). *Insight and Illusion: Wittgenstein on Philosophy and the Metaphysics of Experience*. London: Oxford University Press.

Hall, V. (1936). The effects of time interval on recall. *British Journal of Psychology*, **27,** 41–50.

Hanawalt, N. G. and Demarest, I. H. (1939). The effect of verbal suggestion in the recall period upon the reproduction of visually perceived forms. *Journal of Experimental Psychology*, **25,** 159–74.

Harré, R. (1972). *The Philosophies of Science: An Introductory Survey*. London: Oxford University Press.

Hasher, L., Riebman, B. and Wren, F. (1976). Imagery and retention of free-recall learning. *Journal of Experimental Psychology*: *Human Learning and Memory*, **2,** 172–81.

Hastorff, A. R. and Way, K. S. (1952). Apparent size with and without distance cues. *Journal of General Psychology*, **47,** 181–8.

Hauck, P. D., Walsh, C. C. and Kroll, N. E. A. (1976). Visual imagery mnemonics: Common vs. bizarre mental images. *Bulletin of the Psychonomic Society*, **7,** 160–2.

Hayes, J. R. (1973). On the function of visual imagery in elementary mathematics. *In* Chase, W. G. (ed.) *Visual Information Processing*. New York: Academic Press.

Healy, A. F. (1975). Coding of temporal-spatial patterns in short-term memory. *Journal of Verbal Learning and Verbal Behaviour*, **14,** 481–95.

Healy, A. F. (1978). A Markov model for the short-term retention of spatial location information. *Journal of Verbal Learning and Verbal Behavior,* **17,** 295–308.

Hebb, D. O. (1960). The American revolution. *American Psychologist,* **15,** 735–45.

Hebb, D. O. (1961). Distinctive features of learning in the higher animal. *In* Delafresnaye, J. F. (ed.) *Brain Mechanisms and Learning.* London: Oxford University Press.

Herman, D. T., Lawless, R. H. and Marshall, R. W. (1957). Variables in the effect of language on the reproduction of visually perceived forms. *Perceptual and Motor Skills,* **7,** 171–86.

Hitch, G. and Morton, J. (1975). The unimportance of explicit spatial information in serial recall of visually presented lists. *Quarterly Journal of Experimental Psychology,* **27,** 161–4.

Hollenberg, C. K. (1970). Functions of visual imagery in the learning and concept formation of children. *Child Development,* **41,** 1003–15.

Holmes, V. M. and Langford, J. (1976). Comprehension and recall of abstract and concrete sentences. *Journal of Verbal Learning and Verbal Behavior,* **15,** 559–66.

Holt, R. R. (1964). Imagery: The return of the ostracized. *American Psychologist,* **19,** 254–64.

Holt, R. R. (1972). On the nature and generality of mental imagery. *In* Sheehan, P. W. (ed.) *The Function and Nature of Imagery.* New York: Academic Press.

Holyoak, K. J. (1977). The form of analog size information in memory. *Cognitive Psychology,* **9,** 31–51.

Holyoak, K. J. and Walker, J. H. (1976). Subjective magnitude information in semantic orderings. *Journal of Verbal Learning and Verbal Behavior,* **15,** 287–99.

Horowitz, L. M., Lampel, A. K. and Takanishi, R. N. (1969). The child's memory for utilized scenes. *Journal of Experimental Child Psychology,* **8,** 375–88.

Horowitz, L. M. and Manelis, L. (1972). Towards a theory of redintegrative memory: Adjective–noun phrases. *In* Bower, G. H. and Spence, J. T. (eds) *The Psychology of Learning and Motivation: Advances in Research and Theory,* Vol. 5. New York: Academic Press.

Horowitz, L. M. and Prytulak, L. S. (1969). Redintegrative memory. *Psychological Review,* **76,** 519–31.

Huckabee, M. W. (1974). Introversion-extraversion and imagery. *Psychological Reports,* **34,** 453–4.

Hulicka, I. M. and Grossman, J. L. (1967). Age-group comparisons for the use of mediators in paired-associate learning. *Journal of Gerontology,* **21,** 46–51.

Hunter, I. M. L. (1977). Imagery, comprehension, and mnemonics. *Journal of Mental Imagery,* **1,** 65–72.

Indow, T. and Togano, K. (1970). On retrieving sequence from long-term memory. *Psychological Review,* **77,** 317–31.

James, C. T. (1972). Theme and imagery in the recall of active and passive sentences. *Journal of Verbal Learning and Verbal Behavior,* **11,** 205–11.

Janssen, W. (1976). *On the Nature of the Mental Image.* Soesterberg: Institute for Perception TNO.

Jarvella, R. J. (1970). Effects of syntax on running memory span for connected discourse. *Psychonomic Science,* **19,** 235–6.

Jarvella, R. J. and Herman, S. J. (1972). Clause structure of sentences and speech processing. *Perception and Psychophysics,* **11,** 381–4.

Johnson, D. M. (1939). Confidence and speed in the two-category judgment. *Archives of Psychology,* **241,** 1–52.

Johnson, M. K., Bransford, J. D. Nyberg, S. E. and Cleary, J. J. (1972). Comprehension factors in interpreting memory for abstract and concrete sentences. *Journal of Verbal Learning and Verbal Behavior,* **11,** 451–4.

Johnson-Laird, P. N. (1970). The perception and memory of sentences. *In* Lyons, J. (ed.) *New Horizons in Linguistics.* Harmondsworth: Penguin Books.

Johnson-Laird, P. N. (1974). Experimental psycholinguistics. *Annual Review of Psychology,* **25,** 135–60.

Johnson-Laird, P. N. and Stevenson, R. (1970). Memory for syntax. *Nature,* **227,** 412–3.

Jones, G. V. (1978). Tests of a structural theory of the memory trace. *British Journal of Psychology,* **69,** 351–67.

Jones, M. K. (1974). Imagery as a mnemonic aid after left temporal lobectomy: Contrast between material-specific and generalized memory disorders. *Neuropsychologia,* **12,** 21–30.

Jorgensen, C. C. and Kintsch, W. (1973). The role of imagery in the evaluation of sentences. *Cognitive Psychology,* **4,** 110–16.

Juhasz, J. B. (1972). On the reliability of two measures of imagery. *Perceptual and Motor Skills,* **35,** 874.

Karchmer, M. A. (1974). Proportion of unitization as an index of cued recall level. *Journal of Experimental Psychology,* **103,** 351–7.

Katz, J. J. and Fodor, J. A. (1963). The structure of a semantic theory. *Language,* **39,** 170–210

Katz, J. J. and Postal, P. M. (1964). *An Integrated Theory of Linguistic Descriptions.* Cambridge, Mass.: MIT Press.

Kelly, R. T. and Martin, D. W. (1974). Memory for random shapes: A dual task analysis. *Journal of Experimental Psychology,* **103,** 224–9.

Kenny, A. J. P. (1971). The Verification Principle and the private language argument. *In* Jones, O. R. (ed.) *The Private Language Argument.* London: Macmillan.

Kenny, A. J. P. (1972). To mind via syntax. *In* Kenny, A. J. P., Longuet-Higgins, H. C., Lucas, J. R. and Waddington, C. H. *The Nature of Mind.* Edinburgh: Edinburgh University Press.

Kenny, A. J. P. (1973). *Wittgenstein.* London: Allen Lane.

Kenny, A. J. P. (1975). *Will, Freedom and Power.* Oxford: Blackwell.

Kerst, S. M. (1976). Interactive visual imagery and memory search for words and pictures. *Memory and Cognition,* **4,** 573–80.

Kerst, S. M. and Howard, J. H., Jr (1977). Mental comparisons for ordered information on abstract and concrete dimensions. *Memory and Cognition*, **5,** 227–34.

Kerst, S. M. and Howard, J. H., Jr (1978). Memory psychophysics for visual area and length. *Memory and Cognition*, **6,** 327–35.

Kessel, F. S. (1972). Imagery: A dimension of mind rediscovered. *British Journal of Psychology*, **63,** 149–62.

Kintsch, W. (1972a). Abstract nouns: Imagery versus lexical complexity. *Journal of Verbal Learning and Verbal Behavior*, **11,** 59–65.

Kintsch, W. (1972b). Notes on the structure of semantic memory. *In* Tulving, E. and Donaldson, W. (eds) *Organization of Memory*. New York: Academic Press.

Kintsch, W. (1974). *The Representation of Meaning in Memory*. Hillsdale, N.J.: Lawrence Erlbaum Associates.

Kintsch, W. and Bates, E. (1977). Recognition memory for statements from a classroom lecture. *Journal of Experimental Psychology: Human Learning and Memory*, **3,** 150–9.

Kirkpatrick, E. A. (1894). An experimental study of memory. *Psychological Review*, **1,** 602–9.

Klee, H. and Eysenck, M. W. (1973). Comprehension of abstract and concrete sentences. *Journal of Verbal Learning and Verbal Behavior*, **12,** 522–9.

Knight, R. and Knight, M. (1959). *A Modern Introduction to Psychology*, 6th edn. London: University Tutorial Press.

Kosslyn, S. M. (1973). Scanning visual images: Some structural implications. *Perception and Psychophysics*, **14,** 90–4.

Kosslyn, S. M. (1975). Information representation in visual images. *Cognitive Psychology*, **7,** 341–70.

Kosslyn, S. M. (1978). Measuring the visual angle of the mind's eye. *Cognitive Psychology*, **10,** 356–89.

Kosslyn, S. M., Ball, T. M. and Reiser, B. J. (1978). Visual images preserve metric spatial information: Evidence from studies of image scanning. *Journal of Experimental Psychology: Human Perception and Performance*, **4,** 47–60.

Kosslyn, S. M. and Pomerantz, J. R. (1977). Imagery, propositions, and the form of internal representations. *Cognitive Psychology*, **9,** 52–76.

Kuhlman, C. K. (1960). Visual Imagery in Children. Unpublished doctoral dissertation, Radcliffe College.

Kuhn, T. S. (1970). *The Structure of Scientific Revolutions*, 2nd edn. Chicago: University of Chicago Press.

Kulhavy, R. W. and Heinen, J. R. K. (1974). Imaginal attributes in learning sentence-embedded noun pairs. *Psychological Reports*, **34,** 487–90.

Kurtz, K. H. and Hovland, C. I. (1953). The effect of verbalization during observation of stimulus objects upon accuracy of recognition and recall. *Journal of Experimental Psychology*, **45,** 157–64.

Kusyszyn, I. and Paivio, A (1966). Transition probability, word order, and noun abstractness in the learning of adjective–noun paired associates. *Journal of Experimental Psychology*, **71,** 800–5.

Lambert, W. E. and Paivio, A. (1956). The influence of noun–adjective order on learning. *Canadian Journal of Psychology*, **10,** 9–12.

Lea, G. (1975). Chronometric analysis of the method of loci. *Journal of Experimental Psychology: Human Perception and Performance*, **1,** 95–104.

Lees, R. B. (1960). *The Grammar of English Nominalizations*. The Hague: Mouton.

Likert, R. and Quasha, W. H. (1941). *Revised Minnesota Paper Form Board Test (Series AA)*. New York: Psychological Corporation.

Lindauer, M. S. (1977). Imagery from the point of view of psychological aesthetics, the arts, and creativity. *Journal of Mental Imagery*, **1,** 343–62.

Lockhart, R. S. (1969). Retrieval asymmetry in the recall of adjectives and nouns. *Journal of Experimental Psychology*, **79,** 12–17.

London, P. and Robinson, J. P. (1968). Imagination in learning and retention. *Child Development*, **39,** 803–15.

Lovelace, E. A. and Snodgrass, R. D. (1971). Decision times for alphabetic order of letter pairs. *Journal of Experimental Psychology*, **88,** 258–64.

Luria, A. R. (1973). *The Working Brain*. London: Allen Lane.

Macht, M. and Scheirer, C. J. (1975). The effect of imagery on accessibility and availability in a short-term memory paradigm. *Journal of Verbal Learning and Verbal Behavior*, **14,** 523–33.

McKelvie, S. J. and Gingras, P. P. (1974). Reliability of two measures of visual imagery. *Perceptual and Motor Skills*, **39,** 417–18.

Madigan, S., McCabe, L. and Itatani, E. (1972). Immediate and delayed recall of words and pictures. *Canadian Journal of Psychology*, **26,** 407–14.

Malcolm, N. (1977). *Memory and Mind*. Ithaca, N.Y.: Cornell University Press.

Malpass, R. S., Lavigueur, H. and Weldon, D. (1973). Verbal and visual training in face recognition. *Perception and Psychophysics*, **14,** 285–92.

Mandler, G. (1967). Organization and memory. *In* Spence, K. W. and Spence, J. T. (eds) *The Psychology of Learning and Motivation: Advances in Research and Theory*, Vol. 1. New York: Academic Press.

Marks, D. F. (1972). Individual differences in the vividness of visual imagery and their effect on function. *In* Sheehan, P. W. (ed.) *The Function and Nature of Imagery*. New York: Academic Press.

Marks, D. F. (1973). Visual imagery differences in the recall of pictures. *British Journal of Psychology*, **64,** 17–24.

Marks, D. F. (1977). Imagery and consciousness: A theoretical review from an individual differences perspective. *Journal of Mental Imagery*, **1,** 275–90.

Merry, R. and Graham, N. C. (1978). Imagery bizarreness in children's recall of sentences. *British Journal of Psychology*, **69,** 315–21.

Metzler, J. and Shephard, R. N. (1974). Transformational studies of the internal representations of three dimensional objects. *In* Soiso, R. L. (ed.) *Theories of Cognitive Psychology: The Loyola Symposium*. Hillsdale, N.J.: Lawrence Erlbaum Associates.

Meudell, P. R. (1971). Retrieval and representations in long-term memory. *Psychonomic Science*, **23**, 295–6.

Meudell, P. R. (1972). Short-term visual memory: Comparative effects of two types of distraction on the recall of visually presented verbal and nonverbal material. *Journal of Experimental Psychology*, **94**, 244–7.

Miller, E. (1972). *Clinical Neuropsychology*. Harmondsworth: Penguin Books.

Milner, B. (1965). Visually guided maze learning in man: Effects of bilateral hippocampal, bilateral frontal, and unilateral cerebral lesions. *Neuropsychologia*, **3**, 317–38.

Milner, B. (1966). Amnesia following operation on the temporal lobes. *In* Whitty, C. W. M. and Zangwill, O. L. (eds) *Amnesia*. London: Butterworths.

Milner, B. (1971). Interhemispheric differences in the localization of psychological processes in man. *British Medical Bulletin*, **27**, 272–7.

Moeser, S. D. (1974). Memory for meaning and wording in concrete and abstract sentences. *Journal of Verbal Learning and Verbal Behavior*, **13**, 682–97.

Morelli, G. and Lang, D. (1971). Rated imagery and pictures in paired-associate learning. *Perceptual and Motor Skills*, **33**, 1247–50.

Morris, P. E. (1977). Practical strategies for human learning and remembering. *In* Howe, M. J. A. (ed.) *Adult Learning: Psychological Research and Applications*. London: Wiley.

Morris, P. E. and Gale, A. (1974). A correlational study of variables related to imagery. *Perceptual and Motor Skills*, **38**, 659–65.

Morris, P. E., Jones, S. and Hampson, P. (1978). An imagery mnemonic for the learning of people's names. *British Journal of Psychology*, **60**, 335–6.

Morris, P. E. and Reid, R. L. (1974). Imagery and recognition. *British Journal of Psychology*, **65**, 7–12.

Morris, P. E. and Stevens, R. (1974). Linking images and free recall. *Journal of Verbal Learning and Verbal Behavior*, **13**, 310–15.

Moscovitch, M. (1973). Language and the cerebral hemispheres: Reaction time studies and their implications for models of cerebral dominance. *In* Pliner, P., Kromes, L. and Alloway, T. (eds) *Communication and Affect: Language and Thought*. New York: Academic Press.

Moyer, R. S. (1973). Comparing objects in memory: Evidence suggesting an internal psychophysics. *Perception and Psychophysics*, **13**, 180–4.

Moyer, R. S. and Bayer, R. H. (1976). Mental comparison and the symbolic distance effect. *Cognitive Psychology*, **8**, 228–46.

Moyer, R. S. and Dumais, S. T. (1978). Mental comparison. *In* Bower, G. H. (ed.) *The Psychology of Learning and Motivation: Advances in Research and Theory*, Vol. 12. New York: Academic Press.

Moyer, R. S. and Landauer, T. K. (1967). Time required for judgments of numerical inequality, *Nature*, **215**, 1519–20.

Nappe, G. W. and Wollen, K. A. (1973). Effects of instructions to form common and bizarre mental images on retention. *Journal of Experimental Psychology*, **100**, 6–8.

Neisser, U. (1970). Visual imagery as process and experience. *In* Antrobus, J. S. (ed.) *Cognition and Affect*. Boston: Little, Brown.

Neisser, U. (1972*a*). A paradigm shift in psychology. *Science*, **176**, 628–30.

Neisser, U. (1972*b*). Changing conceptions of imagery. *In* Sheehan, P. W. (ed.) *The Function and Nature of Imagery*. New York: Academic Press.

Neisser, U. (1976). *Cognition and Reality*. San Francisco: W. H. Freeman.

Neisser, U. and Kerr, N. (1973). Spatial and mnemonic properties of visual images. *Cognitive Psychology*, **5**, 138–50.

Nelson, K. E. and Kosslyn, S. M. (1976). Recognition of previously labeled or unlabeled pictures by 5-year-olds and adults. *Journal of Experimental Child Psychology*, **21**, 40–5.

Newcombe, F. (1969). *Missile Wounds of the Brain*. London: Oxford University Press.

Newell, A. (1973). You can't play Twenty Questions with nature and win: Projective comments on the papers of this symposium. *In* Chase, W. G. (ed.) *Visual Information Processing*. New York: Academic Press.

Newell, A. and Simon, H. A. (1972). *Human Problem Solving*. Englewood Cliffs, N.J.: Prentice-Hall.

Nickerson, R. S. (1965). Short-term memory for complex meaningful visual configurations: A demonstration of capacity. *Canadian Journal of Psychology*, **19**, 155–60.

Nielsen, G. D. and Smith, E. E. (1973). Imaginal and verbal representations in short-term recognition of visual forms. *Journal of Experimental Psychology*, **101**, 375–8.

Orne, M. T. (1962). On the social psychology of the psychological experiment: With particular reference to demand characteristics and their implications. *American Psychologist*, **17**, 776–83.

Osgood, C. E., Suci, G. J. and Tannenbaum, P. H. (1958). *The Measurement of Meaning*. Urbana, Ill.: University of Illinois Press.

Owens, A. C. and Richardson, J. T. E. (in press). Mental imagery and pictorial memory. *British Journal of Psychology*.

Paivio, A. (1963). Learning of adjective–noun paired associates as a function of adjective–noun word order and noun abstractness. *Canadian Journal of Psychology*, **17**, 370–9.

Paivio, A. (1965). Abstractness, imagery, and meaningfulness in paired-associate learning. *Journal of Verbal Learning and Verbal Behavior*, **4**, 32–8.

Paivio, A. (1968). A factor-analytic study of word attributes and verbal learning. *Journal of Verbal Learning and Verbal Behavior*, **7**, 41–9.

Paivio, A. (1969). Mental imagery in associative learning and memory. *Psychological Review*, **76**, 241–63.

Paivio, A. (1971*a*). Imagery and deep structure in the recall of English nominalizations. *Journal of Verbal Learning and Verbal Behavior*, **10**, 1–12.

Paivio, A. (1971*b*). Imagery and language. *In* Segal, S. J. (ed.) *Imagery: Current Cognitive Approaches*. New York: Academic Press.

Paivio, A. (1971c). *Imagery and Verbal Processes*. New York: Holt, Rinehart and Winston.

Paivio, A. (1972). A theoretical analysis of the role of imagery in learning and memory. *In* Sheehan, P. W. (ed.) *The Function and Nature of Imagery*. New York: Academic Press.

Paivio, A. (1975a). Coding distinctions and repetition effects in memory. *In* Bower, G. H. (ed.) *The Psychology of Learning and Motivation: Advances in Research and Theory*, Vol. 9. New York: Academic Press.

Paivio, A. (1975b). Imagery and long-term memory. *In* Kennedy, A. and Wilkes, A. (eds) *Studies in Long Term Memory*. London: Wiley.

Paivio, A. (1975c). Imagery and synchronic thinking. *Canadian Psychological Review*, **16**, 147–63.

Paivio, A. (1975d). Neomentalism. *Canadian Journal of Psychology*, **29**, 263–91.

Paivio, A. (1975e). Perceptual comparisons through the mind's eye. *Memory and Cognition*, **3**, 635–47.

Paivio, A. (1976a). Imagery and recall and recognition. *In* Brown, J. (ed.) *Recall and Recognition*. London: Wiley.

Paivio, A. (1976b). Imagery, language, and semantic memory. Research Bulletin no. 385, Department of Psychology, University of Western Ontario.

Paivio, A. (1976c). Images, propositions, and knowledge. *In* Nicholas, J. M. (ed.) *Images, Perception and Knowledge*. Dordrecht: Reidel.

Paivio, A. (1976d). On exploring visual knowledge. Research Bulletin No. 398, Department of Psychology, University of Western Ontario.

Paivio, A. (1978a). Comparisons of mental clocks. *Journal of Experimental Psychology: Human Perception and Performance*, **4**, 61–71.

Paivio, A. (1978b). Dual coding: Theoretical issues and empirical evidence. *In* Scandura, J. M. and Brainerd, C. J. (eds) *Structural/Process Models of Complex Human Behavior*. Leiden: Nordhoff.

Paivio, A. (1978c). Imagery, language, and semantic memory. *International Journal of Psycholinguistics*, **5**, 31–47.

Paivio, A. (1978d). Mental comparisons involving abstract attributes. *Memory and Cognition*, **6**, 199–208.

Paivio, A. (1979). The relationship between verbal and perceptual codes. *In* Carterette, E. C. and Friedman, M. P. (eds) *Handbook of Perception. Vol. IX: Perceptual Processing*. New York: Academic Press.

Paivio, A. and Begg, I. (1971). Imagery and comprehension latencies as a function of sentence concreteness and structure. *Perception and Psychophysics*, **10**, 408–12.

Paivio, A. and Csapo, K. (1969). Concrete-image and verbal memory codes. *Journal of Experimental Psychology*, **80**, 279–85.

Paivio, A. and Csapo, K. (1973). Picture superiority in free recall: Imagery or dual coding? *Cognitive Psychology*, **5**, 176–206.

Paivio, A. and Foth, D. (1970). Imaginal and verbal mediators and noun concreteness in paired-associate learning: The elusive interaction. *Journal of*

Verbal Learning and Verbal Behavior, **9**, 384–90.

Paivio, A. and Okovita, H. W. (1971). Word imagery modalities and associative learning in blind and sighted subjects. *Journal of Verbal Learning and Verbal Behavior*, **10**, 506–10.

Paivio, A., Rogers, T. B. and Smythe, P. C. (1968). Why are pictures easier to recall than words? *Psychonomic Science*, **11**, 137–8.

Paivio, A., Smythe, P. C. and Yuille, J. C. (1968). Imagery versus meaningfulness of nouns in paired-associate learning. *Canadian Journal of Psychology*, **22**, 427–41.

Paivio, A. and Yuille, J. C. (1967). Mediation instructions and word attributes in paired-associate learning. *Psychonomic Science*, **8**, 65–6.

Paivio, A. and Yuille, J. C. (1969). Changes in associative strategies and paired-associate learning over trials as a function of word imagery and type of learning set. *Journal of Experimental Psychology*, **79**, 458–63.

Paivio, A., Yuille, J. C. and Madigan, S. (1968). Concreteness, imagery, and meaningfulness values for 925 nouns. *Journal of Experimental Psychology*, **76** (1, Part 2).

Paivio, A., Yuille, J. C. and Rogers, T. B. (1969). Noun imagery and meaningfulness in free and serial recall. *Journal of Experimental Psychology*, **79**, 509–14.

Parkman, J. M. (1971). Temporal aspects of digit and letter inequality judgments. *Journal of Experimental Psychology*, **91**, 191–205.

Patterson, K. and Bradshaw, J. L. (1975). Differential hemispheric mediation of nonverbal visual stimuli. *Journal of Experimental Psychology: Human Perception and Performance*, **1**, 246–52.

Pellegrino, J. W., Siegel, A. W. and Dhawan, M. (1975). Short-term retention of pictures and words: Evidence for dual coding systems. *Journal of Experimental Psychology: Human Learning and Memory*, **1**, 95–102.

Perensky, J. J. and Senter, R. J. (1970). An investigation of 'bizarre' imagery as a mnemonic device. *Psychological Record*, **20**, 145–50.

Peterson, M. J. (1971). Imagery and the grammatical classification of cues. *Journal of Experimental Psychology*, **88**, 307–13.

Pezdek, K. (1978). Recognition memory for related pictures. *Memory and Cognition*, **6**, 64–9.

Pezdek, K. and Royer, J. M. (1974). The role of comprehension in learning concrete and abstract sentences. *Journal of Verbal Learning and Verbal Behavior*, **13**, 551–8.

Phillips, W. A. and Christie, D. F. M. (1977a). Components of visual memory. *Quarterly Journal of Experimental Psychology*, **29**, 117–33.

Phillips, W. A. and Christie, D. F. M. (1977b). Interference with visualization. *Quarterly Journal of Experimental Psychology*, **29**, 637–50.

Piercy, M., Hécaen, H. and Ajuriaguerra, J. de (1960). Constructional apraxia associated with unilateral cerebral lesions—left and right sided cases compared. *Brain*, **83**, 225–42.

Piercy, M. and Smyth, V. (1962). Right hemisphere dominance for certain nonverbal intellectual skills. *Brain*, **85,** 775–90.

Pinker, S. and Kosslyn, S. M. (1978). The representation and manipulation of three-dimensional space in mental images. *Journal of Mental Imagery*, **2,** 69–83.

Pollock, J. (1970). The structure of epistemic justification. *American Philosophical Quarterly Monograph*, **4,** 62–78.

Pompi, K. F. and Lachman, R. (1967). Surrogate processes in the short-term retention of connected discourse. *Journal of Experimental Psychology*, **75,** 143–50.

Posner, M. I., Boies, S. J., Eichelman, W. H. and Taylor, R. L. (1969). Retention of visual and name codes of single letters. *Journal of Experimental Psychology*, **79** (1, Part 2).

Postman, L. (1975). Verbal learning and memory. *Annual Review of Psychology*, **26,** 291–335.

Postman, L. and Burns, S. (1973). Experimental analysis of coding processes. *Memory and Cognition*, **1,** 503–7.

Potts, G. R. (1972). Information processing strategies used in the encoding of linear orderings. *Journal of Verbal Learning and Verbal Behavior*, **11,** 727–40.

Potts, G. R. (1974). Storing and retrieving information about ordered relationships. *Journal of Experimental Psychology*, **103,** 431–9.

Prentice, W. C. H. (1954). Visual recognition of verbally labeled figures. *Journal of Experimental Psychology*, **67,** 315–20.

Putnam, H. (1973). Reductionism and the nature of psychology. *Cognition*, **2,** 131–46.

Putnoky, J. (1975). Visual, auditory, and tactual modalities of imagery. *Annales, Sectio Paedagogica et Psychologica*, **4,** 57–65.

Pylyshyn, Z. W. (1973). What the mind's eye tells the mind's brain: A critique of mental imagery. *Psychological Bulletin*, **80,** 1–24.

Quinton, A. M. (1973). *The Nature of Things*. London: Routledge and Kegan Paul.

Ratcliff, G. and Newcombe, F. (1973). Spatial orientation in man: Effects of left, right, and bilateral posterior cerebral lesions. *Journal of Neurology, Neurosurgery, and Psychiatry*, **36,** 448–54.

Reese, H. W. (1975). Verbal effects in children's visual recognition memory. *Child Development*, **46,** 400–7.

Reese, H. W. (1977a). Imagery and associative memory. *In* Kail, R. V., Jr and Hagen, J. W. (eds) *Perspectives on the Development of Memory and Cognition*. Hillsdale, N.J.: Lawrence Erlbaum Associates.

Reese, H. W. (1977b). Toward a cognitive theory of mnemonic imagery. *Journal of Mental Imagery*, **1,** 229–44.

Rehm, L. P. (1973). Relationships among measures of visual imagery. *Behavior Research and Therapy*, **11,** 265–70.

Reitman, J. S. and Bower, G. H. (1973). Storage and later recogniton of exemplars of concepts. *Cognitive Psychology*, **4,** 194–206.

Restle, F. (1970). Speed of adding and comparing numbers. *Journal of Experimental Psychology*, **83,** 274–8.

Richardson, A. (1969). *Mental Imagery*. New York: Springer.

Richardson, A. (1972). Voluntary control of the memory image. *In* Sheehan, P. W. (ed.) *The Function and Nature of Imagery*. New York: Academic Press.

Richardson, A. (1977). The meaning and measurement of memory imagery. *British Journal of Psychology*, **68,** 29–43.

Richardson, J. T. E. (1974a). Imagery and free recall. *Journal of Verbal Learning and Verbal Behavior*, **13,** 709–13.

Richardson, J. T. E. (1974b). Review of A. Paivio, *Imagery and Verbal Processes*. *Journal of Literary Semantics*, **2,** 116–20.

Richardson, J. T. E. (1975a). Concreteness and imageability. *Quarterly Journal of Experimental Psychology*, **27,** 235–49.

Richardson, J. T. E. (1975b). Imagery and deep structure in the recall of English nominalizations. *British Journal of Psychology*, **66,** 333–9.

Richardson, J. T. E. (1975c). Imagery, concreteness, and lexical complexity. *Quarterly Journal of Experimental Psychology*, **27,** 211–23.

Richardson, J. T. E. (1975d). Statistical analysis of experiments investigating stimulus attributes. *British Journal of Mathematical and Statistical Psychology*, **28,** 235–6.

Richardson, J. T. E. (1976a). Imageability and concreteness. *Bulletin of the Psychonomic Society*, **7,** 429–31.

Richardson, J. T. E. (1976b). Procedures for investigating imagery and the distinction between primary and secondary memory. *British Journal of Psychology*, **67,** 487–500.

Richardson, J. T. E. (1976c). *The Grammar of Justification: An Interpretation of Wittgenstein's Philosophy of Language*. London: Chatto and Windus for Sussex University Press.

Richardson, J. T. E. (1977a). Functional relationship between forward and backward digit repetition and a non-verbal analogue. *Cortex*, **13,** 317–20.

Richardson, J. T. E. (1977b). Lexical derivation. *Journal of Psycholinguistic Research*, **6,** 319–36.

Richardson, J. T. E. (1978a). Imagery and concreteness in free recall. Paper presented to the London Conference of the British Psychological Society.

Richardson, J. T. E. (1978b). Memory and intelligence following spontaneously arrested congenital hydrocephalus. *British Journal of Social and Clinical Psychology*, **17,** 261–7.

Richardson, J. T. E. (1978c). Mental imagery and memory: Coding ability or coding preference? *Journal of Mental Imagery*, **2,** 101–15.

Richardson, J. T. E. (1978d). Mental imagery and the distinction between primary and secondary memory. *Quarterly Journal of Experimental Psychology*, **30,** 471–85.

Richardson, J. T. E. (1978e). Reported mediators and individual differences in mental imagery. *Memory and Cognition*, **6,** 376–8.

Richardson, J. T. E. (1978*f*). Word-order and imagery in the recall of adjective–noun phrases. *International Journal of Psychology*, **13**, 179–84.

Richardson, J. T. E. (1979). Mental imagery, human memory, and the effects of closed head injury. *British Journal of Social and Clinical Psychology*, **18**, 319–27.

Richardson, J. T. E. (in press). Correlations between imagery and memory scores across stimuli and across subjects. *Bulletin of the psychonomic Society*.

Robinson, J. P. (1970). Effects of verbal and imaginal learning on recognition, free-recall, and aided recall tests. *Journal of Experimental Psychology*, **86**, 115–17.

Rock, I. (1975). *An Introduction to Perception*. New York: Macmillan.

Rock, I. and McDermott, W. (1964). The perception of visual angle. *Acta Psychologica*, **22**, 119–34.

Rohrman, N. L. (1968). The role of syntactic structure in the recall of English nominalizations. *Journal of Verbal Learning and Verbal Behavior*, **7**, 904–12.

Rohwer, W. D., Jr (1966). Constraint, syntax, and meaning in paired-associate learning. *Journal of Verbal Learning and Verbal Behavior*, **5**, 541–7.

Rosenthal, R. (1966). *Experimenter Effects in Behavioral Research*. New York: Appleton-Century-Crofts.

Rumelhart, D. E., Lindsay, P. H. and Norman, D. A. (1972). A process model for long-term memory. *In* Tulving, E. and Donaldson, W. (eds) *Organization of Memory*. New York: Academic Press.

Sachs, J. S. (1967). Recognition memory for syntactic and semantic aspects of connected discourse. *Perception and Psychophysics*, **2**, 437–42.

Sacks, H. V. and Eysenck, M. W. (1977). Convergence-divergence and the learning of concrete and abstract sentences. *British Journal of Psychology*, **68**, 215–21.

Sasson, R. Y. (1971). Interfering images at sentence retrieval. *Journal of Experimental Psychology*, **89**, 56–62.

Sasson, R. Y. and Fraisse, P. (1972). Images in memory for concrete and abstract sentences. *Journal of Experimental Psychology*, **94**, 149–55.

Scapinello, K. F. and Yarmey, A. D. (1970). The role of familiarity and orientation in immediate and delayed recognition of pictorial stimuli. *Psychonomic Science*, **21**, 329–30.

Schnorr, J. A. and Atkinson, R. C. (1969). Repetition versus imagery instructions in the short- and long-term retention of paired associates. *Psychonomic Science*, **15**, 183–4.

Seamon, J. G. and Gazzaniga, M. S. (1973). Coding strategies and cerebral laterality effects. *Cognitive Psychology*, **5**, 249–56.

Segal, S. J. (1971*a*). Preface. *In* Segal, S. J. (ed.) *Imagery: Current Cognitive Approaches*. New York: Academic Press.

Segal, S. J. (1971*b*). Processing of the stimulus in imagery and perception. *In* Segal, S. J. (ed.) *Imagery: Current Cognitive Approaches*. New York: Academic Press.

Segal, S. J. and Fusella, V. (1969). Effects of imaging on signal-to-noise ratio with varying signal conditions. *British Journal of Psychology*, **60**, 459–64.

Segal, S. J. and Fusella, V. (1970). Influence of imaged pictures and sounds on detection of auditory and visual signals. *Journal of Experimental Psychology*, **83,** 458–64.

Segal, S. J. and Fusella, V. (1971). Effect of images in six sense modalities on detection of visual signal from noise. *Psychonomic Science*, **24,** 55–6.

Segal, S. J. and Gordon, P. (1969). The Perky effect revisited: Paradoxical threshold or signal detection error. *Perceptual and Motor Skills*, **28,** 791–7.

Sekuler, R., Rubin, E. and Armstrong, R. (1971). Processing numerical information: A choice time analysis. *Journal of Experimental Psychology*, **89,** 75–80.

Semmes, J., Weinstein, S., Ghent, L. and Teuber, H.-L. (1955). Spatial orientation in man after cerebral injury: 1. Analyses by locus of lesion. *Journal of Psychology*, **39,** 227–44.

Semmes, J., Weinstein, S., Ghent, L. and Teuber, H.-L. (1963). Correlates of impaired orientation in personal and extrapersonal space. *Brain*, **86,** 747–72.

Senter, R. J. and Hoffman, R. R. (1976). Bizarreness as a nonessential variable in mnemonic imagery: A confirmation. *Bulletin of the Psychonomic Society*, **7,** 163–4.

Shallice, T. and Warrington, E. K., (1970). Independent functioning of verbal memory stores: A neuropsychological study. *Quarterly Journal of Experimental Psychology*, **22,** 261–73.

Sheehan, P. W. (1966a). Accuracy and vividness of visual images. *Perceptual and Motor Skills,* **23,** 391–8.

Sheehan, P. W. (1966b). Functional similarity of imaging to perceiving: Individual differences in vividness of imagery. *Perceptual and Motor Skills*, **23,** 1011–33.

Sheehan, P. W. (1967a). A shortened form of Betts' Questionnaire Upon Mental Imagery. *Journal of Clinical Psychology*, **23,** 386–9.

Sheehan, P. W. (1967b). Reliability of a short test of imagery. *Perceptual and Motor Skills*, **25,** 744.

Sheehan, P. W. (1967c). Visual imagery and the organizational properties of perceived stimuli. *British Journal of Psychology*, **58,** 247–52.

Sheehan, P. W. (1972). A functional analysis of the role of visual imagery in unexpected recall. *In* Sheehan, P. W. (ed.) *The Function and Nature of Imagery*. New York: Academic Press.

Sheehan, P. W. (1978). Mental imagery. *In* Foss, B. M. (ed.) *Psychology Survey*, No. 1. London: George Allen and Unwin.

Sheehan, P. W. and Neisser, U. (1969). Some variables affecting the vividness of imagery in recall. *British Journal of Psychology*, **60,** 71–80.

Sheikh, A. A. (1977). Mental images: Ghosts of sensations? *Journal of Mental Imagery*, **1,** 1–4.

Shepard, R. N. (1966). Learning and recall as organization and search. *Journal of Verbal Learning and Verbal Behavior*, **5,** 201–4.

Shepard, R. N. (1967). Recognition memory for words, sentences, and pictures.

Journal of Verbal Learning and Verbal Behavior, **6**, 156–63.

Shepard, R. N. and Chipman, S. (1970). Second-order isomorphism of internal representations: Shapes of states. *Cognitive Psychology*, **1**, 1–17.

Shepard, R. N. and Feng, C. (1972). A chronometric study of mental paper folding. *Cognitive Psychology*, **3**, 228–43.

Shepard, R. N. and Metzler, J. (1971). Mental rotation of three-dimensional objects. *Science*, **171**, 701–3.

Shepard, R. N. and Podgorny, P. (1979). Cognitive processes that resemble perceptual processes. *In* Estes, W. K. (ed.) *Handbook of Learning and Cognitive Processes*. Hillsdale, N.J.: Lawrence Erlbaum Associates.

Singer, J. L. and Antrobus, J. S. (1972). Daydreaming, imaginal processes, and personality: A normative study. *In* Sheehan, P. W. (ed.) *The Function and Nature of Imagery*. New York: Academic Press.

Singer, M. (1973). A replication of Bransford and Franks' (1971) 'The abstraction of linguistic ideas'. *Bulletin of the Psychonomic Society*, **1**, 416–18.

Smith, E. E., Barresi, J. and Gross, A. E. (1971). Imaginal versus verbal encoding and the primary-secondary memory distinction. *Journal of Verbal Learning and Verbal Behavior*, **10**, 597–603.

Spanos, N. P., Valois, R., Ham, M. W. and Ham, M. L. (1973). Suggestibility, and vividness and control of imagery. *International Journal of Clinical and Experimental Hypnosis*, **21**, 305–11.

Spreen, O. and Schulz, R. W. (1966). Parameters of abstraction, meaningfulness, and pronunciability for 329 nouns. *Journal of Verbal Learning and Verbal Behavior*, **5**, 459–68.

Standing, L. (1973). Learning 10,000 pictures. *Quarterly Journal of Experimental Psychology*, **25**, 207–22.

Standing, L., Conezio, J. and Haber, R. N. (1970). Perception and memory for pictures: Single-trial learning of 2,500 visual stimuli. *Psychonomic Science*, **19**, 73–4.

Starker, S. (1974). Two modes of visual imagery. *Perceptual and Motor Skills*, **38**, 649–50.

Stewart, J. C. (1965). An Experimental Investigation of Imagery. Unpublished doctoral dissertation, University of Toronto.

Strawson, P. F. (1959). *Individuals: An Essay in Descriptive Metaphysics*. London: Methuen.

Stromeyer, C. F. and Psotka, J. (1970). The detailed texture of eidetic images. *Nature*, **225**, 346–9.

Teuber, H.-L. (1955). Physiological psychology. *Annual Review of Psychology*, **6**, 267–96.

Teuber, H.-L. (1963). Space perception and its disturbances after brain injury in man. *Neuropsychologia*, **1**, 47–57.

Thurstone, L. L. (1938). Primary mental abilities. *Psychometrika Monographs*, No. 1.

Thurstone, L. L. and Jeffrey, T. E. (1956). *Flags: A test of Space Thinking.* Chicago: Education Industry Service.

Tondo, T. R. and Cautela, J. R. (1974). Assessment of imagery in covert reinforcement. *Psychological Reports,* **34,** 1271–80.

Wagman, R. and Stewart, C. G. (1974). Visual imagery and hypnotic susceptibility. *Perceptual and Motor Skills,* **38,** 815–22.

Walsh, K. W. (1978). *Neuropsychology.* Edinburgh: Churchill Livingstone.

Ward, W. C. and Legant, P. (1971). Naming and memory in nursery school children in the absence of rehearsal. *Developmental Psychology,* **5,** 174–5.

Warren, M. W. (1977). The effects of recall-concurrent visual-motor distraction on picture and word recall. *Memory and Cognition,* **5,** 362–70.

Warrington, E. K. (1971). Neurological disorders of memory. *British Medical Bulletin,* **27,** 243–7.

Watson, J. B. (1913). Psychology as the behaviorist views it. *Psychological Review,* **20,** 158–77.

Watson, J. B. (1914). *Behavior: An Introduction to Comparative Psychology.* New York: Holt, 1914.

Watson, J. B. (1928). *The Ways of Behaviorism.* New York: Harper.

Webber, S. M. and Marshall, P. H. (1978). Bizarreness effects in imagery as a function of processing level and delay. *Journal of Mental Imagery,* **2,** 291–9.

Weingartner, H., Walker, T., Eich, J. E. and Murphy, D. L. (1976). Storage and recall of verbal and pictorial information. *Bulletin of the Psychonomic Society,* **7,** 349–51.

Wells, J. E. (1972). Encoding and memory for verbal and pictorial stimuli. *Quarterly Journal of Experimental Psychology,* **24,** 242–52.

Whitaker, H. A. (1971). *On the Representation of Language in the Human Brain.* Edmonton: Linguistic Research, Inc.

White, K. D. and Ashton, R. (1977). Visual imagery control: One dimension or four? *Journal of Mental Imagery,* **1,** 245–52.

White, K. D., Ashton, R. and Brown, R. M. D. (1977). The measurement of imagery vividness: Normative data and their relationship to sex, age, and modality differences. *British Journal of Psychology,* **68,** 203–11.

White, K., Ashton, R. and Law, H. (1974). Factor analyses of the shortened form of Betts' Questionnaire Upon Mental Imagery. *Australian Journal of Psychology,* **26,** 183–90.

White, K., Sheehan, P. W. and Ashton, R. (1977). Imagery assessment: A survey of self-report measures. *Journal of Mental Imagery,* **1,** 145–69.

Wittgenstein, L. (1953). *Philosophical Investigations.* Oxford: Blackwell.

Wittgenstein, L. (1958). *The Blue and Brown Books.* Oxford: Blackwell.

Wittgenstein, L. (1967). *Zettel.* Oxford: Blackwell.

Wittgenstein, L. (1968). Notes for lectures on 'private experience' and 'sense data'. *Philosophical Review,* **77,** 275–320.

Wollen, K. A. and Lowry, D. H. (1974). Conditions that determine effectiveness of picture-mediated paired-associate learning. *Journal of Experimental Psychology*, **102,** 181–3.

Wollen, K. A., Weber, A. and Lowry, D. H. (1972). Bizarreness versus interaction of mental images as determinants of learning. *Cognitive Psychology*, **3,** 518–22.

Wood, G. (1967). Mnemonic systems in recall. *Journal of Educational Psychology*, **58** (6, Part 2).

Yarmey, A. D. and O'Neill, B. J. (1969). S-R and R-S paired-associate learning as a function of concreteness, imagery, specificity, and association value. *Journal of Psychology*, **71,** 95–109.

Yates, F. A. (1966). *The Art of Memory*. London: Routledge and Kegan Paul.

Yin, R. K. (1969). Looking at upside-down faces. *Journal of Experimental Psychology*, **81,** 141–5.

Yin, R. K. (1970). Face recognition by brain-injured patients: A dissociable ability? *Neuropsychologia*, **8,** 395–402.

Yuille, J. C. (1968). Concreteness without imagery in PA learning. *Psychonomic Science*, **11,** 55–6.

Yuille, J. C. (1973). A detailed examination of mediation in PA learning. *Memory and Cognition*, **1,** 333–42.

Yuille, J. C. and Catchpole, M. J. (1977). The role of imagery in models of cognition. *Journal of Mental Imagery*, **1,** 171–80.

Yuille, J. C. and Paivio, A. (1967). Latency of imaginal and verbal mediators as a function of stimulus and response concreteness-imagery. *Journal of Experimental Psychology*, **75,** 540–44.

Yuille, J. C. and Paivio, A. (1968). Imagery and verbal mediation instructions in paired-associate learning. *Journal of Experimental Psychology*, **78,** 436–41.

Yuille, J. C. and Paivio, A. (1969). Abstractness and recall of connected discourse. *Journal of Experimental Psychology*, **82,** 467–71.

Yuille, J. C., Paivio, A. and Lambert, W. E. (1969). Noun and adjective imagery and order in paired-associate learning by French and English subjects. *Canadian Journal of Psychology*, **23,** 459–66.

Yuille, J. C. and Ternes, W. (1975). Attention and modality specific interference as determinants of short-term verbal and visual retention. *Canadian Journal of Psychology*, **29,** 360–74.

Author Index

Subject Index